www.wadsworth.com

www.wadsworth.com is the World Wide Web site for Wadsworth and is your direct source to dozens of online resources.

At www.wadsworth.com you can find out about supplements, demonstration software, and student resources. You can also send email to many of our authors and preview new publications and exciting new technologies.

www.wadsworth.com
Changing the way the world learns®

From the Wadsworth Series in Mass Communication and Journalism

General Mass Communication

Journalism

Photojournalism and Photography

Public Relations and Advertising

Research and Theory

CREATIVE STRATEGY IN ADVERTISING

EIGHTH EDITION

A. JEROME JEWLER
BONNIE L. DREWNIANY
School of Journalism and Mass Communications
University of South Carolina, Columbia

Australia • Canada • Mexico • Singapore • Spain
United Kingdom • United States

THOMSON

WADSWORTH

Publisher: Holly J. Allen
Assistant Editor: Shona Burke
Editorial Assistant: Laryssa Polika
Senior Technology Project Manager:
    Jeanette Wiseman
Senior Marketing Manager: Kimberly Russell
Marketing Assistant: Andrew Keay
Advertising Project Manager: Shemika Britt
Senior Project Manager, Editorial Production:
    Paul Wells
Print/Media Buyer: Karen Hunt
Permissions Editor: Stephanie Lee
Production Service: Melanie Field, Strawberry Field
    Publishing

Text Designer: Kathleen Cunningham
Copy Editor: Betty Duncan
Cover Designer: Laurie Anderson
Cover Image: man with shopping basket,
    ImageSource Photography; interconnected
    targets, Brandtner Staedeli / Solus Images; stack
    of magazines & CDs, Digital Vision Photography;
    woman in heels with shopping bag, PhotoAlto
    Photography
Cover Printer: Thomson West
Compositor: TBH Typecast, Inc.
Printer: Thomson West

Printed in the United States of America
1 2 3 4 5 6 7 08 07 06 05 04

For more information about our products, contact us at:
Thomson Learning Academic Resource Center
1-800-423-0563

For permission to use material from this text or product, submit a request online at **http://www.thomsonrights.com**. Any additional questions about permissions can be submitted by email to **thomsonrights@thomson.com**.

Library of Congress Control Number: 2003116833

ISBN 0-534-62510-X

Thomson Wadsworth
10 Davis Drive
Belmont, CA 94002-3098
USA

Asia
Thomson Learning
5 Shenton Way #01-01
UIC Building
Singapore 068808

Australia/New Zealand
Thomson Learning
102 Dodds Street
Southbank, Victoria 3006
Australia

Canada
Nelson
1120 Birchmount Road
Toronto, Ontario M1K 5G4
Canada

Europe/Middle East/Africa
Thomson Learning
High Holborn House
50/51 Bedford Row
London WC1R 4LR
United Kingdom

{ This book is dedicated to the memory of Dr. Alan Fried. }

Contents

Preface

Advertising is about problem solving. For instance:

- An airline faces stiff new competition. The competitor has shorter flights and an advertising budget that's triple the size of your client's.
- The leading brand of ketchup has been around for more than 100 years. Everyone knows the brand and likes it. The problem is people aren't using as much ketchup as they once did.
- A city with a cold climate wants to get college students to spend their spring break with them rather than at a warm beach resort.
- An opera company has a dwindling audience. How can they convince people that opera isn't dull and boring?

These are the types of problems you'll be expected to solve. The answers don't come instantly but through a process. You start by gathering information about your client, its competitors, and the target audience. What do consumers think about your client? What rational or emotional arguments can you make to get them to think differently? Once you have a handle on these issues, it's time to brainstorm about ways to deliver the message. After you come up with dozens of ideas (or more), one solution will rise to the top as the answer to your client's problem. Then, and only then, will you be ready to write and design the ads.

This book will take you through the creative problem-solving process. And if you're wondering how the problems listed above were solved, read on. The answers are found throughout this book.

Chapter 1 defines creativity in advertising. You'll learn that creating effective advertising isn't as easy as it appears. It's not just about getting noticed or coming up with a clever slogan. Nor is it about creating ads that amuse your friends. It's about understanding how your client's brand fits into the lives of its target audience.

Chapter 2 addresses the ever-changing marketplace. This chapter will help you understand how to reach ethnic minorities, older people, and other groups that are often ignored by advertisers.

Chapter 3, fact-finding, begins the creative process. You'll learn what types of questions to ask and where to go digging for the answers. Then Chapter 4 guides you through the process of taking information, adding your own insight, and coming up with a strategic plan for creativity. You'll take the strategy statement you learn to write in Chapter 4 and come up with ideas in Chapter 5. These aren't actual ads; they're just thoughts that will guide you to finished executions.

Chapter 6 begins the more tactical approach. Here you'll learn how to write effective copy for print ads. Chapter 7 tells you how to communicate your ideas visually. Chapter 8 explores radio commercials, and Chapter 9 talks about television. Chapter 10 delves into the magic of direct marketing, and Chapter 11 provides insight into Internet advertising.

Chapter 12 looks at areas outside of advertising, including public relations, sales promotion, social marketing, and guerilla marketing. You'll find that many solutions to your clients' problems include alternatives to traditional advertising.

Chapter 13 explores methods to sell your ideas to clients, and Chapter 14 explores your ultimate sales pitch—you.

As you look at the examples in this book, you'll see that I included a broad range of clients. A few of the campaigns have mega-sized budgets, but many have budgets that are a mere fraction of what the competition spends. Some of the ads were created by global agencies headquartered in New York and Los Angeles. Others are from smaller markets such as Greenville, South Carolina; Silver Spring, Maryland; and Syracuse, New York.

You'll see that, although the clients and budgets may vary, the problem-solving process remains the same. You'll find that the success of a campaign doesn't depend upon how much you spend but by how much you know about the brand and consumer and how well you can communicate that knowledge.

I would like to thank the following people who helped make this edition possible: Holly Allen, Publisher; Paul C. Wells, Senior Editorial Production Project Manager; Melanie Field, Strawberry Field Publishing; and Betty Duncan, copyeditor. I would also like to thank the following reviewers whose insight have helped improve this edition: Stephen A. Banning, Louisiana State University; Robert F. Lauterborn, University of North Carolina, Chapel Hill; Cassandra Reese, Ohio University; Ann Rittenhouse, Pennsylvania State University; Peter S. Sheldon, University of Illinois at Urbana-Champaign; and Hazel Warlaumont, California State University, Fullerton. Thanks also goes to Elaine Jones who helped proofread this book.

A tremendous debt of gratitude goes to my friend, mentor, and colleague, A. Jerome Jewler. Every page of this book, as well as every lecture I give, has his influence on it.

I am grateful to my colleagues at the School of Journalism and Mass Communications at the University of South Carolina who supported my efforts as I went on sabbatical to work on this edition. Also, I would like to thank my colleagues at the S. I. Newhouse School of Public Communications at Syracuse University who gave me a creative environment in which to write the book while I was on sabbatical. And, of course, I owe a great debt of gratitude to my students who, after all, are the reason for this book.

I hope you enjoy reading this book as much as I did writing it. I hope it inspires you to do great creative work.

Bonnie L. Drewniany

About the Authors

A. JEROME JEWLER received the 2000 Distinguished Advertising Educator Award presented by the American Advertising Federation. He is a distinguished professor emeritus in the School of Journalism and Mass Communications, University of South Carolina, Columbia, where he began teaching undergraduate and graduate courses in 1972. He is a graduate of the University of Maryland, with a BS in Journalism and an MA in American Civilization. He worked as an advertising copywriter before beginning his teaching career.

He taught briefly at the University of Tennessee; spent a summer with McCann–Erickson, Ltd., London, as a visiting professor; spent another summer in research at the Center for Advertising History of the Smithsonian Institution; and another summer teaching creative strategy to nineteen American students in England.

He has served as codirector for instruction and faculty development for the University of South Carolina college success course and has led workshops on teaching at more than 25 colleges and universities. He and John Gardner are the coeditors of *Your College Experience,* a nationally known college success text.

Jewler enjoys retirement by serving as vice president of a community theater, visiting heart patients at a local hospital, and introducing school groups to the wonders of history as a docent at the South Carolina State Museum.

BONNIE L. DREWNIANY is an associate professor in the School of Journalism and Mass Communications, University of South Carolina, Columbia. She has an MBA from Rutgers University with a concentration in Marketing, and a BS from Syracuse University, with a concentration in Mass Communications.

Prior to joining the University of South Carolina, she was a visiting professor at Syracuse University's S. I. Newhouse School of Public Communications. She also taught as an adjunct at Parsons School of Design, Rutgers University, and Seton Hall University. During the spring of 2003, she returned to Syracuse University and worked on the revision of this book while teaching advertising campaigns at the Newhouse School.

Her professional experience includes ten years with the R. H. Macy Corporation, where she was advertising copy director for the New Jersey division. She has also freelanced for F. A. O. Schwartz, Fortunoff's, and American Express.

Her research interests include advertising's portrayal of minorities, women, and older people. Her findings have been published in the *Wall Street Journal* and various academic publications. She serves on the Academic Committee of the American Advertising Federation and on the ADDY Committee of the Columbia Advertising Club. She spends her summers in Massachusetts.

CREATIVITY:
UNEXPECTED BUT RELEVANT SELLING MESSAGES

A commercial shows a middle-aged couple talking in bed. The wife says that she fears they're drifting apart because he doesn't talk to her in that "special" way anymore. He explains, "But we were younger then. We were in college." She doesn't buy it. To appease her, he cuddles close to her. You expect to hear him whisper sweet nothings in a low, sexy voice. Instead, he warbles like Donald Duck: "I love you. I love you very, very much." She giggles. The title card reads "Magic Happens. Disney."

This Disney commercial is a wonderful example of creativity in advertising. It contains the human truth that relationships get stale over time and need to be refreshed. It's unexpected. You think that the husband is going to sound like Barry White, but instead he sounds like a cartoon character. And it has a selling idea that makes the Disney brand relevant to its audience.

Creativity Defined

Creative ads make a relevant connection between the brand and its target audience and present a selling idea in an unexpected way. Let's examine components of the definition.

Creative ads make a relevant connection between a brand and its target audience. A brand is much more than a name, logo, or clever slogan. It's a collection of experiences that exist in consumers' minds. Creative director Ann Hayden explains, "I'm convinced that people—all people—want to buy

How do you encourage advertisers to be more creative in their newspaper ads? Mike Hughes, president of the Martin Agency, suggested that the Newspaper Association of America advertise. Mike's idea was to reach creative people by means of what they read—the pages of daily newspapers. Mike said that creative people are willing to listen to people they respect. Hence, he suggested a campaign called "How to Write a Newspaper Ad," written by advertising agency creative legends. Mike wrote the ad shown here. Be sure to read the other ads in the feature Tips & Tactics in Chapters 4–7.

Courtesy of the Newspaper Association of America.

Figure 1-1
Some people are a bit intimidated by ballet and think it's just for high-society snobs. This campaign shows average folks can get a kick out of watching ballet performances.

The new ballet will have quite an effect on you.

The Greenville Ballet Association is now the South Carolina Ballet.
Come see the difference at an all new Nutcracker, December 14-15.
For tickets, call the Peace Center Box Office: 864.467.3000 or order online at www.peacecenter.org.

SOUTH CAROLINA BALLET

Courtesy of South Carolina Ballet.

from people. Customers want to know who you are, your habits, your values. They want to be able to predict you. They need to trust you. If they connect with you on some kind of human basis, and believe they have something in common with you, they will give you vast permission to sell them things that make them happy."[1]

The Disney commercial reminds viewers that magic is important to everyone, regardless of age. Another Disney spot shows a mother with her

---

[1] From the Saatchi & Saatchi Business Communications Web site, 1999.

Figure 1-1 (continued)

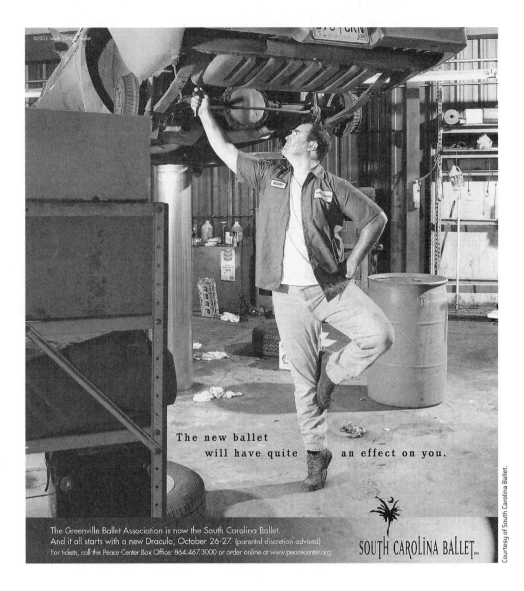

The new ballet will have quite an effect on you.

The Greenville Ballet Association is now the South Carolina Ballet.
And it all starts with a new Dracula, October 26-27. (parental discretion advised)
For tickets, call the Peace Center Box Office: 864.467.3000 or order online at www.peacecenter.org.

SOUTH CAROLINA BALLET.sm

daughter and baby boy. They enter a crowded elevator and the daughter tells
the strangers about her trip to Disney. She's so enthusiastic about the trip
that it sounds as if they just returned, but the mother explains they took the
trip a year ago. The daughter tells everyone they got all types of souvenirs
from the trip, including her baby brother. The strangers grin. The mother
explains, "We all had a good time."

Creative ads present a selling idea. The selling idea can be something
tangible, such as Cheer will keep your clothes from fading. Or it can be
intangible, like the way ballet can change your life (see Figure 1-1). The
method of presenting the selling idea can be rational, emotional, or a combination of both. Because competitors can copy most products and services,
emotional selling points are usually more powerful than rational ones.

Figure 1-1 (continued)

The new ballet will have quite an effect on you.

Creative ads are unexpected. Look at the ad for Stren fishing line in Figure 1-2. The agency could have shown a man reeling in a giant fish. However, that would be so expected that it would blend in with all the other ads for fishing products. Instead, the close-up of man's split pants catches you off guard and makes you wonder what the ad is all about. Meanwhile, the copy, "The most dependable fishing line in the world," delivers the selling message and helps the visual make perfect sense.

Sadly, too many ads fail to meet the above criteria for creativity. Many ads are so bland that they get lost in the clutter. Others beat you senselessly over the head with the message, "Save! Save! Save!" Others entertain but fail to say anything relevant about the brand. And others try to shock you with messages that are rude, crude, and lewd.

Figure 1-2
How do you convince customers that your fishing line is really, really strong? The obvious way would be to show a giant fish that's just been hooked. But that's been done before. This ad from Carmichael Lynch for Stren is unexpected but relevant.

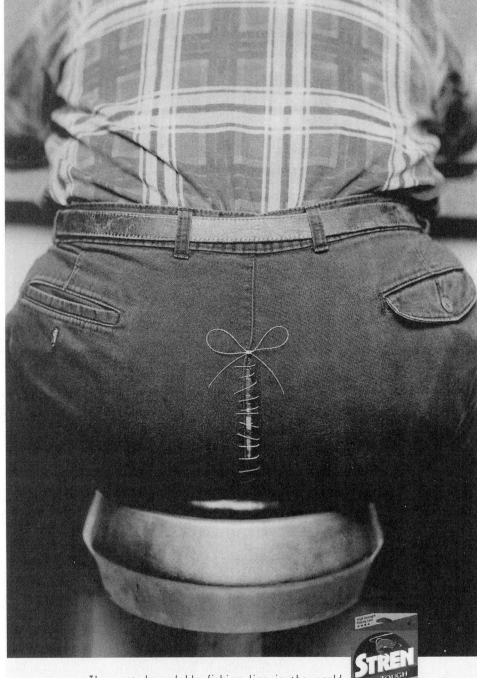

That's Entertainment, but Is It Advertising?

Rance Crain, president and editorial director of Crain Communications, Inc., quoted a letter to the editor from a father: "My 6½-year-old son cut through the mayhem of murderous lizards, a digitally reincarnated Elvis and dancing tomatoes to offer an unwitting, but telling, indictment of Super Bowl ads: 'These commercials are cool. Not like the regular ones where they're trying to sell you something.'"[2]

Like that little boy, most viewers love Super Bowl commercials because of their use of humor, celebrities, and ad critters. Unfortunately, the viewers don't always express their enthusiasm for the commercials at the cash register. Super Bowl commercials are hardly unique in this regard—some of the most popular commercials of all time have been tremendous flops in terms of sales. So does this mean you should avoid humor, celebrities, and ad characters in your ads? No. But it does mean you should use them strategically.

Humor

Consider this TV commercial: An amateur stage production shows two children lost in the forest. The good fairy appears from overhead and starts floating toward them. "Not to fear, little children. I will helpppp—" THUD! She plummets to the stage. Tag line: "Should have used Stren. Stren. The most dependable fishing line in the world." The humor takes us by surprise and shows a situation that we can empathize with. It communicates a relevant, unexpected, and memorable message about the product. It gives us a reason to buy. It works.

Here are some tips on how to use humor in advertising:

1. *Know the difference between humor and jokes.* A joke is a one-shot deal. Once you hear the punch line, it's not as funny the second time. And when you hear the same joke a bunch of times, it can become downright tedious. Humor, by contrast, is subtler and often contains nuances that make you want to see and hear it again and again. Many humorous commercials actually get funnier the more times that you see them.

   A comedy club understood the difference between jokes and humor when it created a delightful radio spot that promoted what they were selling: laughter. The spot recorded various types of laughter—the chuckle, the giggle, the cackle, the sputtering burst, the snort, and so on. You could hear the spot over and over and laugh each time because the laughter became contagious.

---

[2] Remarks by Rance Crain to the Columbia Advertising and Marketing Federation, Columbia, SC, 17 March 1998.

2. *Relate to the human experience.* One of the things that made the comedy club spot so amusing was that listeners could identify people they knew who laughed like that. The spot made a relevant human connection. Allen Kay—whose advertising agency, Korey, Kay & Partners, has won numerous awards for its humorous ads—believes in having a "sense of human." As Kay told *Agency* magazine, "We spell humor h-u-m-a-n. It includes a lot of ironies in life that people recognize and realize and makes them say, 'Yeah, I've been there.'"[3]

3. *Make sure the humor is central to your product message.* Have you ever been so captivated by a commercial that you could repeat almost every detail of it—except for the name of the product it was trying to sell? If the product is obscured by the humor, the ad has flopped. To work, humor must be central to the message you're trying to communicate.

4. *Understand your audience's sense of humor.* Your ads should reflect the tastes, aspirations, and sensibilities of its intended audience. Just because you and your friends find something hysterical doesn't mean the rest of the world will. In fact, people may even be insulted by it. So be sure to test your humor on members of your target audience. Figure 1-3 reflects the sense of humor of its thrill-seeking audience.

5. *Avoid humor that's at the expense of others.* Making fun of ethnic groups, the disabled, and the elderly will very likely backfire on you. A car company offended African Americans by running an ad in *Jet* magazine that stated, "Unlike your last boyfriend, it goes to work in the morning." And a discount clothing store offended Jewish people by saying, "Dress British. Think Yiddish."

6. *Have fun with your product, but don't make fun of it.* Self-deprecating humor can work if you turn your supposed shortcomings into an advantage. Motel 6 does this brilliantly. They don't try to hide their lack of amenities but rather flaunt it. At Motel 6, you're not going to get fancy soaps, European chocolates, or fluffy bathrobes. Instead, you'll get a comfortable room at a comfortable price. See the BriefCase in Chapter 8 for examples of this long-running campaign.

7. *Don't assume that your audience is stupid.* Think of it this way: Would you rather buy something from someone who apparently views you as an idiot or from someone who seems to appreciate your intelligence? Absolut vodka saw a phenomenal growth in its sales following the use of smart, subtle humor in its print ads.

---

[3] Robyn Griggs, "Grinning in the Dark," *Agency,* Fall 1998, pp. 16–17.

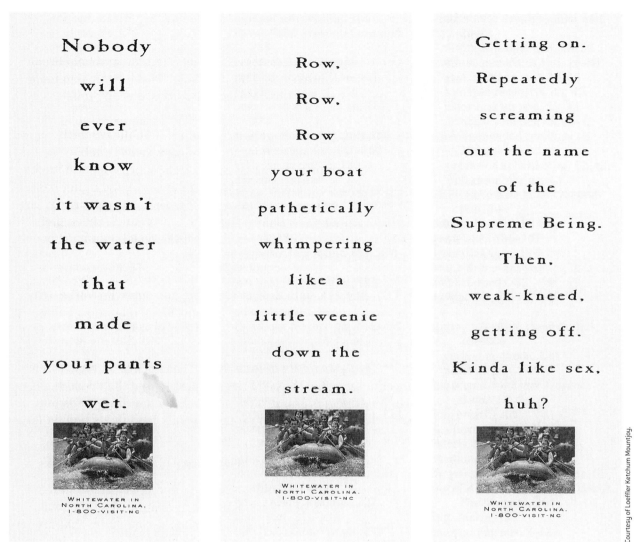

Figure 1-3
The joy. The jolts. The jitters. If you've ever gone whitewater rafting, you'll agree that these ads capture the experience. And if you haven't ever tried it, go soon—it'll clear the cobwebs from your brain.

Celebrity Endorsements

Some of the most popular commercials feature a who's who of pop culture. Superstars like Britney Spears and Jennifer Lopez sing the praises of products. Supermodels Tyra Banks, Naomi Campbell, and Cindy Crawford make any product look good. And sports stars like Tiger Woods, Serena Williams, and Yao Ming score big with advertisers and viewers.

There are numerous advantages to using celebrities, including the following:

- *They have stopping power.* Celebrities attract attention and help break through the clutter of other ads. The "Got Milk?" print campaign made milk seem cool by showing hundreds of celebrities sporting milk mustaches.

- *They're likable.* Companies hope that the admiration the celebrity enjoys will be transferred to them. Catherine Zeta-Jones gave T-Mobile "instant credibility" according to T-Mobile president Bob Moore who admitted, "I wonder secretly, if we had the best ads in the world and didn't have Catherine, would they have worked as well? Catherine's celebrity is getting our ads talked about."[4] Before signing on a celebrity, check their "Q" score, which is a measure of the popularity and appeal of famous people. You can get information at www.qscores.com.

- *Their unique characteristics can help communicate the selling idea.* Seven-foot five-inch basketball star Yao Ming appears with Verne Troyer ("Mini-Me") in ads promoting Apple's 12- and 17-inch laptops. Yao is shown with the smaller screen while Verne has the big screen. The two celebrities help further the selling idea—size—in a dramatic way.

- *They're perceived as experts in their fields.* The trick is to make a relevant connection between the celebrity's expertise and the brand being advertised. An athlete is a natural spokesman for sporting goods but doesn't seem very credible when promoting junk food that's high in fat and calories.

Before you think a celebrity is the answer, consider these drawbacks:

- *They're expensive.* Many top athletes, actors, and musicians command contracts in the millions of dollars. Smaller companies shouldn't even dream of spending this type of money, nor should companies that are trying to promote their low prices. Even large companies should think twice before plopping down millions of dollars. A Super Bowl commercial for Pepsi showcased Britney Spears doing musical numbers from bygone eras. The commercial, which aired in 2002, cost $5.8 million and was ranked the third-lowest spot among the 52 ads rated by *USA Today*'s annual Super Bowl Ad Meter.[5]

- *They're often a quick fix, not a long-term strategy.* Celebrities go in and out of fashion, and as their popularity level shifts, so does their persuasiveness. Look at a *People* magazine from a decade or two ago. How many of the former superstars are still super popular?

---

[4] Eleftheria Pappis, "Man of the Moment," *Adweek,* 3 March 2003, p. 35.
[5] Theresa Howard, *USA Today* Web site, 22 April 2002.

- *They may lack credibility.* Sixty-three percent of respondents in a study published in *Advertising Age* said that celebrities are "just doing it for the money," and 43 percent believed celebrities "don't even use the product."[6]

  A commercial for Champion sportswear shows images of obnoxious professional basketball players. One dribbles a ball imprinted with the front of a dollar bill. The voice-over inquires, "When did the logo on your shoe become more important than the heart on your sleeve? When did the word 'renegotiate' move from the business page to the sports page? Where have all the champions gone?" The images on the screen change to plain folks playing football and running just for fun. The voice-over continues, "You'll find us in places where the lights don't flash, and the only contract you sign is with yourself. We are the champions. . . ."

- *They may endorse so many products that it confuses people.* Tiger Woods got into hot water for bouncing a Titleist golf ball on the wedge of a Titleist golf club while shooting a Nike commercial.

- *They can overshadow the message.* Although a celebrity may draw attention to an ad, some consumers focus their attention on the celebrity and fail to note what's being promoted. In one spot, Yao Ming tries to pay for a souvenir from New York City by writing a check. The cashier responds, "Yo," pointing to a sign that says "no checks." Yao corrects her, "Yao." They go back and forth with the Yo, Yao routine and the spot closes with a brief pitch for Visa's check card. The commercial is a clever spin on the "Who's on First" routine. The audience will likely remember Yao's name, but it's not as certain they'll remember which credit card company paid for the ad. The Visa brand name could easily have been made dominant if the cashier had asked the Chinese athlete to show his visa and passport and he presented his Visa check card instead.

- *Bad press about the celebrity can hurt the sponsor.* Nutella dumped Kobe Bryant as their spokesman after the basketball star was accused of raping a woman. Kmart canceled its contract with golfing veteran Fuzzy Zoeller after he joked about Tiger Woods eating fried chicken and collard greens. And O. J. Simpson, once one of the most popular endorsers, probably won't be asked to appear in any commercials in the future. "Having a highly-paid, highly visible celebrity endorser is like having an expensive beach home on the Florida coast. It's swell, if you don't mind lying awake all night worrying about approaching storms," says Bob Garfield, ad critic at *Advertising Age.*[7]

[6] Dave Vadehra, "Celebs Remain Entertaining, if Not Believable," *Advertising Age,* 2 September 1996, p. 18.
[7] Bob Garfield, "Champion Forgoes Endorser and Scores a Couple of Points," *Advertising Age,* 14 July 2003, p. 29.

At least initially, you should avoid using celebrities in your ads because it's very unlikely you'll have that type of budget on your first account. Also, it doesn't show original thinking. Your portfolio should show how you can solve problems creatively, not how a famous personality can do it.

Advertising Trade Characters

Giggling doughboys. Talking dogs. Dancing raisins. All of these whimsical characters have pitched products and ideas over the years. Creative guru Ted Bell notes that characters like the Jolly Green Giant and Colonel Sanders are part of the "fabric" of their companies and consumers have an emotional attachment to them even after they've been on hiatus for a while. "You see the Colonel, and it's instant recognition, with no explanation necessary. When the old characters reappeared, the new cynical audience actually seemed to like them. Younger consumers enjoyed them because they were corny and campy; for older viewers, they had nostalgic appeal."[8]

Done right, the character will communicate a selling feature. Snap, Crackle, and Pop reinforce the unique sound the cereal makes when milk is added to Kellogg's Rice Krispies cereal. Smokey Bear convinces children and adults to prevent forest fires. The AFLAC duck has made us aware of a thing called supplemental insurance.

Perhaps the best thing about animated characters is the control you have over them. Unlike a celebrity, they're not going to get caught shoplifting, molesting a minor, or saying something stupid in public. Because they don't get older, they can appeal to different generations of consumers. Smokey Bear, Tony the Tiger, and the Jolly Green Giant are more than 50 years old. The Quaker Oats man has been around since 1887 (his cholesterol level must be great!).

Still, many creative directors find advertising trade characters to be gimmicky, cutesy, and old-fashioned. In many cases, they're right. Unless the character can help make a connection to the brand, don't consider it. Like using humor and celebrities, advertising trade characters must be relevant to the consumer and the brand. Also, keep in mind that just because people love your character, it won't necessarily mean they love your brand. Most people loved the singing sock puppet from Pets.com but few understood why they needed to order pet supplies over the Internet. The loveable sock puppet is now traded on eBay as a collector's item.

[8] Warren Berger, *Advertising Today* (London: Phaidon Press, 2001), p. 285.

Ethical and Legal Issues

How Far Will You Go to Be "Creative"?

Ask yourself these questions about advertising:

Should profit or prudence prevail when surveys indicate that women, Hispanic Americans, and African Americans are prime targets for cigarettes and alcohol at a time when most consumers are consuming less of both?

Should a commercial for a popular pain reliever reveal that the reason "more hospitals choose our brand" is that it is supplied at a reduced price?

Should consumers, who have no medical background, be told to ask physicians about specific brands of prescription drugs?

Should an automobile maker show a sports car outracing a jet plane in an age when speeding motorists are killed daily?

Should advertisers cast television commercials using such imperatives as "she should be blond—or if brunette, not too brunette, and pretty but not too pretty," or "midwestern in speech, middle-class looking, gentile," or "if we're using blacks, make them upscale"?

Is even a mock representation of violence and domination appropriate in commercial speech?

What about sexual innuendo? If sex sells, should there be any limits?

Myths and Stereotypes

Try as they may to avoid perpetuating negative values in the context of a message, a number of advertisers, intentionally or not, cause certain consumers to feel they're not "good enough" or "pretty enough" or "successful enough." As you read the following messages, decide which parts are myths and which parts contain some truth. Do you see any consequences—positive or negative—from using them to sell a product or service?

The children: Let's be sure our children get all the things we didn't (more games and toys, fancier clothes, more exotic vacations, and so on).

Men and women: For men, it's smart to be strong and sensible, to work hard for success, to rein in emotions. Of course, women can cry.

The materialistic ideal: What you are depends to a large extent on the products and services you own and use, as opposed to your values, personality, ethics, and interests.

Technology: The more technology, the better the life, so be sure your TV is theater quality in terms of both screen size and sound.

The egalitarian ideal: We're all in this together.

HOW TO DESTROY AN AD IN FIVE EASY STEPS

Ohrbach's, a bargain clothing store in New York, was famous for its witty ads, which were created by the legendary Bill Bernbach. One of its most famous ads showed a cat, wearing a woman's hat and clenching a long cigarette holder, above the headline "I found out about Joan." The copy continued, "The way she talks, you'd think she was in Who's Who. Well! I found out what's what with her. Her husband owns a bank? Sweetie, not even a bank account. Why that palace of theirs has wall-to-wall mortgages! And that car? Darling, that's horse-power, not earning power. They won it in a fifty-cent raffle! Can you imagine? And those clothes! Of course she does dress divinely. But really . . . a mink stole, and Paris suits, and all those dresses . . . on his income? Well darling. I found out about that too. I just happened to be going her way and I saw Joan come out of Ohrbach's!"

The ad clearly meets our definition of creativity. It's unexpected, relevant, bonds with its customers, and has a selling idea. But think what might have happened if Ohrbach's management insisted that Bernbach put more "sell" into the message. Here's one scenario:

1. Let's include the store name in the headline, just in case customers miss it at the bottom of the ad.

2. Let's tell customers they'll save at Ohrbach's. Make the headline bigger. And the cat smaller. And be sure to include the price of the hat.

3. Let's tell customers how much they'll save in 72-point type. And let's have the word "SAVE" in a starburst. Make sure we have a giant 'X' through the suggested retail price of the hat and blow up the Ohrbach's price.

4. You know, customers might think all we sell is hats. Let's list all the other things we sell.

5. Let's drop the cat and run a huge savings headline. After all, customers care about themselves. Not about some dumb cat. Let's add a sense of urgency. Say something like, "Today only!" And in the body copy, let's run some examples of the savings customers will find.

Bernbach's ad positioned the store as a fantastic place to save money on good fashions. What did our "revisions" do to that message? They destroyed it.

The elitist dream: We're not all in this together! Other people need to be smart to keep up with me.

What's good for America: You're unpatriotic if you drive a Honda, shave with a Braun, or drink French wine. (Used only to sell American brands, of course.)

Foreign is better: Wine, food, clothes, cars, you name it. If it has a foreign accent, it must be better than a domestic brand.

The perfect host: If you're not the perfect cook, decorator, party host, and so on, what's wrong with you?

Sex: No matter what the question is, sex is the answer. All it takes is brand X to make you irresistible. Use it and you will be loved; when it doesn't work, it's your fault.

Fear and guilt: You'll be offensive if you don't use this deodorant. You'll lose your home if you don't have the proper protection. You're a goof if you dress like one.

Being "real"—the denial of fantasy: This one is tricky because the advertiser seems to be leveling with you. "We know advertising is full of tricks," they seem to be saying, "so we're going to level with you." (But are they really?)

Regulations

Advertisers can go too far in their attempts to be creative. In some cases, consumers get so outraged they start a boycott. Also, the media may choose not to run an ad they find offensive as *Elle* magazine did when it ran a blank page instead of running a Benetton ad that showed a man dying of AIDS. Sometimes the issue of taste is stretched so far that it breaks the law. A Sam Adams radio promotion on the Opie & Anthony show rewarded people for having sex in public. One couple was arrested for doing so near worshipers in New York's St. Patrick's Cathedral, and this led to the cancellation of the syndicated radio show and a federal investigation.[9]

Here are other regulations you should know before you create ads:

1. *Know the difference between puffery and deception.* The legal definition of puffery is "an exaggeration or over-statement expressed in broad, vague, and commendatory language, and is *distinguishable* from mis-descriptions or false representations of specific characteristics of a product and, as such, is not actionable."[10] For instance, an ad for spaghetti sauce may claim it's "as good as mom's." Few people would believe this to be a statement of fact. And, if your mom is a bad cook, you may actually hope it *isn't* true!

---

[9] Hillary Chura, "Sam Adams Unlikely to Be Hurt by Scandal," *Advertising Age,* 2 September 2002, p. 3.

[10] J. Thomas Russell and W. Ronald Lane, *Kleppner's Advertising Procedure* (Upper Saddle River, NJ: Prentice Hall, 2002), pp. 635–636.

2. *If you make a claim, be prepared to substantiate it.* You may be tempted to promote a health benefit or state that your product is better than another company's. Before you do this, be aware that the Federal Trade Commission (FTC), the Food and Drug Administration (FDA), and the National Association of Attorney Generals require that you can substantiate your claims. If you can't, they can order you to do a variety of things, including running corrective advertising.

   Competitors can sue if your ad "misrepresents the nature, characteristics, qualities, or geographic origin of his or her or another person's goods, services, or commercial activities." John Deere & Co. stopped MDT Products from using the John Deere logo in a disparaging manner. And Wilkinson Sword was ordered to pay Gillette $953,000 in damages after making deceptive superiority claims.

3. *Don't copy creative ideas from other campaigns.* Regardless of what you may have heard, imitation is not always the most sincere form of flattery. Nike forced Volkswagen to pull a print ad that used an "Air Jorgen" headline because it was too close to Nike's "Air Jordan" trademark.

4. *Don't copy other people's likeness.* Tom Waits won a $2.4-million lawsuit against Frito-Lay and ad agency Tracy Locke after they used someone who sounded like Waits in a radio campaign for Doritos. Vanna White won $400,000 from Samsung after it used a female robot dressed in an evening gown and blond wig, standing in front of a letter board.

5. *Respect other companies' trademarks.* Tony the Tiger and the Exxon tiger coexisted peacefully for more than 30 years. But when Exxon started using its tiger to sell food, Kellogg's sued for infringement of its tiger trademark.

6. *Watch what you say in front of children.* Advertising claims that may be perfectly suitable for adults may be unacceptable for children. A Post Grape Nuts commercial was deemed unfair because a spokesman compared the "natural goodness" of Grape Nuts to the wild nuts and berries he picked in the woods. The message was unacceptable since some nuts and berries found in the wild are poisonous and children might not tell the difference.

   Also, don't use cartoon characters to promote an adult product such as beer or cigarettes. Joe Camel and the Budweiser frogs joined Santa Claus and Mickey Mouse in a list of characters widely recognized by children. As you can imagine, children's rights advocates had a problem with this.

The Creative Challenge

Good advertising doesn't come easily. Anyone can dash off an ad in minutes; you see or hear those every day in print, on radio or TV, in your mailbox, on billboards, and on the Internet. And anyone can come up with an idea that's

Figure 1-4

Most guitar ads feature musicians in contorted positions or are filled with technical jargon. Taylor Guitar ads follow a different strategy. They state, "Taylor Guitars—handcrafted from the finest materials to give the sweetest sound." The copywriter could have run the strategy statement as a headline. But, like all talented artists, he brought it to a new level.

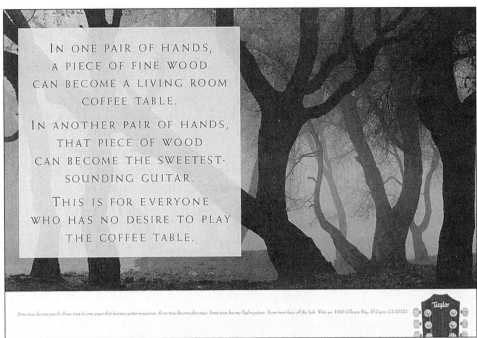

IN ONE PAIR OF HANDS,
A PIECE OF FINE WOOD
CAN BECOME A LIVING ROOM
COFFEE TABLE.

IN ANOTHER PAIR OF HANDS,
THAT PIECE OF WOOD
CAN BECOME THE SWEETEST-
SOUNDING GUITAR.

THIS IS FOR EVERYONE
WHO HAS NO DESIRE TO PLAY
THE COFFEE TABLE.

Copy reads: Some trees become pencils. Some trees become paper that becomes guitar magazines. Some trees become shoe trees. Some trees become Taylor guitars. Some trees have all the luck. Write us: 1940 Gillespie Way, El Cajon, CA 92020.

rude and offensive, but unless the idea relates to the selling message and to the intended audience, it'll be a flop.

Creative advertising makes a relevant connection with its target audience and presents a selling idea in an unexpected way. The relevance comes from the facts, whereas the unexpected connection is the inspiration of the writer and art director—the added ingredient that gets the message noticed. That's what this book is all about: identifying the advertising problem, gathering the facts, and—through a process of critical and creative thinking—adding your own insight to create a memorable ad that not only commands attention but also delivers the right message to the right audience in a language they understand and accept (see Figure 1-4).

Look at some of the ads in this book. See if you can identify the unexpected element in each ad and see if it passes the test for relevance. Note whether the idea of entertainment has fused with the factual message so that you now want to read the ad. Did the people who created the ad do everything possible to attract the audience that they were seeking? Or did they sacrifice a good idea to a funny punch line or an outrageous statement or image? That is, did the entertainment content intrude on the message or reinforce it?

Figure 1-4 (continued)

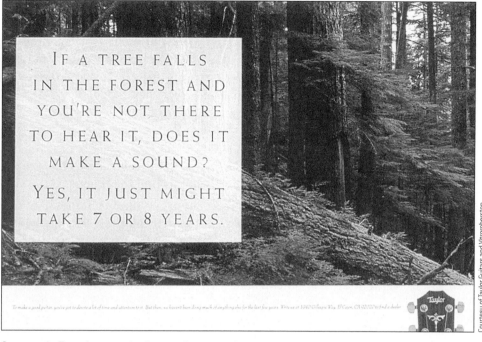

Copy reads: To make a good guitar, you've got to devote a lot of time and attention to it. But then, we haven't been doing much of anything else for the last few years. Write us at 1940 Gillespie Way, El Cajon, CA 92020 to find a dealer near you.

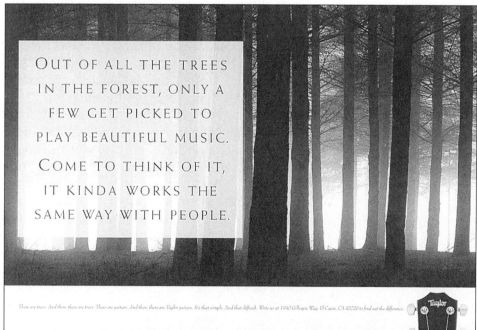

Copy reads: There are trees. And then, there are trees. There are guitars. And then, there are Taylor guitars. It's that simple. And that difficult. Write us at 1940 Gillespie Way, El Cajon, CA 92020 to find out the difference.

Suggested Activities

1. Take inventory of the number of advertising messages you see or hear in a single day. How many did you count, how many do you remember vividly, and what were some of the more unusual places in which you found advertising?

2. Find examples of advertisements that you believe (a) promise "miracles" through products, (b) offer stereotypes of people to sell products, (c) play on fears to convince us to buy, (d) state questionable "truths," and (e) are in bad taste. What could the advertisers have done to eliminate such qualities without diminishing the impact of the selling message?

3. Although some might argue that it's impossible to be creative about ordinary products, advertising professionals will retort, "Boring is no excuse!" Writer James Gorman takes nearly three magazine pages exploring the charm of the lowly pencil. In part, he writes:

   Remember pencils? Remember the smell of cedar shavings, the pleasure of writing on clean paper with that first, sharp point, the sense of guilt and personal inadequacy that comes from seeing the gnawed and stubby evidence of your own anxiety neurosis next to some obsessive's long, sharp points and untoothed hexagonal pencil bodies? I had forgotten about pencils until recently, when I overdosed on computers and decided I needed a rest cure. Pencils. Do people still use them? Are there living pencil devotees? Or have the laser printer and the felt tip pen conquered all?[11]

   Gorman adds that he called the Pencil Makers Association in Moorestown, New Jersey, and discovered that "pencils are doing fine." U.S. companies make about 2 billion pencils each year, he learned. He also discovered that pencils got their start in 1564, when a large graphite deposit was uncovered in England. Gradually, folks figured out what to put around the graphite, what to mix it with, and how to cook it to make it stronger and better for writing. Ernest Hemingway and Walt Whitman used pencils, not pens or typewriters. So did Vladimir Nabokov and Herbert Hoover. Henry Thoreau ran a family pencil-making business. Finally, Gorman learned that "you could eat one every day without harming yourself," mainly because the "lead" in a pencil is not lead at all but graphite.

   If Gorman can take three full pages to entertain you about pencils, can you create a single advertisement to provide the pencil with a personality so appealing that readers will clamor for more pencils? Try it.

[11] "Pencil Facts," from James Gorman, adapted from *Wigwag,* February 1990. Used by permission.

4. Find an ad in a national magazine, or describe a commercial from radio or TV. Critique it using the following guidelines:

   a. Does the ad gain your attention without confusing you? Would it stand out in a magazine or newspaper full of ads (or on television or radio, as the case may be)?

   b. Does the ad show empathy with the target audience? Is the target clearly defined? Is there a sense of involvement—that is, does the ad make you exclaim, "That's me they're talking about"?

   c. Does the ad clearly communicate the key benefits? Is there a reason to consider purchase, whether rational or emotional, overt or implied? If implied, is it clear enough?

   d. Does the ad use a memorable device to make you remember something important? Is there a line or phrase in the copy that is especially outstanding?

   e. Does the ad make you feel positive about the product, the ad, the manufacturer, and yourself?

   f. Is there anything about the ad, however small, that might be improved? How could it be improved?

Search Online! Discovering More About Creativity

Use InfoTrac® College Edition to discover more about creativity. Try these phrases and others for Key Words and Subject Guide searches: *creativity, creative thinking, creative and relevant, divergent thinking, humor, celebrity endorsement, advertising myths, advertising stereotypes, advertising and society.*

For more information about creativity in advertising, go to:

> Ad Forum: www.adforum.com
>
> Clio Awards: www.clioawards.com

For more information about ethics, issues, and regulations, go to:

> Advertising Educational Foundation: www.aded.org
>
> Bad Ads: www.badads.org
>
> Better Business Bureau: www.bbb.org
>
> Children's Advertising Review Unit: www.caru.org
>
> Federal Trade Commission: www.ftc.gov
>
> Food and Drug Administration: www.fda.gov

BRIEFCASE

Icelandair and BWI Take the Travail Out of Travel

Check out a bunch of airline ads and what do you see? Pictures of smiling flight attendants. Relaxed passengers stretched out in spacious seats. Breathtaking views of exotic destinations. And planes. Lots of planes, all flying high above the clouds. Yikes! So many airline ads look the same.

So how do you break through the monotony? And what do you do when you're a small airline and you're facing new competition? That's the challenge Icelandair gave to Nasuti & Hinkle when SAS airlines started offering direct flights to Scandinavia from Dulles Airport, a competitive threat to approximately 20 percent of Icelandair's Baltimore Washington International (BWI) airport business.

Nasuti & Hinkle discovered that SAS was planning to spend roughly $1 million on advertising—more than three times what Icelandair had available to spend. Also, Icelandair acknowledged that SAS had a better product in terms of flying time to Scandinavia. But none of this discouraged the Nasuti & Hinkle team because they had a secret weapon—personal experience. They knew firsthand what it was like to fly from the various Washington area airports since their agency is located in Silver Spring, Maryland. They decided to concede the immediate Dulles geographic area business and assumed that the Baltimore business was safe. That left what they called the "swing" areas that are roughly equidistant to the two airports—Alexandria and Arlington, Virginia; Bethesda and Silver Spring, Maryland; and Washington, DC.

Executives at Nasuti & Hinkle knew that the weak link in the entire Washington-to-Scandinavia SAS chain was one their traveling target audience knew all too well—the starting point in Washington. At the time, as now, air travel in and out of Dulles is not as easy as it might be. With no parking near the terminal and its system of shuttles to a midfield terminal, just getting to the aircraft is a chore.

Their strategy was simple—Dulles Airport—and the creative focused on how flying to Scandinavia from BWI on Icelandair is much easier and more

With special thanks to Woody Hinkle of Nasuti & Hinkle.

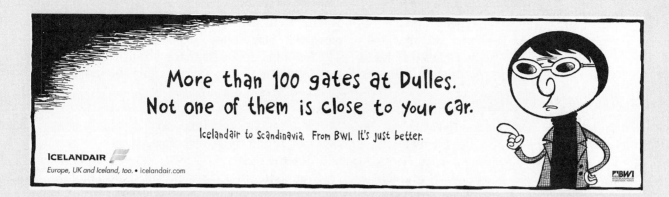

convenient than from Dulles with all its attendant aggravations. The target audience was primarily composed of Scandinavians who were living in the United States but flew back to Scandinavia for business or to visit.

With a limited budget, Nasuti & Hinkle focused all of their media dollars into radio (see the accompanying 60-second radio spot "People Mover"), Metro subway car cards, and signs on bus backs, staggered to stretch their budget as far as possible. With a primarily Scandinavian target audience, they used a very Scandinavian look to the signs, enlisting a well-known Swedish cartoonist to create a signature character for Icelandair. Headlines included, "Scandinavians were made for snowmobiles. Not shuttle buses." and "Scandinavia doesn't seem so far away when you leave from BWI." They even ran some messages entirely in Swedish, the dominant language in Scandinavia. Through friends, they found a copywriter in Sweden who translated (and in the case of radio, rewrote) their creative for a Swedish audience.

After their two-month effort, Icelandair was able to more than hold onto its market share for flights to Scandinavia. In fact, their market share actually increased a few points despite the arrival of SAS in the marketplace.

See how Nasuti & Hinkle solved another challenge for Icelandair in the BriefCase found in Chapter 11.

"People Mover" :60 radio

WOMAN: Well, see I *like* those people mover things. The airport buses that take you from the terminal to the other terminal where the plane actually is.

I mean I *really* like it. Off balance . . . crowded bus . . . bumping up against all kinds of people! Ahhhh!

So now that I can fly to Scandinavia from Dulles I'm . . . wow! When I fly BWI on Icelandair—well, at BWI there's more flights a week than Dulles. But the plane's right at the terminal, and there's a parking garage right there next to it so—no bus!

But now I can ride two—one from satellite parking and then—the other one! That's *twice* as many people. Close up!

ANNCR: Icelandair to Scandinavia and Europe from BWI. Garage parking. Convenience. Daily flights. Unless you're some kind of freak, it's just better. Call Icelandair at 800-223-5500 or visit Icelandair.com.

DIVERSITY:
TARGETING AN EVER-CHANGING MARKETPLACE

Effective advertising makes relevant connections with its target audience. To be successful, advertisers must understand, respect, and embrace the diversity of American consumers (see Figure 2-1). Today, 30 percent of Americans are people of color.[1] In some cities, former minorities collectively are now the majority. Los Angeles and Miami are more than 60 percent Hispanic, African American, and Asian American.[2] In California, Hispanics, Asians, Pacific Islanders, and African Americans now exceed 50 percent of the state's population.[3]

The buying power of ethnic Americans is growing dramatically. The Selig Center for Economic Growth at the University of Georgia predicts the combined buying power of minorities in the United States will exceed $1.5 trillion by 2008, more than triple the 1990 level of $456 billion.[4] Furthermore, ethnic groups currently dominate the purchases of numerous products and services. For example, African Americans buy 55 percent of M&M/Mars' Snickers bars, and Western Union's biggest customers are ethnic groups transferring money to Latin America and Asia.[5] Not only that, but white

---

[1] 2000 U.S. Census.
[2] Laurel Wentz, "Reverse English," *Advertising Age,* 19 November 2001, p. S2.
[3] Saul Gitlin, "Ground Shifts in California," *Advertising Age,* 25 September 2000, p. 78.
[4] Jeffrey M. Humphreys, "The Multicultural Economy 2003," *GBEC,* Second Quarter 2003, p. 2.
[5] Wentz, "Reverse English," p. S1.

Figure 2-1
These powerful ads convince people that the Greenville Hospital System truly cares about each of its patients. Sixty-four percent of respondents preferred the hospital after being exposed to the ads, up from 43 percent prior to the ad campaign.

Figure 2-1 (continued)

consumers, particularly those ages 12–34, are increasingly influenced by the fashion, dining, entertainment, sports, and music tastes emerging from minority communities, from hip-hop to salsa-flavored ketchup.[6]

Interesting things are happening to the age of Americans, too. The median age of the U.S. population in 2000 was 35.3 years, up from 32.9 in 1990. This rise reflects a 4-percent decline in numbers among 18- to 34-year-olds and a 28-percent increase in 35- to 64-year-olds, according to the U.S. Census.[7]

These figures should make it quite clear that advertisers must understand the attitudes and behaviors of an ever-changing marketplace. So how do you reach these important segments?

African Americans

African Americans are 36.7 million strong and have an annual purchasing power of $646 billion.[8] Unlike many of their white counterparts, African Americans love to shop. *American Demographics* reports that 43 percent of African Americans find it "fun and exciting" to shop for clothes whereas only 35 percent of white Americans feel the same way.[9] Furthermore, a study conducted by Mediamark Research found 58 percent of African American consumers say they enjoy wearing the latest fashions, compared with 46 percent of Asians and Hispanics, and 36 percent of whites.[10]

American Demographics magazine reports that African Americans have two priorities in their budget: buying food to eat with the family at home and buying clothes and personal care items to help them look their best. According to the report, African American households devote 75 percent more than the average American household on pork and poultry, 50 percent more on cereals and processed vegetables, and 33 percent more on beef, fresh milk, and processed fruits. They spend 47 percent more than the average American on personal care products, 67 percent more on apparel for boys and girls ages 2–15, and 33 percent more on laundry and cleaning supplies. When it comes to housing, they spend 91 percent more on rented dwellings, 52 percent more on telephone services, and 25 percent more on television, radio, and sound equipment than the average American household.[11]

The median income for African American households is $29,470, which is considerably less than the $42,228 median income of the population as a whole. Part of this may be attributed to the fact that African Americans lag

[6] Stuart Elliott, "Campaigns for Black Consumers," *New York Times,* 13 June 2003, nytimes.com.
[7] "Nation's Median Age Highest Ever," U.S. Census press release, 15 May 2001.
[8] Rebecca Gardyn and John Fetto, "Race, Ethnicity and the Way We Shop," *American Demographics,* February 2003, p. 31.
[9] Ibid., p. 31.
[10] Ibid., p. 32.
[11] Alison Stein Wellner, "Our True Colors: The Multicultural Market Is Fast Becoming a Multibillion Dollar Marketplace," *American Demographics,* November 2002, p. S6.

behind the U.S. average in academic attainment. Just 4.8 percent of the African American population holds advanced degrees, compared to 8.9 percent for the population as a whole. However, *American Demographics* reports that over the past decades African American educational attainment has improved markedly, and it is likely that this trend will continue.[12] If it is true that income follows education, then this market will be even more important to advertisers in the future.

Hispanic Americans

The nation's 38.8 million Hispanic Americans represent 13.5 percent of the U.S. population, making them the nation's largest minority group.[13] By 2007, the Hispanic population is expected to grow to nearly 42 million, according to MapInfo projections.[14] Not only is the Hispanic population gaining strength in numbers, but so is their spending power. Hispanics' economic clout has risen from $222 billion in 1990 to $653 billion in 2003, and the Selig Center for Economic Growth predicts that it will reach $1,014 billion in 2008.[15]

Hispanics originate from many different places, including Mexico, Cuba, Puerto Rico, Central and South America, and Europe. The majority live in major cities, particularly Los Angeles, New York City, and Miami, and when it comes to advertising, the majority prefers to read and hear ads in Spanish. According to Strategy Research Corp., 55 percent of Hispanics prefer to see ads in Spanish, 30 percent would choose English, and 13 percent don't have a preference between the two languages.[16] However, Christy Haubegger, the founder and former publisher of *Latina,* says, "Income is closely correlated with language ability. It's rare to see an affluent household that is Spanish-dependent."[17] (See Figure 2-2.)

As a result of the diversity of their roots, Hispanic Americans have varied tastes in food, clothing, and music. Advertisers should pay attention to these cultural subtleties, as Coca-Cola did when it ran three versions of an ad for Hispanics. Each ad featured the Coca-Cola logo and a can of Coke, along with the words "y su comida favorita" (and your favorite meal). But the food next to the Coke was changed to reflect different cultural preferences. Tacos were featured for the western Mexican American segment, pork loin for the southeastern Cuban American segment, and arroz con pollo (chicken and rice) for the northeastern Puerto Rican segment.

---

[12] Ibid., p. S7.
[13] "Hispanic Population Reaches All-Time High of 38.8 Million, New Census Bureau Estimates Show," U.S. Department of Commerce news release, 18 June 2003.
[14] Wellner, "Our True Colors," p. S8.
[15] Humphreys, "The Multicultural Economy 2003," p. 6.
[16] Wentz, "Reverse English," p. S2.
[17] Laurel Wentz, "Cultural Cross Over," *Advertising Age,* 7 July 2003, p. S2.

Figure 2-2
People from all over the country have stories about loved ones who were killed by a drunk driver. This urgent plea to stop friends from driving drunk runs in English and Spanish to reach all segments of Hispanic Americans.

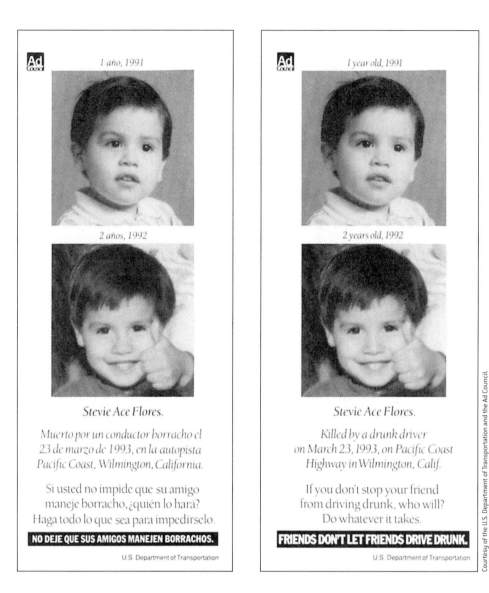

Although it's complex, the Hispanic American market is attractive to advertisers. *American Demographics* reports that Hispanics allocate 100 percent more of their budget on apparel for babies, 67 percent more on apparel for girls, 33 percent more for apparel for boys, and 22 percent more for apparel for men than the average American household. When it comes to food, Hispanics spend 75 percent more on pork and fresh fruits and vegetables. And like African Americans, they spend 91 percent more on rented dwellings than the average American household.[18]

---

[18] Wellner, "Our True Colors," p. S9.

Part of the reason for these expenditures is that Hispanic Americans tend to have larger families, with almost 3.5 people per household compared to the national average of just over 2.5.[19] To reach Hispanics successfully, advertisers should recognize the importance placed on the family and tradition. A radio station learned this lesson after it promoted a sweepstakes that offered a prize of two tickets to Disneyland and received a limited response from Hispanics. The reason? Hispanics didn't want to choose which family members should go.

Marketers must also pay close attention to the ages of their target groups. Nearly 70 percent of the Hispanic population is under age 35, representing more than $300 billion in purchasing power.[20] As you might expect, age plays a major role in shaping attitudes, styles of dress, and choice of music. But there's an interesting twist: The younger generation of Hispanics is often more in tune with their ancestry than their parents are. A special *Newsweek* poll reports those over age 35 are more likely to identify themselves as American, whereas those under age 35 are more likely to identify themselves as Hispanic or Latino. To reach Hispanic American youths, advertisers should stop thinking in terms of Generation X or Y and instead think Generation Ñ. Bill Teck, who coined the term Generation Ñ, explains: "If you know all the words to [the merengue hit] 'Abusadora' and 'Stairway to Heaven,' if you grew up on cafe, black beans and 'Three's Company,' . . . if you're thinking of borrowing one of your father's guayaberas, . . . you're Generation Ñ."[21]

Asian Americans

Although Asian Americans represent only 3.6 percent of the U.S. population, they are the nation's fastest-growing and most affluent minority group. The median income for Asian American households is $53,635, which is significantly higher than the $42,228 median income of all U.S. households. Asian Americans are also better educated than the overall U.S. population. Forty-four percent of Asian Americans have at least a bachelor's degree, compared to 24 percent of the general U.S. population. Furthermore, 17 percent have an advanced degree, compared to the national average of 9 percent.[22]

Despite the affluence of this market, advertisers have been slow to target Asian Americans because of the complexity of their varied languages and cultures. Many nationalities are included in this minority group, among them Chinese, Japanese, Korean, Filipino, Vietnamese, and Asian Indian. And there's not a common language among them. People of Chinese origin, the

---

[19] "While U.S. Households Contract, Homes Expand," AmeriStat release, March 2003.
[20] Mireya Navarro, "Advertisers Carve Out a New Segment," *New York Times,* 22 May 2003, nytimes.com.
[21] John Leland and Veronica Chambers, "Generation Ñ," *Newsweek,* 12 July 1999, p. 53.
[22] Wellner, "Our True Colors," p. S2.

largest subgroup, speak dozens of different dialects, with Mandarin, Cantonese, and Taiwanese being the most common. Elliot Kang of Kang & Lee Advertising explains, "If your father is Japanese and your mother is Korean and you lived in Taiwan and then your parents got divorced, moved to Los Angeles and your father took up with the Filipino woman next door and married her—well, that's almost like being Asian American."[23]

As you can imagine, horror stories about advertisers who have inadvertently alienated this market abound. Marlene L. Rossman points to a number of such stories. One advertiser wished Chinese Americans a "Year New Happy" rather than a "Happy New Year." Another used Korean models to target the Vietnamese community, oblivious to the fact that the two groups rarely look anything alike. And a footwear manufacturer depicted Japanese women performing foot binding; as Rossman observed, this not only stereotyped Japanese people as "Shogun" characters but also displayed the company's ignorance about Asian cultures, given that foot binding was practiced exclusively in China.[24]

InterTrend Communications, an agency specializing in the Asian market, offers the following tips on their Web site. From Japan: It's bad luck to write your name in red ink and good luck to dream about Mt. Fuji. From Vietnam: Never take a picture with only three people in it because it is very unlucky for all. From China/Taiwan/Hong Kong: Don't give clocks as gifts to Chinese people because they are a symbol of death and try to avoid dining with seven dishes because it symbolizes a funeral meal. From Korea: Never shake your foot because it drives out good fortune. Colors and numbers have special meaning. Red means prosperity, happiness, and luck to the Chinese, Japanese, and Vietnamese. White means death and bad fortune to the Vietnamese and Chinese. The number 7 means wealth to the Japanese and luck to Koreans. The number 8 means wealth and luck to the Chinese.

Although each nationality has distinct cultures and traditions, there are two important commonalities: the importance of family and tradition. In Asian cultures, it is inappropriate to call attention to oneself; therefore, tactful ads targeted at Asian Americans don't show an individual standing out from the crowd or achieving personal gain by using the product. Instead, culturally conscious ads focus on how the family or group benefits. With the great importance placed on tradition, "new and improved" claims are far less effective than those that stress a company's or product's many years of excellence.

Native Americans

The estimated 2.5 million Native Americans make up less than 1 percent of the nation's population, and nearly 42 percent earn less than $25,000 annu-

---

[23] Marketing to a New America Conference, New York City, 22 May 1996.
[24] Marlene L. Rossman, *Multicultural Marketing: Selling to a Diverse America* (New York: American Management Association, 1994).

ally.[25] As a result of their small size and limited spending power, few marketing efforts are aimed at this group.

Although companies don't often target this group in advertising campaigns, they use Native American names and symbolism. For example, Chrysler uses the name "Cherokee" for one of its jeeps, Land O' Lakes butter features a Native American on its package, and fans of the Atlanta Braves buy toy tomahawks to show their team support. Ironically, "Crazy Horse" malt liquor was named after the Sioux leader who was opposed to alcohol consumption among his people. Needless to say, these images are insulting to Native Americans.

Gail Baker Woods, author of *Advertising and Marketing to the New Majority,* points to the fact that Native Americans are becoming better educated and that tribes have begun to develop their own businesses and to use their land as an economic resource. If, as Woods says, these economic and educational trends continue for Native Americans, "marketers will surely find them in their search for new consumers."[26]

The Selig Center for Economic Growth seems to concur with Woods' prediction. Native American buyer power rose to $45.2 billion in 2003, up from $37.2 billion in 2000 and $19.3 billion in 1990. The Selig Center predicts that Native American buying clout will reach $63.1 billion in 2008.[27] Furthermore, the Survey of Minority-Owned Business Enterprises, released by the Census Bureau in 2001, showed that the number of Native American–owned firms increased more than 12 times faster than the number of U.S. firms and their receipts rose 4.5 times faster than those of all firms.[28]

How to Reach Ethnic Minorities

Savvy advertisers know several methods for reaching ethnic minorities:

1. *Feature minorities in starring roles, not just in the background.* In addition to making a positive connection to the ethnic group portrayed, research shows that general audiences favorably receive advertisements featuring minorities. Luke Visconti, partner at Diversity Inc., explains, "A white audience will say, 'That's a nice picture of a mother and child' and an African-American audience will say, 'Ahhh, an African-American mother and African-American child; this product gets me.'"[29]

2. *Seek the opinions of people who hail from the culture you are targeting.* However, be aware that traditional research methods may not work. For

[25] Wellner, "Our True Colors," p. S18.
[26] Gail Baker Woods, *Advertising and Marketing to the New Majority* (Belmont, CA: Wadsworth, 1995), p. 50.
[27] Humphreys, "The Multicultural Economy 2003," p. 4.
[28] Ibid.
[29] Stuart Elliott, "Campaigns for Black Consumers," *New York Times,* 13 June 2003, nytimes.com.

DIVERSE GOOFS: TRANSLATING AMERICAN ADVERTISING INTO OTHER LANGUAGES

- When Braniff Airlines touted its upholstery by saying "Fly in leather," it came out in Spanish as "Fly naked."

- Coors' slogan "Turn it loose" means "Suffer from diarrhea" in Spanish.

- When Vicks first introduced its cough drops in Germany, they discovered that Germans pronounce *v* as *f*, which made their trade name reminiscent of the German word for sexual penetration.

- Puffs tissues learned its lesson in Germany, too. "Puff" in German is a colloquial term for a brothel.

- The Chevy Nova never sold well in Spanish-speaking countries, perhaps because "No va" means "It does not go."

- When Pepsi's old campaign, "Come Alive. You're in the Pepsi Generation," was translated into Chinese, it announced that "Pepsi will bring your ancestors back from the grave."

- GM's "body by Fisher" translated, in some languages, into "corpse by Fisher," something you would not want associated with automotive design.

- Coke discovered problems in China when they used Chinese characters that, when pronounced, sounded like "Coca-Cola" but meant "Bite the wax tadpole."

example, a survey written in English won't get results that are representative of all American households because 15 percent of the U.S. population doesn't speak English at home. In addition, many immigrants are uncomfortable giving out information to strangers over the telephone or through the mail.

3. *Be sensitive to nuances in language.* It's not enough merely to translate the English copy of a campaign into another language. Frank Perdue found this out the hard way when someone unfamiliar with regional slang translated the line "It takes a tough man to make a tender chicken" into Spanish. The translation came out something like, "It takes a sexually stimulated man to make a chicken affectionate." For some other examples of mistranslations, see the box above.

   Spanish words can have different meanings, depending on national heritage. The word *bichos,* for example, means "bugs" to Mexicans and "a man's private parts" to Puerto Ricans. Imagine you were writing an ad for an insecticide and weren't aware of this little subtlety! Also, be aware of different uses of English words because they can mean different things to different groups. For example, sales of Stove Top stuffing improved among African Americans after the company realized this group uses the word "dressing," rather than "stuffing."

4. *Show the diversity of each group.* Advertisers from a few decades ago were guilty of showing light-skinned African American models in fashion ads and dark-skinned African Americans in ads promoting services. Their botched attempt to be inclusive helped further stereotyping.

5. *Learn about their heritage.* It's important to show respect for ethnic holidays, whether it's the Chinese New Year, Kwaanza, or Cinco de Mayo. It's also important to pay close attention to details and learn about preferences in food, icons, customs, and clothing. For example, McDonald's was praised for a commercial that featured a celebration that looked like a

simple birthday party to most viewers but was recognized by Hispanics as the quinceañera, the celebration of a girl's coming of age at 15.

The 50-Plus Market

Today, 38 percent of American adults are over age 49, and that group is expected to grow to 47 percent by 2020, according to the U.S. Census Bureau. Furthermore, those in the 50-plus population control 55 percent of the discretionary income in the United States and account for the majority of personal assets—upwards of 80 percent of the money in savings and loans and 70 percent of the net worth of U.S. households. The Federal Reserve Board reports family net worth peaks between the ages of 55 and 74, at an average of about $500,000.[30] (See Figure 2-3.)

Some of these older, affluent consumers choose to spend a portion of their wealth on second or third residences, luxury goods, or vacations. According to recent statistics, the 50-plus population purchases 48 percent of all luxury cars, 37 percent of all spa memberships, and 80 percent of all luxury trips. The Travel Industry Association of America estimates that people age 55-plus account for $130 billion in travel spending and 80 percent of luxury travel. "The name of the game is not $59 hotel rooms but $15,000 cruises," Richard M. Copland, president of the American Society of Travel Agents told the *New York Times*.[31]

Despite the wealth and spending power of older Americans, advertisers remain youth obsessed. "For a lot of brands we work with, it's sexier to advertise to the younger consumers who are trendier, much more fashion-forward, very social and very in the public eye," Melissa Pordy, senior VP-director at Zenith Media, told *Advertising Age*.[32]

Other marketers believe it's important to reach younger consumers who aren't yet brand loyal, rather than go after older consumers who are more set in their ways. However, a study conducted by AARP and Roper ASW found that brand loyalty varies more by product category than by age. For example, 18 percent of consumers ages 18–44 were brand loyal to a particular airline, compared to 17 percent in the 45 to 54 age bracket, 22 percent for those 55–64, and 17 percent for people 65 and older. DVD/video players had a 27 percent brand loyalty among 18- to 44-year-olds, 23 percent among those 45–54, 18 percent among those 55–64, and 22 percent among consumers 65 and older.[33]

Ignoring the older market is bad enough, but some advertisers even go so far as to insult older people by portraying them as doddering and senile.

---

[30] Peter Francese, "Older and Wealthier," *American Demographics,* November 2002, pp. 40–41.
[31] Harriet Edelson, "Appealing to Older Travelers' Wanderlust, and Wallets," *New York Times,* 25 May 2003, nytimes.com.
[32] Hillary Chura, "Ripe Old Age," *Advertising Age,* 13 May 2002, p. 16.
[33] Ibid., p. 16.

Figure 2-3
The king of rock 'n roll lives in the hearts of many people, particularly those in the 50-plus set. This humorous ad laughs with the audience, not at them. After all, the last time someone saw Elvis, he couldn't fit into his uniform, either.

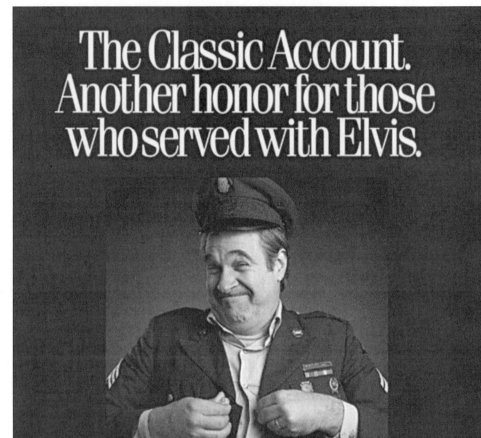

The Classic Account. Another honor for those who served with Elvis.

If you're turning 50, you may have buttoned on a uniform about the time Elvis helped to defend us.

Whether you did—or whether it still fits—isn't the point, of course. It's that now South Carolina National has a banking package that fits you very well.

And the only requirement is that you're 50 or older.

If you are, you're eligible for free checking, free checks, free travelers checks and money orders.

Interest on every dollar in your account. Discounts on a safe deposit box. A special Health Care CD. And more.

You can even apply for a special SCN Palmetto VISA® card.

Our Classic Account is the kind of honor most banks won't offer till you turn 55. But we figure it's time someone gave special consideration to the generation that grew up with rock 'n roll.

See your SCN banker. Or call Ann Singer at 1-800-922-5560. (771-3939 in Columbia.)

FLEXBANKING℠
South Carolina National
Equal Opportunity Lender. Member FDIC.

Courtesy of Flex Banking.

Fifty-six percent of respondents in an *Adweek* Online Web poll agreed that when seniors appear in advertising it's usually as an unflattering stereotype.[34] A commercial for Midas was pulled after the company received complaints from adults of all ages. In the commercial, an older woman learns about Midas' lifetime guarantee, takes off her shirt and asks, "What can you do with these?" A commercial for Boost Mobile showed an old man falling off a skateboard. The supertitle on the screen explains the joke, "Boost Mobile. Designed for young people. But it's just more fun showing old people."

Tips to Reach the Older Market

1. *Don't think of older people as just one market.* Think about some of the older people you know: grandparents, neighbors, professors, and community leaders. Chances are these people are quite different from one another. They have different political views, different senses of humor, different lifestyles, and so on. Like any group, the older population is composed of people with varied incomes, education levels, ethnic backgrounds, and life experiences. Using one message to reach all these people is about as absurd as saying one message will work for all people ages 18–49.

2. *Don't specify age.* Research has shown most older people feel younger than their birth certificate indicates. As Bernard Baruch said, "To me, old age is fifteen years older than I am." Several years ago, an advertising campaign featured the claim "the first shampoo created for hair over 40." It bombed. The problem? Younger people refused to buy a product aimed at older people, and older people didn't want to be reminded they had older hair.

3. *Cast models who reflect the way your audience feels.* Use models who portray an upbeat, positive image, not those who reinforce the negative stereotypes of frailty and senility. But don't go to the opposite extreme. Although you may be tempted to show a person in his 80s who bungee-jumps, most older people won't identify with this portrayal.

   Cast models who represent the age your audience feels. Remember how you identified with the "big" kids when you were younger? Well, the opposite is true as you get older. Most older people see themselves as ten to fifteen years younger than their birth certificates indicate. Therefore, use models who are younger than your target audience.

4. *Tell the whole story.* Although commercials with fast editing cuts and very little copy may appeal to younger audiences, older audiences prefer a narrative style, with a beginning, a middle, and an end. As Grey Advertising summed it up, this generation is MGM, not MTV.

---

[34] Jack Feuer, "Pride and Prejudice," *Adweek,* 28 October 2002, p. 9.

When writing copy, give facts, not fluff. After years of shopping, older people are not going to be fooled into buying your product simply because you tell them that it's "new" or "the best." After all, these folks remember product flops, and they want facts to back up your claims. Give them a compelling reason to try your product, and they'll be willing to read lengthy copy or listen to a detailed pitch.

5. *Set your type in at least 12-point to make it more legible.* Ad legend Jerry Della Femina joked about small type on packages to make his point at a creative conference, "I rubbed bath gel into my beard and followed it with shampoo, thinking it was conditioner."[35]

6. *Don't remind older people of their vulnerability.* It's a fact of life: Arthritis, high blood pressure, heart problems, and other ailments bother more older people than younger people. However, older people know they have aches and pains without being reminded by you. Rather than dwell on the problems, your advertising should show how your product offers solutions.

7. *Show older people as they are, happy with themselves.* Show them enjoying life, playing with their grandchildren, volunteering their time, starting new hobbies, and learning new things. Advertisements for Fox Hill Village, a retirement community in Massachusetts, used to show smiling retirees on balconies admiring the beautiful landscape. But when the community ran a series of ads featuring Ben Franklin, Clara Barton, Noah Webster, and other individuals who became famous during their later years, inquiries went up 25 percent.

8. *Try an ageless approach.* Lee Lynch, founder and CEO of Carmichael Lynch, points to Harley-Davidson's campaign where the rider is faceless, allowing people to project themselves into the image, regardless of age.[36]

People with Disabilities

An estimated 50 million Americans have disabilities, and nearly 10 million are disabled enough that they need help with activities of daily living.[37] Once nearly invisible in ads, people with disabilities are starting to have starring roles. McDonald's showed that people with disabilities can work and be productive citizens through a heartwarming commercial narrated by an employee named Mike, who has Down syndrome. Wal-Mart's advertising features employees and customers in wheelchairs, and one of their TV commercials stars a hearing-impaired employee signing to a deaf customer.

---

[35] "The Fine Print," *Adweek,* 25 November 2002, p. 34.
[36] Eleftheria Parpis, "Shades of Gray," *Adweek,* 28 October 2002, p. 19.
[37] Martin Krossel, "Selling to the Disabled Can Mean More Than Ads," *New York Times,* 20 November 2001, p. C4.

Although many people praise these ads, some question the motives behind them. Bob Garfield, a critic for *Advertising Age,* states that jumping from not showing people with disabilities at all to portraying them as super-human or as tokens does not help them or the advertiser in the long run. Screenwriter Mark Moss, who ended up in a wheelchair after a diving accident, told the *Boston Globe,* "Advertisers know that using people with disabilities is politically correct and a viable way to catch people's attention. I look at the phenomenon like I do politicians kissing babies. It's good for the babies . . . it's good for the politicians . . . but we can't be blamed for looking at it with cynicism."[38]

As with any target group, it's important to ask group members what they think. For example, a major fast-food chain ran a newspaper ad with the headline "Introducing our new easy-to-read menu," which was printed over a design that looked like Braille. A blind student appropriately asked, "Why didn't they actually print the ad in Braille? If they printed it on a heavier stock and inserted it into the paper, then I could keep it for future reference."

Gays and Lesbians

The policy of "Don't ask, don't tell" reaches far beyond the U.S. military. Even the all-knowing U.S. Census Bureau doesn't ask. As a result, there are varying opinions on this market's size, but it is estimated to be between 6 and 10 percent of the population.[39] Annual spending power is estimated to be $450 billion, according to Witeck-Combs Communications.[40]

Data from gay publications illustrate the importance of this market to advertisers. Six in ten readers of gay and lesbian newspapers have household incomes over $60,000, and *The Advocate* reports the median household income for their readers is $90,000.[41] Furthermore, Simmons notes that this market segment is exceptionally loyal, with 89 percent reporting they would buy products or services that advertised in gay publications. A spokesman for Hiram Walker & Sons confirmed this, telling *Advertising Age,* "I have a file of letters an inch or two thick from gay consumers thanking us and vowing their loyalty. A straight consumer wouldn't take the time and say thank you for validating us."[42]

Another plus to advertisers is what Stephanie Blackwood, cofounder of Double Platinum, calls the "*Will & Grace* spillover." She explains, "First, an upscale gay male in New York City or Los Angeles buys a new product. He then influences his urban, educated female friends, who may work in the

---

[38] Maggie Farley, "Ads with a Soul Touch Untapped Market," *Boston Globe,* 6 July 1992, p. 10.

[39] Nicci Brown and Margaret Costello, "Surveying an Untapped Market," *Syracuse University Magazine,* Spring 2002, p. 13.

[40] Claire Atkinson, "Marketers Warm Up to Gay Audience," *Advertising Age,* 4 August 2003, p. 26.

[41] Sandra Yin, "Coming Out in Print," *American Demographics,* February 2003, p. 20.

[42] Nancy Coltun Webster, "Playing to Gay Segments Opens Doors to Marketers," *Advertising Age,* 30 May 1994, pp. 5–6.

fields of communications, fashion or the media, to buy that product. These women, in turn, talk to each other about what to buy, where to eat and even what to buy a boyfriend or father, influencing purchase choices. The result: What began as a gay-targeted marketing campaign becomes an efficient and affordable way to promote a product in the mainstream."[43]

Lessons That Apply to All Segments

Whatever group you are targeting, certain basic principles apply, including the following:

1. *Look at the whole person, not one demographic characteristic.* To understand your target audience, you must factor in other demographic aspects, as well as psychographic issues such as values, attitudes, personality, and lifestyle. For example, a middle-aged Hispanic American business executive living in the suburbs is likely to have very different attitudes from an inner-city Hispanic American youth living below the poverty line or a single, working Hispanic American mother earning minimum wage. Second- or third-generation Americans have different views than recent immigrants. African Americans who formed their core values before the 1960s will have one outlook, those who were a part of the civil rights movement will have another, and teenagers will have still another.

2. *Avoid stereotypes.* Taco Bell offended Mexican Americans with its border search commercial because it looked like a search for illegal immigrants. The state of Pennsylvania offended Chinese Americans with its state lottery promotion that featured the line "No tickee—no money." Dow Chemical insulted African Americans with a commercial in which a robust black woman exclaimed, "Ooh-wee!" because it was a reminder of the black mammy stereotype. Native American activists protested when a brewer tried to introduce a malt liquor called "Crazy Horse." Unfortunately, this list of insulting ads could go on and on. Your job is to change that.

   Be wary even of "positive" stereotypes. Not all African Americans are great athletes, musicians, or dancers, yet advertising often portrays them this way. Likewise, not all Asian Americans are good at math or science. In fact, when figure skater Kristi Yamaguchi won the Olympic gold medal, the *New York Times* printed an anonymous comment: "We are not all math or science wizards or laundry operators or restaurant owners, but skaters, architects, writers. And more. And less." The same holds true for every group that you'll ever want to reach in your advertising.

3. *Laugh with them, not at them.* Humor does have a place—if it doesn't rely on insulting stereotypes. To test whether your humor might be

[43] Yin, "Coming Out in Print," p. 19.

insulting to some group, consider replacing one of the characters with a person from a different market segment. For example, if you wanted to make sure customers remembered your client's name, you might be tempted to create a humorous commercial featuring an older person who is hard of hearing and needs to have everything repeated, as Country Time Lemonade did. Or you might feature an older woman who keeps forgetting the name and needs to be constantly reminded, as another company did. However, would it be as funny if a young, physically active college student couldn't hear or remember the name? Probably not. What if you replaced the older woman with a college student who was high on drugs? Would it be a fair portrayal of college students? Of course not.

4. *Make relevant ties to their special causes.* Consider donating a portion of your sales to causes that are dear to their hearts, such as AIDS research, the Council on Aging, the Special Olympics, the Rape Crisis Center, the Native American Arts Foundation, the Sickle Cell Disease Foundation, the United Negro College Fund, or ASPIRA, a scholarship fund for Hispanics. However, make it a long-term commitment, not a one-shot deal.

5. *Test your ads on a member of the target audience.* You may find an embarrassing mistake in time to correct it before it runs. For example, the Publix grocery chain might have saved itself from the embarrassment of wishing their customers "a quiet, peaceful Yom Kippur" right below an announcement of a sale on center cut pork chops and fresh pork shoulder picnics if they had double-checked with someone who is Jewish.

6. *Show diversity in your ads.* As America becomes more diverse, it's not only the right thing to do but also the smart thing to do. Figure 2-4 is a good example of an ad that reaches a diverse audience.

Suggested Activities

1. Watch 2 hours of prime-time television and record the way the groups mentioned in this chapter are portrayed. How many are in starring roles? How many reflect stereotypes? What products are they selling?

2. Compare print ads for fashion, liquor, and travel that appear in general-interest magazines (such as *Cosmopolitan, Vogue, Sports Illustrated,* and *Newsweek*) to those that appear in special-interest magazines (such as *Essence* and *Ebony,* which target African Americans; *Latina* and *People en Español,* which target Hispanic Americans; and *New Choices* and *Modern Maturity,* which target older people). Are the ads similar? If not, comment on the differences in visuals and text that appear to reflect different targeted audiences.

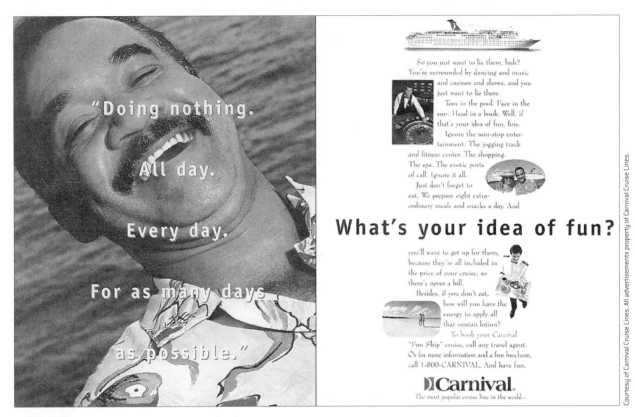

Figure 2-4
Carnival Cruise Lines realizes that people's idea of fun is quite diverse. While you might view the campaign as a prime example of niche marketing, in reality it expands the target audience each time it asks, "What's *your* idea of fun?"

3. Choose an ad (such as for toothpaste, soap, or potato chips) and redo the ad to appeal directly to an ethnic minority.

4. Create an ad selling jeans to people over age 50.

5. Look at automobile ads from recent decades and comment on the changes in the way people are portrayed. (Your library should have bound editions of back issues of magazines such as *Time* and *Newsweek*.)

Search Online! Discover More About Targeting

Use InfoTrac College Edition to discover more about diversity. Try these phrases and others for Key Words and Subject Guide searches: *ethnic consumers, ethnic buying habits, African American consumer, Hispanic American consumer, Asian American consumer, Native American consumer, 50-plus consumer, disabled consumer, gay and lesbian consumer.*

Figure 2-4 (continued)

For more information about diversity in the United States, visit the following Web sites:

U.S. Census: www.census.gov

Economic trends: www.selig.uga.edu

Asian market: www.intertrend.com

Hispanic market: www.hispanicbusiness.com *and* www.ahaa.org

Gay market: www.commercialcloset.com

Older market: www.aarp.org

Tide en Español

Some brands linger for decades and slowly fade into obscurity. But if you take a brand and continually extend it with new technologies, forms, and benefits without losing sight of the original, you can run with it for years.

Procter & Gamble has done this with Tide detergent, now celebrating more than 50 years as the leader in its category. Tide has endured because, as a corporate spokesperson puts it, "It is kept up-to-date, meeting consumer needs and doing so in ways that provide steadily improving performance and value." Of course, advertising must keep pace with such changes. A 1953 advertisement for Tide—showing an apron-clad woman high kicking with joy as she holds a box of Tide—was headlined, "You never had it so clean. Never before Tide was it possible to get your family wash so clean." Great positioning for its time, but we're in a new millennium, remember?

Women work outside the home today. They need to manage home and family as well as workplace tasks. With flextime, some work extra hours each day so that they can take a day off during the week to shop, do laundry, and catch the school play. This takes planning. Lots of it. Choosing a detergent brand is a comparatively minor issue in their lives, but time is of the essence.

So the new Tide ads speak to today's woman. They speak with humor, because she appreciates it. They acknowledge that life is full of problems, some of which their detergent can solve. They don't promise results; they imply them: "Recess. Gym class. Food fights. Any questions?" reads one in English.

Idiomatic phrases don't translate well. So for its Hispanic campaign, the words, as well as the language, are different:

"La salsa se baila, no se viste" translates as "Salsa is meant to be danced, not worn," which plays on the fact that salsa is also a dance.

"¿Para que usar la servilleta cuando existe la camiseta?" translates as "Why do you need a napkin when you have a T-shirt?"—a play on the Spanish words servilleta (napkin) and camiseta (T-shirt).

Courtesy of Conhill Advertising.

A third ad uses the rhyme "De la cuchara a la boca, se cae la sopa" ("From the table to the mouth, the soup spills out"), which is an old saying used to teach table manners to children.

The campaign, without merely translating English copy, has the same smart tone as the general-market campaign, but was obviously created for the Hispanic market.

Using the person's life as the context of the message can be a strong way to maintain top-of-mind awareness, especially for established brands. In any language, Tide has proved that.

FACT FINDING:
THE BASIS FOR EFFECTIVE CREATIVE WORK

3

An ad for Chippers Funeral Home in Perth, Australia, features a close-up of an elephant's eye with a tear streaming down. The headline reads, "It Is Not Uncommon To See Elephants Weep Openly At Funerals." The copy goes on to describe the "humanity" that elephants extend to dying members of their family. When an elephant dies, the extended family circles it. Slowly, with their heads hanging gloomily, they walk around the body several times before standing still. The bereaved then place branches, leaves, and clumps of grass on the body of their dead relative to form a grave. Occasionally, the elephants also weep.

This poignant ad didn't just write itself. It happened because the agency, Vinten Browning, researched the difficult subjects of death and grieving before writing a single word.

Whether you're trying to understand how people grieve or how people wash their laundry, research is one of the most important stages in advertising. Thorough searches can help you discover what makes people "tick," uncover new uses for products, learn about new market areas, and spot new trends. By doing a complete job in the research stage, you'll find it's much easier to come up with the big idea and write convincing copy. As advertising legend Ed McCabe shares, "When you are ready to write, it should be automatic, fueled by knowledge so comprehensive that advertising almost writes itself. Only with absolute knowledge of a subject can you

QUESTIONS THAT MAY LEAD TO THE BIG IDEA

INDUSTRY
Who is the brand leader?

How long have they held that position?

What are the trends in the industry?

Does your brand set the trends or follow them?

Are there any pending issues (for example, legislation or mergers) that may affect your brand's future?

How does the nation's economic and diplomatic climate affect sales?

Are there any emerging industries that may affect sales in the future?

COMPANY
How long has the company been in business?

What are the high and low points in the company's history?

What is the corporate philosophy?

How has the media covered the company?

How is the company involved in the community?

Is the company known for its product innovations?

Who are key personnel/managers?

Which company employees have direct contact with customers?

How many brands does your company offer?

How important is your brand to the company?

BRAND
What do current customers feel about your brand?

To what extent does your brand match up with consumers' needs, wants, problems, and interests?

In what ways does your brand exceed consumer expectations?

CONSUMER ANALYSIS
What are the demographic characteristics of the current customers? Competitive customers? Prospects (emerging users)?

What are the geographic characteristics?

What are the psychographics?

When and how often do consumers use the product?

When and how often do consumers buy the product?

How do they use the end product/service?

How do they make the buying decisions?

What information is most important?

Where do they get their information?

Who are your best customers?

COMPETITION
What are competitors doing for the same service/product?

How can we do it better?

What do competitors' previous advertising campaigns look like?

What worked? What didn't?

How do consumers perceive the current campaigns?

---

hope to transcend the banality of mere facts and experience the freedom of insight."[1]

So where do you start?

Step 1: State Your Question(s)

Before you do your research, you need to define the question or problem you're investigating. For example, you may want to know who is the most likely prospect for the product. What real or perceived differences make your brand better than a competitor's? How should this be communicated? How do customers perceive the current campaign? By carefully defining your question(s), you avoid gathering irrelevant information and wasting time. (See the box above for additional questions you may want answered.)

---

[1] Warren Berger, *Advertising Today* (London: Phaidon Press Limited, 2001), p. 120.

Step 2: Dig Through Secondary Sources

Once you've got a clear statement of the question, look for answers from information that already exists in company records, trade associations, libraries, and on Web sites.

Company Records

Annual reports   In addition to financial data, an annual report contains information about the corporate philosophy, the competition, and future goals. However, even any bad news in such reports usually has an optimistic slant to it. Therefore, annual reports should be primarily used as a starting point.

Customer profiles   If you've ever filled out a product warranty card, entered a sweepstakes, applied for a credit card, or sent for a rebate, you've supplied important information, such as your age, sex, income, education, family size, and living situation (see Figure 3-1). You may also have been asked to state how you learned about the product, where you bought it, and whether you have owned that brand before. Your answers become part of a database that helps marketers know how to reach you and others like you.

Public relations files   The public relations department collects press clippings and satisfied-customer letters that are sometimes so glowing that they warrant being reprinted as an ad. And, with a bit of inspiration, even negative publicity can be turned to the client's advantage. For example, after the media ran stories claiming that Leona Helmsley was a tyrant to her hotel employees, her advertising agency turned her insistence on perfection into a positive attribute. One ad showed letters from satisfied guests with the headline "She knows people talk about her. She'll even show you what they say."

Technical reports   Granted, much of the information in these reports may sound like gobbledygook to the average reader, but you never know when you'll happen on the perfect line. For instance, Harley Procter uncovered the "99 and 44/100% pure®" claim for Ivory soap from a chemist's report, and David Ogilvy wrote an ad for Rolls Royce using an engineer's statement: "At 60 miles an hour the loudest noise in this new Rolls Royce comes from the electric clock." But don't think you'll get instant results. Ogilvy spent three weeks reading about Rolls Royce before he wrote his classic ad. Procter had to do a little math to arrive at the famous slogan. The chemist reported that the ingredients that did not fall into the category of pure soap equaled 56/100%, hardly a line that would help sell a product for more than 100 years. Figure 3-2 shows how facts can make interesting reading.

Web site   The company's Web site is a great starting point because it gives an overview of the history of the organization, profiles key employees, highlights its product line, and allows customers to ask questions, download tips, play games, and so on. Much like an annual report, the Web site presents the

Figure 3-1

A classic warranty card designed for manufacturers by the Polk Company, one of the nation's leading information gatherers, indicates the scope and nature of data that a majority of consumers are willing to share with companies. The form allows space for "Product & Purchase Related Questions" on the left side, but the balance of the questions (usually answered by an overwhelming majority of recipients), cover demographics, lifestyles, shopping habits, and ownership or preferences for pets, computers, Internet services, and large/tall sizes, among other things. Imagine how valuable such information might be, not only to the company whose product the consumer purchased but also for thousands of other companies that use Polk's data services.

Figure 3-1 (continued)

Please send products and
other correspondence to:

||| ||

Multi-Dimensional Intelligence™

**PO BOX 17XXXX
DENVER CO 80217-XXXX**

Standard 7.3

(7/96)

Please fold here.

19. To help us understand our customers' lifestyles, please indicate the interests and activities in which *you* or *your spouse* enjoy participating on a *regular* basis.

01. ☐ Bicycling	21. ☐ Automotive Work	41. ☐ Our Nation's Heritage
02. ☐ Golf	22. ☐ Electronics	42. ☐ Real Estate Investments
03. ☐ Physical Fitness/Exercise	23. ☐ Home Workshop/Do-It-Yourself	43. ☐ Stock/Bond Investments
04. ☐ Running/Jogging	24. ☐ Recreational Vehicles	44. ☐ Mutual Funds
05. ☐ Snow Skiing	25. ☐ Listen to Records/Tapes/CDs	45. ☐ Entering Sweepstakes
06. ☐ Tennis	26. ☐ Avid Book Reading	46. ☐ Casino Gambling
07. ☐ Camping/Hiking	27. ☐ Bible/Devotional Reading	47. ☐ Science Fiction
08. ☐ Fishing	28. ☐ Health/Natural Foods	48. ☐ Wildlife/Environmental Issues
09. ☐ Hunting/Shooting	29. ☐ Photography	49. ☐ Dieting/Weight Control
10. ☐ Power Boating	30. ☐ Home Decorating/Furnishing	50. ☐ Science/New Technology
11. ☐ Horseback Riding	31. ☐ Attending Cultural/Arts Events	51. ☐ Self-Improvement
12. ☐ Sailing	32. ☐ Fashion Clothing	52. ☐ Walking for Health
13. ☐ House Plants	33. ☐ Fine Art/Antiques	53. ☐ Watching Sports on TV
14. ☐ Grandchildren	34. ☐ Foreign Travel	54. ☐ Community/Civic Activities
15. ☐ Needlework/Knitting	35. ☐ Cruise Ship Vacations	55. ☐ Home Video Games
16. ☐ Flower Gardening	36. ☐ Travel in USA	56. ☐ Motorcycles
17. ☐ Vegetable Gardening	37. ☐ Gourmet Cooking/Fine Foods	57. ☐ Watch Cable TV
18. ☐ Sewing	38. ☐ Wines	58. ☐ Home Video Recording
19. ☐ Crafts	39. ☐ Coin/Stamp Collecting	59. ☐ Moneymaking Opportunities
20. ☐ Buy Pre-Recorded Videos	40. ☐ Collectibles/Collections	60. ☐ Current Affairs/Politics

20. Using the numbers in the above list, please indicate your 3 most important activities: |__|__| |__|__| |__|__|

21. Please check all that apply to your household.

01. ☐ Shop by Catalog/Mail	06. ☐ Own a Compact Disc Player	11. ☐ Subscribe to an Online/Internet Service
02. ☐ Member of Frequent Flyer Program	07. ☐ Own a Camcorder	12. ☐ Own an IBM or Compatible Computer
03. ☐ Donate to Charitable Causes	08. ☐ Have a Dog	13. ☐ Own an Apple/Macintosh Computer
04. ☐ Wear Women's Large/Tall Sizes	09. ☐ Have a Cat	14. ☐ Own a CD-ROM
05. ☐ Wear Men's Large/Tall Sizes	10. ☐ Own a Cellular Phone	15. ☐ Speak Spanish at Home

Thanks for taking the time to fill out this questionnaire. Your answers will be used for market research studies and reports. They will also allow you to receive important mailings and special offers from a number of fine companies whose products and services relate directly to the specific interests, hobbies, and other information indicated above. Through this selective program, you will be able to obtain more information about activities in which you are involved and less about those in which you are not. Please check here if, for some reason, you would prefer *not* to participate in this opportunity.

If you have comments or suggestions about our product, please write to:
Customer Service • XXYZZ Inc. • 123 Road Ave. • Anywhere, USA 12345

Please seal with tape. Do not staple.

Figure 3-2
Facts can be fun, particularly if they have an unexpected twist at the end.

company's best face. Therefore, keep in mind you'll need to do additional digging to uncover insights for your campaign.

Trade Associations

Name a trade or area of interest, and there's bound to be an association for it, staffed with knowledgeable people. Some of the more offbeat associations include the Flying Funeral Directors of America, the Committee to Abolish Legal-Sized Files, and the International Barbed Wire Collectors Association.

There's even an association of associations, the American Society of Association Executives. To find an association for your client's product or service, refer to the *Encyclopedia of Associations* published by Gale, available at most libraries.

Libraries

A good place to start is with a guidebook to business information, such as *Business Information Sources,* the *Handbook of Business Information,* and *Marketing Information: A Professional Reference Guide.*

Indexes to articles in periodicals   You probably used the *Readers' Guide to Periodical Literature* in high school. It's a good index of articles from general-interest magazines, but it's not likely to list much on advertising or in-depth product coverage. Therefore, you'll want to consult the following:

- *Business Periodicals Index* is a subject index of more than 300 business journals including *Advertising Age, Adweek, American Demographics, Journal of Advertising Research, Marketing Communications, Sales and Marketing Management,* and the *Wall Street Journal.*
- *Communication Abstracts* is arranged by subjects such as advertising, mass communications, journalism, and public communication.
- *Guide to Industry Special Issues* is an index of special issues of regularly published business journals including *Advertising Age* and *Adweek.*
- *Topicator* is a classified index of journals in the fields of advertising, communications, and marketing.

Sources of statistical information   The U.S. Government Printing Office publishes thousands of books and pamphlets, many of which are available at your library. A quick way to find these publications is in the *Subject Bibliography Index,* which lists more than 15,000 different government publications. Specific sources of statistical information include the following:

- *County and City Data Book* gives information on states, counties, and cities in the United States on a variety of subjects including education, labor, income, housing, and retail and wholesale trade.
- *Statistical Abstract of the United States* is considered the "bible" of social, political, industrial, and economic statistical information of the United States. It contains information on everything from the retail sales of men's fragrances to the number of eye operations performed.
- *U.S. Census* is totally updated every ten years and provides population, ancestry, marital status, education, geographic mobility, occupation, income, and other demographic data. One of the few things it doesn't report, because of the constitutional separation of church and state, is religious data.
- *U.S. Industrial Outlook* gives statistics on the current situations and long-term prospects for approximately 50 major industries.

Syndicated market data   A number of research companies offer subscribers a detailed look at the lifestyles and shopping habits of various U.S. markets. Here's a sample:

- *Editor and Publisher Market Guide* gives market information on U.S. and Canadian cities in which a daily newspaper is published. It includes data on population, number of households, disposable personal income, and retail sales.

- *Information Resources, Inc.* (IRI) is a syndicated tracking service that integrates scanner sales, feature ad, and coupon, display, and price data from supermarkets, drugstores, and mass merchandisers.

- *Lifestyle Market Analyst* breaks down the U.S. population geographically and demographically and includes information on the interests, hobbies, and activities popular in each geographic and demographic market.

- *MediaMark Research* (often referred to as MRI) provides information on heavy, medium, and light users of various product categories and specific brands and gives the media usage patterns of these groups.

- *Nielsen National Marketing Survey*, available through A. C. Nielsen Company, provides share-of-market data for products sold in supermarkets, drugstores, and mass merchandisers.

- *Prizm,* available through Claritas, classifies each zip code into one of 62 lifestyle clusters, with descriptors such as "Red White & Blues" and "New Homesteaders."

- *Scarborough Research* surveys 75 markets and provides information about local consumer-shopping patterns, demographics, and lifestyle activities.

- *Simmons Study of Media and Markets* (SMRB) is one of the most widely used sources of product usage and media audience data. Similar to MRI, SMRB provides market information on 750 product and service categories.

- *Survey of Buying Power* ranks zip code areas in special characteristics such as Asian American population, children under 5 years of age, and households in mobile homes. It also gives 5-year projections and percentage of change for population, buying income, and retail spending in all U.S. counties.

- *VALS 2,* developed by SRI, groups consumers into eight categories: (1) Actualizers are successful, sophisticated, active, take-charge people who have high self-esteem; (2) experiencers are young, vital, impulsive, and rebellious and seek variety, excitement, and the offbeat; (3) strivers seek motivation, self-definition, and approval from others; (4) fulfilleds are mature, satisfied, well-educated professionals; (5) achievers are successful, work-oriented, in control of their lives, and respectful of authority; (6) believers are conservative, have deeply rooted moral codes, and modest income and education; (7) makers are suspicious of new ideas and unimpressed by physical possessions; and (8) strugglers are poor, ill educated, and low skilled.

Computer databases and online services Your library subscribes to a variety of services that enable you to access information from all over the world. Here are a few that are useful for business searches:

- *ABI-Inform* provides coverage of business and management periodicals. Areas covered are advertising, competitive intelligence, new product development, marketing, and sales promotion.
- *Business Periodicals on Disc* contains citations with abstracts to articles appearing in more than 900 business periodicals.
- *Compact Disclosure* contains complete Securities and Exchange Commission (SEC) filings for 12,500 publicly held companies.
- *InfoTrac Business Index* contains more than 3 million citations, some with complete articles from more than 1000 business journals and news sources.
- *Lexis-Nexis* provides full text documents from more than 5600 news, business, legal, and reference publications.
- *Newspaper Abstracts* is an index, with abstracts, to the *Wall Street Journal, New York Times, Los Angeles Times, Boston Globe, Atlanta Constitution/Journal, Chicago Tribune, Christian Science Monitor,* and *USA Today.*

Web Sites

The following is a sampling of Web sites that contain information useful to advertisers:

- *Advertising Research Foundation* (www.arfsite.org) gives a synopsis of past issues of the *Journal of Advertising Research* and lets you purchase reprints online.
- *Business Researcher's Interests* (www.brint.com) offers more than 2000 links to online research tools, including newspapers, full-text databases, online libraries, and free reports.
- *BusinessWire* (www.businesswire.com) is an electronic distributor of press releases and business news.
- *Census Bureau* (www.census.gov) allows you to search the U.S. Census Bureau database, read press releases, check the population clock, and listen to clips from its radio broadcasts.
- *CNN Money* (www.money.cnn.com) is the Web site for CNN's business and finance.
- *Guerilla Marketing Online* (www.gmarketing.com) lets you review marketing tips and examine case studies.
- *Hoover's Online* (www.hoovers.com) provides a database of detailed profiles for publicly traded companies.

- *Research-It!* (www.iTools.com) allows you to search through directories of more than 50,000 specialized topics.
- *Stat-USA* (www.stat-usa.gov) offers access to databases on business- and trade-related subjects.
- *World Advertising Research Center* (www.warc.com) allows users to locate studies in advertising and marketing that have been published anywhere in the world through its search engine.

Most business publications have electronic versions, including the following:

- *Advertising Age* (www.adage.com)
- *Adweek* (www.adweek.com)
- *American Demographics* (www.demographics.com)
- *Business Week* (www.businessweek.com)
- *Forbes* (www.forbes.com)
- *Fortune* (www.fortune.com)
- *Media Life* (medialifemagazine.com)

Step 3: Conduct Primary Research

Once you've exhausted the secondary sources, you will likely find you still have unanswered questions that warrant primary research. Here's where observation, focus groups, surveys, and experiments come in.

Firsthand Experience

Try it. Taste it. Touch it. Hear it. Smell it. What were your perceptions of the product before you used it? How about now that you've used it? Try the competition. What are the competitors' weaknesses? Your client's strengths? Why would you choose to buy your client's brand?

Firsthand experience gives you important insights that may lead to the big idea. The idea for the memorable line "Two scoops of raisins in a box of Kellogg's Raisin Bran" came from an art director who emptied a box of the cereal onto his kitchen table and counted the raisins.

However, be careful not to assume that everyone thinks or behaves the same way you do. You may have a more sophisticated understanding of the product, you may have a bias toward your client, or you may not be part of the target market. Therefore, other research methods are essential.

Surveys

Surveys, one of the most common primary-research methods, ask current or prospective customers questions about product usage, awareness of ad campaigns, attitudes toward competing brands, and so on. Surveys are conducted online and by mail, telephone, or personal interview.

Whichever method you use to conduct your survey, be certain to test the survey on a small sample to ascertain whether there are leading or ambiguous questions. When a team of advertising students wanted to determine people's awareness level of the American Red Cross slogan "Help Can't Wait," they tested a survey that asked respondents to match five nonprofit organizations to five slogans. Almost all the slogans were correctly matched. But did this mean people really knew the "Help Can't Wait" slogan, or was it a fluke? To find out, the students conducted another test, using seven slogans and five organizations. The results were quite different. The fictitious slogan "The Life Blood of America" was matched to the Red Cross by 65 percent of respondents. Why the different results? In the first survey, respondents could guess the correct answer through the process of elimination. The second survey prevented the respondents from covering a genuine lack of awareness.

The structure of your question can also give different results. In the American Red Cross example, respondents were given a multiple-choice question, an example of a closed-end question. As you may imagine, the results may be even more dramatic if the students chose to use an open-ended question where the respondents are asked to answer in their own words.

In addition to checking for ambiguous and misleading questions, keep the following points in mind when you design a survey:

1. Keep the survey short.
2. Use simple language.
3. Include complete instructions.
4. Put easy-to-answer questions first.
5. Ask general questions before detailed ones.
6. Save potentially embarrassing questions, such as about income, for the end.

Focus Groups

Invite five to ten people who are typical of your target market to discuss their feelings about your product. You'll want to get permission to record the session, and you will need a moderator who encourages everyone to speak and who keeps the discussion on track. Because participants are urged to say what's on their minds, important issues may be uncovered.

Focus-group participants complained about the scratchy tags sewn inside undershirts. So Hanes did something about it. They introduced the tagless T-shirt that promises no itch. Commercials feature men wriggling, squirming, and contorting themselves while Hanes spokesman, Michael Jordan, looks on and says, "It's gotta be the tag," in a spin on his famous Nike line, "It's gotta be the shoes." Consumers immediately responded. Sales of tagless

T-shirts ran 30 to 70 percent ahead of their tagged counterparts within 2 months after the campaign launch.[2]

Target wanted to tap into the $210 billion business generated by college students who buy everything from microwave ovens to shower loofahs for their dorms. To gain some insight, Target hired research firm Jump Associates who in turn invited incoming college freshmen and students with a year of dorm living under their belts to a series of "game nights" at high school graduates' homes. Jump created a board game that involved issues associated with going to college. The game led to informal conversations and questions about college life. As the students were talking, Jump researchers were observing on the sidelines, and video cameras were recording it all. The findings from the sessions helped inspire the Todd Oldham Dorm Room product line. Among the offerings was a laundry bag with instructions on how to do the laundry printed on the bag. Although other retailers' back-to-school sales were so-so at best, Target's sales increased 12 percent.[3]

Although focus groups can uncover some interesting attitudes, keep in mind this research method reflects the opinions of only a few people. Some critics wonder about the quality of information that can be gathered from a 2-hour session that involves ten people, in which each person has 12 minutes to speak. Others wonder about the types of people who willingly give up their personal time in return for a modest incentive. Still others complain that the traditional focus-group setting of a conference room with a two-way mirror is like studying wildlife at a zoo. To determine whether you've really uncovered something important, you'll need to back up your focus-group findings with other research such as in-depth interviews.

Interviews

One-on-one interviews usually last from 30 minutes to 2 hours and can uncover important insights, particularly if they're conducted in a natural setting. If you want to learn someone's opinions about camping, go to a campsite. Want to know someone's preferences in pizza? Then conduct your interview at a pizza shop. Before the interview starts, ask the participant for permission to record the interview to ensure accuracy. Also remember this is an interview, not a two-way conversation, so you should do very little talking and should refrain from giving personal opinions.

Ask a lot of questions when you're interviewing consumers. Always remember that they may not want to reveal the real reasons why they do or don't like a product. A mother in England told a market researcher that milk was best for her children but soda pop was terrible. Then he asked what she

---

[2] Stuart Elliott, "Campaign Spotlight: Hanes Says Goodbye to the Tag," *New York Times,* 10 December 2002, nytimes.com.

[3] Alison Stein Wellner, "The New Science of Focus Groups," *American Demographics,* March 2003, pp. 29–33.

bought for them, and she replied, "Soda pop. They hate milk." What could you do with this information if you had to sell milk?

Projective Techniques

Consumers may not come right out and tell their true feelings about a brand in a survey, focus group, or interview. Perhaps it's because they don't want to offend you. Perhaps they haven't articulated the reason in their own minds and therefore have a difficult time explaining it. Perhaps they want to avoid appearing irrational or vain. For example, if you ask people why they bought an expensive imported luxury car, you may be given rational explanations about the car's safety record and resale value. However, if you ask the participants to describe the type of person who owns the expensive imported luxury car, you may learn it's about showing off or getting even.

Using projective techniques, researchers ask respondents to sketch drawings, tell tales, finish sentences, do word associations, create collages, and match companies with animals, colors, places, and types of music in order to understand consumers' subconscious attitudes toward products. These techniques sometimes uncover surprising motives for behavior.

When Grey Advertising asked a group of consumers to imagine long-distance telephone carriers as animals, AT&T was described as a lion, MCI as a snake, and Sprint as a puma. Grey used these insights to position Sprint as the one that could "help you do more business," rather than mimicking the savings approach of the competition.

Goodby, Silverstein & Partners asked luxury-car owners to draw the way they feel about their cars. Most of the drivers of the BMW, Mercedes, Infiniti, and Lexus drew the outside of the cars. Porsche owners, by contrast, rarely drew the car. Instead, the point of view was from the driver's seat, showing winding roads. This exercise gave the agency the idea to emphasize the fun you'll have while driving a Porsche.

Although projective techniques may uncover information that would be missed with other research methods, it's important to keep in mind that they are expensive to use on a per-respondent basis and require the expertise of trained psychologists.

Observation

Go to a store and observe customers interacting with your brand. How much time do they spend reading your brand's label? Looking at the price? Examining other brands? If you have permission from the store manager, ask the customers why they chose a particular brand, when and how often they usually buy it, and how they use it.

Better yet, try to observe consumers using your brand in a natural setting. Sunbeam sent researchers with video cameras to hang out with the guys around the backyard barbeque grill before introducing a new line of Coleman gas grills. By listening in on the conversations, the team gathered a key insight: A gas grill isn't really a tool that cooks the hamburgers and hot dogs. Rather, "it's the centerpiece of warm family moments worthy of a summer highlights reel." So, rather than promote the Coleman grill in terms of size, BTUs, and accessory options, Sunbeam designed the grill to evoke nostalgia for the warm family experience. The marketing strategy positioned grilling as "a relaxing ritual where the grilling area is the stage." The result: The Coleman Grill did $50 million in sales in its first year, making it one of the most successful launches in Sunbeam's history.[4]

One of the more offbeat methods of observation came from an archaeologist who found that studying people's garbage might uncover hidden truths. Several marketing researchers have adopted this method and discovered some rather interesting things, such as the fact that cat owners read more than dog owners.

Experiments

This research method answers questions about cause and effect. Suppose you want to compare the attitudes of a group of people who saw your ad with a group who didn't. Did the people who saw your ad have a more favorable impression of your client? Were they more knowledgeable about the brand? And so on.

Want to uncover opinions about product usage? Give participants your product to use for a week and then ask them to discuss their experiences in a focus group. The planners at Goodby, Silverstein & Partners chose a "deprivation strategy" to understand people's feelings about milk. Participants were asked to go without milk for a week before attending a focus-group session. At first, the participants didn't think it would be difficult, but the week without milk proved otherwise. The idea for the famous two-word line "Got Milk?" came out of the responses from the focus-group participants who had been deprived of milk for a week.

Online Research

Conducting surveys, interviews, and focus groups online is fast and inexpensive. It also allows you to reach people who would not be willing to travel to a facility for a focus group or may feel uncomfortable giving responses about sensitive issues in person. But there are disadvantages, too. One individual can provide multiple responses to a single survey. Someone not in your target audience can respond; you may think you're interviewing a 20-something single female when in fact you're interviewing a 60-year-old married man. Also, you don't have the advantage of nonverbal cues such as tone of voice, expressions on face, and body language.

---

[4] Allison Stein Wellner, "Watch Me Now," *American Demographics,* October 2002, pp. S1–S8.

Using Multiple Research Methods

Each research method has its unique advantages and disadvantages. Therefore, researchers will often use more than one approach to find the answers to their questions. Kraft, the makers of DiGiorno Pizza, used seven research firms to conduct surveys, focus groups, taste tests, and copy tests to learn the best way to position their brand. Surveys and focus groups found that people wanted a frozen pizza with a fresh-baked taste but so far hadn't found one in the stores. In blind taste tests, DiGiorno scored highest among frozen brands and placed second only to one carryout pizza. With this information, the creative team came up with the theme "It's not delivery . . . It's DiGiorno."

The ads creatively addressed the research findings, but still a question remained: Were the spots effective? To find out, Kraft ran a quantitative copy test to measure the effectiveness of the spots. Roughly 64 percent of the respondents recalled the spot's main message of "fresh-baked taste" whereas an average commercial scored about 24 percent. The ad also generated strong brand identification, with 52 percent recalling the DiGiorno name. And finally, one other set of figures proved the success of the big idea: Three years after its introduction, it's the second best-selling frozen pizza.[5]

Step 4: Interpret the Data

You can collect mountains of data, but it's useless if you don't know how to interpret your findings. For example, your research may uncover some negative opinions about your client. An almost immediate reaction would be to try and change these perceptions. However, this may not be the best move. For example, Sabena Qualitative Research developed a perceptional map whereby customers evaluated stores on best/worst value and most/least up-to-date in fashions. Talbots was placed in the best value/least up-to-date quadrant. At first glance, you might be tempted to do something to make Talbots seem more up-to-date. In fact, the company tried that a number of years ago, introducing flashier colors and more current styles. Guess what? Sales dropped because the store's customers wanted classics, not the latest fashions. Talbots quickly went back to what it does best, and its loyal customers are happy once again.

Future Steps in the Process

After the information is gathered, the account executive or planner will prepare a creative brief, also known as a creative strategy statement, to give to the writer and artist (this will be discussed in detail in Chapter 4). The cre-

---

[5] Sara Eckel and Jennifer Lach, "Intelligence Agents," *American Demographics,* March 1999, p. 58.

ative team will use this information as inspiration to develop numerous ideas or creative concepts (discussed in Chapter 5). To ensure that the ideas are on strategy, the agency may do some concept testing with members of the target audience to get their reaction before the ads run. As you can imagine, this can help agencies avoid making costly mistakes.

Concept testing is particularly useful for new product ideas and new approaches for existing products. However, some top creators of ads warn that the more an advertising idea is tested and manipulated on the basis of consumer research, the more watered down it becomes.[6] Social researcher Hugh Mackay warns, "If you show someone an ad and get them to talk about it as if they are on some kind of consumer jury, almost certainly what you'll get is a spurious art director's or amateur copywriter's assessment."[7] But Mackay concedes, "If the planner, writer, art director and client are in disagreement or are experiencing doubt, testing ads would be appropriate. But the testing should be as naturalistic as possible and always done in homes. If it's a print ad, don't get a group discussion and hold it up. Give it to them in the context of a magazine or paper, ask them to look at it overnight and come back tomorrow for a chat."[8]

Common Mistakes in Research

Research is a valuable tool, but it's not foolproof. Here are some common mistakes:

- *Asking the wrong questions.* Before Coca-Cola introduced New Coke in 1985, it conducted numerous focus groups, which showed people preferred the taste of the new soft drink to the old one. The research led the company to change its 100-year-old formula. However, consumers revolted, and Coca-Cola had to reintroduce its old flavor. The problem was that consumers were not told that the original Coca-Cola might be eliminated.

- *Believing everything people tell you.* Jon Steel, director of account planning and vice chairman at Goodby, Silverstein & Partners, points to the problem of people saying the "right" thing: "To hear people talk in focus groups, and indeed to believe the answers they give in larger, more reliable quantitative surveys, one would think that Americans are the cleanest living, healthiest race on the planet. They all eat well, they work out, and cholesterol levels are universally low."[9]

- *Not testing to see if the data are relevant to your client's problem.* The ad agency for Jell-O found that consumers were interested in lighter

[6] Warren Berger, *Advertising Today* (London: Phaidon Press Limited, 2001), p. 470.
[7] Jim Aitchison, *Cutting Edge Advertising* (Singapore: Prentice Hall, 1999), p. 29.
[8] Ibid., p.30–31.
[9] Jon Steel, *Truth, Lies & Advertising: The Art of Account Planning* (New York: Wiley, 1998), p. 83.

desserts, so it positioned Jell-O as a light, tasty dessert that won't fill you up. Sales declined. The problem wasn't that the data were erroneous. It was that the data didn't apply to Jell-O's core consumers, who thought of desserts as the fun part of the meal. Sales increased when the agency repositioned the brand as fun: "Make Jell-O gelatin, and make some fun."

- *Biasing the results.* To be reliable, your research must be repeatable; that is, the same questions or research techniques must produce similar results, regardless of who conducts the study. However, a variety of factors can bias results. For example, with *interviewer bias,* the person interviewing respondents gives cues (smiles, frowns) that suggest one answer is better than another. With *sample bias,* the sample doesn't represent a good cross section of the target audience. Thus, if you wanted to investigate whether teenagers like an advertising campaign, you wouldn't test it on a weekday morning at a shopping mall because the target market would be (or at least should be!) in school, not at the local mall. With *source bias,* the source of the research message influences the answer. People aim to please, so they may say only nice things about company XYZ if they know the person asking the questions works for XYZ. With *nonresponse bias,* questions aren't answered because they're too difficult, confusing, personal, and so on.

- *Not studying someone who is typical of your audience.* Bill Oberlander warns against focus groups: "Anybody who's going to cut out an hour and a half of their time on a Thursday night to go to a very small, fluorescently lit, stale cookied, bad coffee'd room to talk about how they consume mosquito-bite ointment in their lives, I think those people are losers."[10]

Suggested Activities

1. Select two cities from different parts of the country (for example, New York and New Orleans), and prepare a report of their similarities and differences in shopping habits, food preference, income levels, home ownership, number of children in the family, and so on.

2. Observe how your target audience uses the product you're about to advertise. If you're selling golf balls, go to a golf course and watch players in action. If you're selling a detergent, go to a self-service laundry and observe how the people load their machines. If you're selling dog food, watch friends feeding their pets. What did you notice? Were there any surprises? Any common rituals? What insights can help direct your advertising?

---

[10] Aitchison, *Cutting Edge Advertising,* p. 26.

3. Play a game with friends. Choose a product category (such as cars, jeans, or perfume) and write the names of different brands within the product category on index cards (each index card will have a different brand name). Distribute a card to players and ask them to describe their brand as if it were a person, without revealing the brand name. (To get them started, you might give them some questions to answer, such as what would the brand do for a living? Where would it live? What kind of movies would it like? What kind of books? Magazines? TV shows? Who's their best friend? How would they dress? What kind of hairstyle would they have?) Then ask other players to guess the brand that's being described. What did you discover?

4. Choose one of the following categories and use the library and Web to assemble as much information as you can about the product category; who uses it, what industry trends are, which are the top brands in the market, how products differs, how the product is used, and where the category is headed in the future.

Adult Personal Care

Toothpaste
Mouthwash
Shampoo
Personal-care soaps
Hand and body cream
Deodorants/antiperspirants
Electric shavers

Remedies

Athlete's foot remedies
Indigestion aids

Household Supplies

Cleaners
Glass cleaners
Fabric softeners
Charcoal
Air freshener sprays

Baked Goods, Snacks, Desserts

Frozen yogurt
Frozen desserts
Cookies
Crackers

Meat and Prepared Meals

Frozen pizza
Mexican foods
Prepared dinners

Beverages

Instant iced tea
Energy drinks
Bottled water and seltzer

Soup, Fruits, Vegetables

Canned or jarred soup
Flavored/seasoned rice

Search Online! Discovering More About Fact Finding for Creative Excellence

Use InfoTrac College Edition to discover more about fact finding for creative excellence. Try these phrases and others for Key Words and Subject Guide searches: *market research, creative research, advertising research, secondary research + advertising, advertising resources + Internet, marketing resources + Internet, focus group, marketing survey, projective techniques + research.*

In addition to the Web sites listed in this chapter, the following sites will give you access to a comprehensive set of links and articles about advertising:

University of Texas: http://advertising.utexas.edu/world

World Advertising Research Center: www.warc.com

BRIEFCASE

Bell Helmets: Courage for Your Head

How did Goodby, Silverstein & Partners create the remarkable campaign you see on these pages for its client, Bell Helmets? First, by finding out as much as they could about the company and the market. From the start, it was evident that the target consumers were divided into two groups: the "adult biker enthusiast" and the "young biker," whose mother usually participated in the choice of helmet once she managed to convince her youngster to wear one.

Through firsthand research, the agency team found that mass merchants (instead of independent bike shops) were selling the majority of bike helmets, that the market was growing steadily due to new helmet laws, and that people perceived all helmets to be alike, with the result that prices and profit margins were being pushed downward.

From their San Francisco offices, the agency team drove into the hills north of the city to ask mountain bikers how they chose a helmet. Back in the city, they interviewed youngsters in one focus group who biked regularly and then interviewed their mothers in a separate focus group.

"We were amazed that, young or adult, most bikers had no idea what brand of helmet they were wearing," admits Mary Sturvinou, Goodby's strategic planner on the Bell Helmets account. One person, when asked to name the brand, actually said, "What does it say on my helmet?"

In the focus groups with children and their mothers, the agency team learned that the majority of youth helmets were purchased at toy and discount stores. "If a store sells it as a bicycle helmet, it must be okay" was the general attitude among these groups. When youngsters were given a variety of brands to examine and asked to pick the helmet they liked best, brand names were of little consequence. Many referred to their choice as the "youth" brand because the word appeared on the package to indicate the helmet size!

But when the agency team visited the Bell Helmets factory, they were impressed with the lengths to which Bell went to test the safety of each

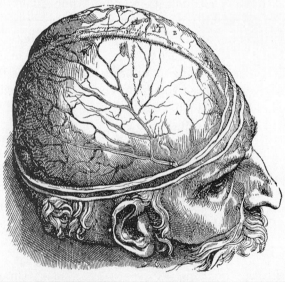

A HELMET THOUGHTFULLY DESIGNED BY ENGINEERS, CRAFTSMEN AND DEAD GUYS.

Product Development Engineer, Tom Stone

Industrial Designer, Michele Saward

VP of Research & Development, John Doe

You know what our designers contributed. It's sitting down there in the form of that Fusion In-Mold, SandBlast™ finish 16-vent Psycho Pro, featuring our Full Nelson™ fit system (named after a particularly snug wrestling hold).

You can probably guess what our engineers and craftsmen contributed. For forty years, they have been pioneering helmet structure and safety by tenaciously developing their own unique crash and burn tests (and standards)

No hallucinogens were used in the designing of our new Pro Series. (As far as we know.)

in their own unique research facility.

Then there's the dead guys. They seem to require a bit more of an explanation. Their contribution has been more along the lines of a spongy grayish thing called a brain. You see, to figure out what happens in a real accident, we need to determine what happens to the brain. Crash test dummies don't have brains. So, we used cadavers to test how the G-forces of an impact effect the old cerebellum. We worked with brain surgeons from the

St. Louis Medical Center, running crash tests with electrodes hooked up to the brains of, well, dead guys. Of course, no one else does this sort of thing.

Anyway, we've learned a lot.

For starters, no other helmets on the market are better than ours. Which is probably why no company has sold nearly as many helmets. And why 22 out of the top 33 IndyCar drivers and hundreds (too many to count, in fact) of professional cyclists prefer Bell.

As well as most dead guys.

COURAGE FOR YOUR HEAD. BELL HELMETS

---

model. They learned that a number of Indy racers who had crashed had credited Bell Helmets with saving their lives.

What next? Goodby's brief on the case sets several important goals, including the following: (1) Correct the perception that all helmets are created equal and (2) begin reversing youngsters' perceptions that "helmets equal corrective shoes," by making Bell top of mind in a category with no real brand registration. Another insight from the team was that the link between the most serious road racer and the 8-year-old child just learning to skate or bike is the spirit (or coolness) of their sport. Everyone wants the freedom and courage to pursue their sport to its fullest, even if they never actually exercise this opportunity.

The strategy was a natural outgrowth of this line of thinking: Bell Helmets are the safest you can buy. Bell allows you to pursue your sport to its fullest. To the trade, the message was, "Only Bell has been here for 40 years and, thanks to their tradition of testing, will be here 40 years from now."

In brainstorming sessions, the team agreed that Bell should be a star in a field that had little brand awareness. "Bell should own helmets," said one of the Goodby folks. And someone else added, "When you wear a helmet you can trust, it gives you the courage you need to tackle a sport all the way." Writer Paul Venables jumped from that thought to the idea that Bell Helmets were "courage for your head," which became the tag line for the campaign. With Jeremy Postaer's unusual use of heavy borders, bold headlines, and screened body copy, the two-page magazine ads stood out instantly. Television spots echoed the same theme, using grainy footage of bikers, racers, and other daredevils crashing their vehicles as a gentle whistler fills the soundtrack to suggest that "these guys are cool because they've protected their heads." In between the action shots, full-screen titles completed the story, and the signoff used a full-screen Bell Helmets logo followed by a helmet wrapping itself around a model of the human brain with the chin strap locking into place as the announcer stated, "Bell Helmets: Courage for your head." (See Figure 9-1 for a copy of one of these scripts.)

The result? Bell's total market share increased 8 points in eight months in a shrinking market (from 40 to 48 percent). Distribution in independent bike stores increased where Bell had anticipated a decline. In qualitative research, the team discovered that after exposure to the advertising, youngsters did not feel as negative about wearing helmets while parents felt very strongly that "there must be a difference in helmet quality" and "I should buy the best."

Amazing what first-rate strategic planning, exhaustive research, and creative thinking can do, isn't it?

STRATEGY:
A ROADMAP FOR THE CREATIVE TEAM

4

John Lyons talks about strategy as

> *a carefully designed plan to murder the competition. Any premise that lacks a killer instinct is not a strategy. Any premise that doesn't reflect or include a consumer's crying need is not a strategy. Any premise embalmed in stiff, predictable language is not a strategy. Any premise that addresses the whole world, women 3 to 93, is not a strategy. Any premise interchangeable with that of another product is not a strategy. The true test of an advertising strategy is to let another human being read it. If that person can't say yes, that's me, or yes, I need that, or yes, that's my problem—throw it away.*[1]

Strategy is the way you plan to sell the product, not the words and images you use to do so. Strategy consists of identifying what you need to say even before you've found the right way to say it. But mere facts do not a strategy make. To the facts you must add your insight—you must see connections that no one else has noticed. Strategic planning is the stage between fact gathering and the big idea. Think of your strategy as a roadmap for the client and creative team—it will map out the direction the advertising campaign should take. But it'll be the job of the creative team to describe the scenery.

[1] John Lyons, *Guts: Advertising from the Inside Out* (New York: AMACOM, 1987), p. 124.

Jeff Goodby, co-chairman/creative director at Goodby, Silverstein & Partners has won just about every advertising prize imaginable. Just read his opening line and you'll see why he's considered one of the most creative minds in this country. Be sure to read the other ads in feature Tips & Tactics in Chapters 1, 5–7.

Courtesy of the Newspaper Association of America.

HOW TO WRITE A NEWSPAPER AD
BY JEFF GOODBY

Great newspaper ads are like leaving a flaming bag of **DOG POOP** on someone's doorstep. They have a naughty, vandalistic side to them, tripped off **KA·BOOM** on unsuspecting victims. I've watched across the subway train as someone opened the paper and got closer to something I'd written. It was like ringing the doorbell and finding a BUSH to hide behind. To get this effect, you **HAVE TO BE TOUGH**. Ask yourself: **"WOULD I REALLY READ THIS?"** *NOT* read it because it's pretty good for an enterprise software ad. But **WOULD I EVER** **REALLY** READ IT? **THIS** IS ISSUE # **1**. *NOT* "Are we saying the right thing?" **NOT** "WILL PEOPLE believe us?" **THIS** "Can you imagine forgetting to ask this?/Well, just open any newspaper, AMIGO. All too often we get it **TECHNICALLY** right. **BUT** we don't get it read. WE skip the art. And the **ART** is the part that gets people to **LOOK**.

SHOW OUTRAGEOUS THINGS that don't belong there. **SHOCK PEOPLE** with a new logic. use the speech of fish. IN OTHER WORDS, **PRESUME** people will pay attention to SOMETHING GOOD. **PRESUME** they have a sense of *humor*. PRESUME they **GET ART**. If we **ALL** do this, it will become very difficult to find which newspaper page we want to wrap the fish in.

I WILL LIKE THAT DAY.
You will too.

JEFF GOODBY IS CO-CHAIRMAN/CREATIVE DIRECTOR & FOUNDER OF GOODBY SILVERSTEIN IN SAN FRANCISCO. HE HAS WON ALMOST EVERY AWARD IMAGINABLE MANY TIMES OVER, INCLUDING AN ATHENA HONORING THE BEST NEWSPAPER ADVERTISING IN THE COUNTRY. TO SEE EXAMPLES OF HIS AGENCY'S WORK & OTHER GREAT NEWSPAPER ADS, VISIT www.naa.org.

Newspaper Association of America
THIS MESSAGE IS BROUGHT TO YOU BY THE NEWSPAPER ASSOCIATION OF AMERICA AND THE PUBLISHING NEWSPAPER.

Figure 4-1
DuPont thinks of farmers as spiritual pragmatists. By sharing the farmers' values and positioning DuPont agricultural products as an extension of them, this campaign seeks to promote the DuPont brand through trust and empathy.

For example, farming is more than a job or even a profession. It is a way of life. Farmers will tell you they farm because they love working outdoors, because they relish being their own boss, because they can raise their families in a good environment, and because they get deep satisfaction from making things grow, from being a part of "God's miracle."

At the same time, farmers are businesspeople. Managing millions of dollars in assets and making a profit is no easy task. So, in addition to loving the life they lead, farmers are intensely interested in practical solutions to problems associated with farming. What this all boils down to is that farmers are "spiritual pragmatists." And it was this insight that became the basis of the print campaign shown in Figure 4-1. By sharing the farmers' values and positioning DuPont agricultural products as an extension of them, the agency sought to promote the DuPont brand through trust and empathy and to create preference for DuPont products in an area in which true functional competitive advantages are difficult to achieve or discern.

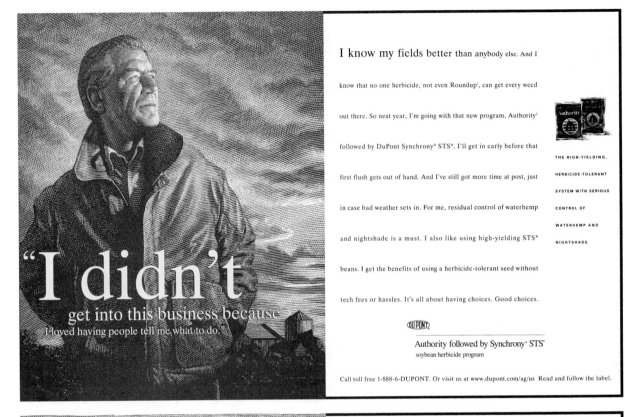

I know my fields better than anybody else. And I know that no one herbicide, not even Roundup¹, can get every weed out there. So next year, I'm going with that new program, Authority² followed by DuPont Synchrony® STS®. I'll get in early before that first flush gets out of hand. And I've still got more time at post, just in case bad weather sets in. For me, residual control of waterhemp and nightshade is a must. I also like using high-yielding STS® beans. I get the benefits of using a herbicide-tolerant seed without tech fees or hassles. It's all about having choices. Good choices.

THE HIGH-YIELDING, HERBICIDE-TOLERANT SYSTEM WITH SERIOUS CONTROL OF WATERHEMP AND NIGHTSHADE.

DUPONT

Authority followed by Synchrony® STS®
soybean herbicide program

Call toll free 1-888-6-DUPONT. Or visit us at www.dupont.com/ag/us Read and follow the label.

Living a life that's reserved for a very few. Doing what's right. That's why I farm. I'm always looking for flexible, new solutions. Like DuPont Basis Gold®. I can use it in a one-pass, total post, or as part of a two-pass program following a preemergence product like new LeadOff™ corn herbicide from DuPont. Either way, Basis Gold® controls emerged weeds and grasses even if it doesn't rain. And when it does, the residual protects me all the way to harvest. Plus, Basis Gold® can be used on virtually any corn, so I can plant whatever works best on my land. I like having these choices—especially the option to do it my way.

IN ANY KIND OF WEATHER, ON ANY KIND OF CORN, IT CONTROLS MY GRASS AND BROADLEAF WEEDS.

DUPONT

Basis Gold®
corn herbicide

Call toll free 1-888-6-DUPONT. Or visit us at www.dupont.com/ag/us Read and follow the label.

O'Toole's Three-Point Approach to Strategy

John O'Toole, former chairman of FCB Communications and former president of the American Association of Advertising Agencies, says you should consider three things when determining a strategy:

1. *Who or what is the competition?* To set your brand apart, you need to know what other brands are saying. You also need to be aware that your competition may go beyond the product category. For example, the competition for home exercise machines includes diet supplements and health clubs, not just other machines. It probably also reflects a preference for running or swimming and any number of other related things.

2. *Who are you talking to?* Are you targeting users of another brand? Consumers who've never used any brand in your category? Consumers who use a related product but might be persuaded to switch to yours? Perhaps you're targeting your current customers, urging them to buy your brand more often or simply to remain brand loyal. Or perhaps you're targeting gatekeepers, the people who influence the purchasing decision for your target audience. Ally & Gargano targeted many audiences in its campaign for Federal Express. As agency president Amil Gargano explained, "We focused on expanding the market with the target moving from management to every department of American business including secretaries, mailroom personnel and trainees. No one was spared."[2]

   Many strategy statements describe customers in demographic terms: age, sex, marital status, income, occupation, owner or renter, user or nonuser of product category, and so on. But demographics alone cannot help the creative team of copywriter and art director really see and understand the person they're trying to reach. To illustrate the point, account planner Jon Steel reminds us that the group of "men aged 35 and over with large household incomes" includes Bill Clinton, Billy Graham, Michael Jackson, Donald Trump, Bob Dole, and a large number of drug dealers. Much more meaningful is a profile of that person's lifestyle including values, leisure-time activities, attitudes toward work and family, and the stresses of everyday life. Steel describes the demographic information as the "skeleton" and the lifestyles and values as the "body and soul."[3]

   Sometimes different segments of your target audience will have such diverse interests that you'll need to create separate advertising campaigns. Check out the ads in Figure 4-2. Notice how they speak to people who want to relax while on vacation. Now peek ahead to Figure 6-1. These ads appeal to people who want to discover new things during their vacations.

---

[2] Bernice Kanner, *The 100 Best TV Commercials . . . and Why They Worked* (New York: Times Books, 1999), p. 35.
[3] Jon Steel, *Truth, Lies & Advertising: The Art of Account Planning* (New York: Wiley, 1998).

Figure 4-2
Notice how few words are needed to communicate that North Carolina is the perfect place to escape from the hassles of every-day life. Now take a peek ahead to Figure 6-2 and notice the different approach that's used for people who want to explore every nook and cranny of the state. The long copy in Figure 6-1 is perfect for vacationers who want to learn as much as they can about their destination. And the lack of copy in the ads shown here is perfect for vacationers who just want to "veg out."

1-800-VISIT NC   www.visitnccoast.com   AOL Keyword: VISITNC

NORTH CAROLINA
A better place to be

Figure 4-2 (continued)

Figure 4-2 (continued)

3. *What do you want them to know, understand, and feel?* Describe how your brand touches one or more of the basic human needs: to be popular, to feel attractive and wanted, to obtain material things, to enjoy life through comfort and convenience, to create a happy family situation, to have love and sex, to wield power, to avoid fear, to emulate those you admire, to have new experiences, or to protect and maintain health. As creative director John Stingley observes, "The basic motivations of people never really change. That's why Shakespeare is still relevant today. Human history pretty much boils down to the influence of love, sex, greed, hunger, and insecurity."[4]

Rather than communicating a rational benefit, which is fairly easy for competitors to copy, try for an emotional appeal. "Women don't buy lipstick, they buy hope," Revlon founder Charles Revson once told his staff. Likewise, Clairol Herbal Essence shampoo isn't about removing dirt and oil from hair; it's about sex appeal. Porsche sports cars aren't about getting from point A to point B; they're about power and status and one-upmanship. Consider this comment from a Porsche owner: "There's nothing practical about it. I live in the United States where the law says I have to drive fifty-five miles an hour. It doesn't have room for my kids and my luggage. And that's exactly why I love it."[5] Notice how this consumer insight is reflected in the following headline for Porsche:

TOO FAST

DOESN'T BLEND IN

PEOPLE WILL TALK

DDB Needham's Focus on Basic Human Needs

The DDB Needham agency explores the emotional and rational rewards of using products in the process of defining its strategy. Cheese, for example,[6] offers the following rewards:

- *In-use rewards:* Is convenient (practical), offers a new taste (sensory), earns the gratitude of the family (social), and contributes to the belief that you're a good cook (ego satisfaction)

- *Results-of-use rewards:* Helps build strong bones (practical), makes you feel better (sensory), makes you look good to others (social), and contributes to the belief that you're a good parent (ego satisfaction)

---

[4] The Designers and Art Directors Association of the United Kingdom, *The Copywriter's Bible* (Switzerland: Roto Vision SA, 1995), p. 163.
[5] Jim Aitchison *Cutting Edge Advertising* (Singapore: Prentice Hall, 1999). p. 45.
[6] Adapted from a presentation by Doug Walker at the University of South Carolina, 17 October 1999.

- *Incidental-to-use rewards:* Provides low-cost nutrition (practical), makes no mess (sensory), adds variety to party refreshments (social), and makes you feel like a smart shopper (ego satisfaction)

Which benefits do you think are the most important to mothers? To college students? To professionals? To people living on Social Security?

McCann–Erickson's Role-Playing Approach

The McCann–Erickson agency suggests that you get inside the head of your consumer by acting as if you were that person, writing your responses to the first six questions here in the consumer's "voice" and the final question in your own voice.

1. Who is our target?
2. Where are we now in the mind of this person?
3. Where is our competition in the mind of this person?
4. Where would we like to be in the mind of this person?
5. What is the consumer promise, the "big idea"?
6. What is the supporting evidence?
7. What is the tone of voice for the advertising?

Writing partially in the first person to arrive at a strategy for reaching parents, the initial thinking for Bell Helmets (see the BriefCase in Chapter 3) probably went something like this:

1. *Who is our target?* "Hi. I'm Lena Emoto. I work full time as an accountant, and my husband, Ray, is a mechanical engineer. We have two growing children: Michelle, 9, and Bobby, 12. And are they busy kids! Dropping in at their friends' houses practically every day. Biking up to the corner convenience store to buy a slush drink. I'm lucky that they can take care of themselves after school and that their bikes allow them some mobility. But I sometimes worry about that. After all, the streets can be dangerous. Thank goodness I've convinced them to wear helmets, even though they originally fought me on it."

2. *Where are we now in the mind of this person?* "Sure, there are lots of brands of helmets. I didn't spend much on theirs because they all looked pretty much alike to me. They also looked like they'd protect their heads in case they fell or hit something. So while we almost shelled out big bucks for a higher-priced brand, Ray's car needed a major repair job, and with all we spent for school supplies and clothing, we decided it wasn't necessary to buy an expensive helmet just for riding in the neighborhood."

3. *Where is our competition in the mind of this person?* "As I said, most brands look about the same. We found two great-looking helmets for about thirteen bucks each. So far, they've been okay. Why spend more than you need? Clothes and shoes cost enough as it is."

4. *Where would we like to be in the mind of this person?* "At first I thought it was dumb to spend more on a bicycle helmet. Then I heard about Bell Helmets, how they make them with such care, how they test them, how they're practically indestructible, and how they've saved the lives of professional and amateur racers."

5. *What is the consumer promise, the "big idea"?* "They say Bell Helmets are thoroughly tested for safety. So when my kids wear one, they can enjoy biking, and I don't have to worry so much about them getting a bad head injury."

6. *What is the supporting evidence?* "Bell pioneered the field of helmet safety. They're first with racecar helmets, and now with bike helmets, too. They invented their own safety tests, which they still conduct in their own labs. They sell more helmets than any other company, and Bell is the helmet of choice for more racecar drivers and pro cyclists than any other brand. I discovered that by reading their ad."

7. *What is the tone of voice for the advertising?* Make parents think about spending money on a helmet in terms of safety, not status. Use humor to make a sobering statement.

An Account-Planning Approach

Merry Baskin, former chair of the Account Planning Group, describes the role of an account planner as a combination of market researcher, data analyst, qualitative focus-group moderator, information center, bad cop (to account management's good cop), new product development consultant, brainstorming facilitator, target audience representative/voice of the consumer, soothsayer/futurologist, media/communications planner, strategic thinker/strategy developer, writer of the creative brief, think-piece polemicist, social anthropologist, insight miner, and knowledge applicator.[7]

In a nutshell, account planners serve as liaisons between the creative team and the consumer. They use surveys, focus groups, one-on-one interviews, observation, and projective techniques to uncover human truths, brand insights, and emerging cultural trends. These insights are summarized in creative briefs and presented to the copywriter and art director to help them get into the mind-set of the target audience (see Figure 4-3). John Stingley says,

> *In many ways, creating advertising is the same discipline as acting. You must start by mentally discarding your own identity. You have to become the people you are communicating with. Internalize their interests, joys, fears, tastes, even biases. Often it means mentally and emotionally becoming someone you would never in a million years be like yourself.*[8]

---

[7] Merry Baskin, "What Is Account Planning?" Account Planning Group Web site, apg.org.uk.
[8] The Designers and Art Directors Association of the United Kingdom, *The Copywriter's Bible* (Switzerland: Roto Vision SA, 1995), p. 163.

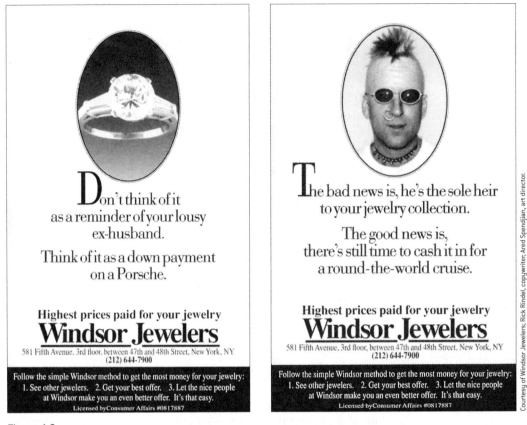

Figure 4-3
You need to get into the mind-set of your customers, as Windsor Jewelers does here. Notice that they didn't say something dumb like, "Trade in your treasured family heirlooms for cash." After all, they understood that people have a hard time parting with family treasures. These ads make it simple.

Account planner Lauren Tucker says a creative brief must address the following:

1. *The role of advertising.* Why are you advertising? What is the problem that advertising can solve? How will the client benefit? How will consumers benefit?

2. *Target audience.* Describe the consumer in a way that gives insight into how they think and feel about your brand. For example, Margaret Morrison[9] asks you to consider the difference among the following descriptions:

   - Mothers with children under 12 years old.

---

[9] Margaret A. Morrison, Eric Haley, Kim Bartel Sheenhan, Ronald E. Taylor, *Using Qualitative Research in Advertising: Strategies, Techniques and Applications* (Thousand Oaks, CA: Sage, 2002), pp. 112–115.

- Mothers, with children under 12 years old, who probably do not prepare many meals from scratch but generally use a variety of packaged goods as the basis for their meals. These moms may be users of products such as jarred spaghetti sauce and packaged dinners, and they may also be users of foods purchased from the deli counter of their grocery store. They are also busy and highly involved in the lives of their children.

- Mothers who consider themselves creative and somewhat adventurous in the kitchen but need to balance their creativity with the demands of the picky eaters in the family.

Morrison's first example provides very little information to the creative team about what motivates the target consumer. The second example provides quite a bit of information but no real inspiration. Morrison notes this description is likely to fit virtually every mother with children under 12 years old in the United States. The third example creates a vivid picture in the mind of everyone reading the creative brief. It describes what is unique and different about the mothers who are in the target audience compared to the other mothers who may fit the profile demographically but not psychographically.

3. *Key insight*. Bill Bernbach once said, "At the heart of an effective creative philosophy is the belief that nothing is so powerful as an insight into human nature, what compulsions drive a man, what instincts dominate his action, even though his language so often can camouflage what really motivates him."[10]

   The insight may come through observation, such as the fact that people tend to pull Oreo cookies apart and lick the cream filling before biting into the cookie. It may also come from what consumers say in interviews and focus groups. For example, the statement "I might as well apply this donut to my hips" led to NutriGrain's creative concept that shows people wearing giant donuts around their waists.

4. *Benefit*. Define your benefit in human terms. For example, "Tide cleans the dirt your family gets into" not "Tide cleans better than other brands."

5. *Brand personality/brand promise*. For example, the Motel 6 brand is honest. Simple. Unpretentious. Good-humored. And commonsensical.

6. *Mandatories*. Bank ads must contain financial disclosure information. A retailer may insist that all ads include the address and the store hours.

In addition to the written creative brief, you may wish to include clips of TV programs the consumer watches, download music they like, create a scrapbook of their hobbies, make a montage of photos that represent what they do in an average day, and so on.

[10] Baskin, "What Is Account Planning?"

Stating the Strategy

Each agency approaches strategy from its own unique perspective. Whichever approach is used, the strategy must be carefully stated so that it gives the creative team direction and inspiration. Although you may have gathered reams of data, only include what's relevant to solving the advertising problem in your strategy statement. Kevin Dundas describes two opposite extremes:

> *The urge to fill that piece of paper with detail, data, fact, and hearsay is unbelievably tempting. I recall a senior planner handing me a brief for sign-off and proudly stating, "Let's see the creatives get out of that one." It was a great piece of strategic thinking, but as a stepping-off point to a creative team it was DOA.*
>
> *Equally, I have had planners shuffle into my office embarrassed to reveal the one-page summation of a mountain of strategizing and positioning work for their brand. "It's too simple and obvious; it is what the brand has always stood for." More than likely this is a good position to take; why challenge or rewrite a position like refreshment or performance or safety? The genius, of course, lies in how the planner has configured or retextured the brand proposition for today's target audience.*[11]

As you write your strategy statement, try to write as visually as you can so that the writer and artist will almost see and hear the consumer in their minds. But keep the statement brief. Kenneth Roman and Jane Mass argue that if you can't fit the information onto one page, the chances of getting it all into a 30-second commercial are slight.[12]

Linking Strategy with the Thinking/Feeling and High/Low-Importance Scales

Advertising agency Foote Cone & Belding has created a strategy model based on two basic facts: (1) Some purchasing decisions are based more on logic whereas others are based more on emotions, and (2) some purchasing decisions may involve extensive deliberation whereas others are made with little or no thought. Visualize this model as a grid with four quadrants (see Figure 4-4).

- *Quadrant 1: Thinking/High Importance.* Also called the informative model, this approach assumes that the consumer needs a great deal of information because of the importance of the product and logical issues concerning it. Many campaigns for automobiles, digital cameras, comput-

---

[11] Kevin Dundas, "A Passion for Advertising," *Agency,* Summer 1998, p. 38.
[12] Kenneth Roman and Jane Maas, *The New How to Advertise* (New York: St. Martin's Press, 1992), p. 5.

Figure 4-4
The Foote Cone & Belding strategy-planning model ranks consumer purchasing decisions in terms of high versus low importance and thinking versus feeling.

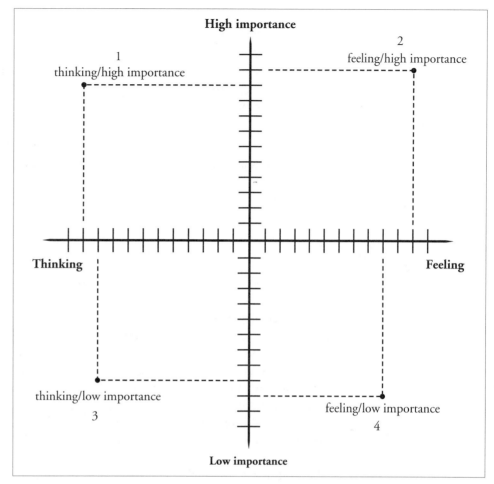

ers, and home entertainment systems fit this category. Long copy, specific information, and perhaps a demonstration might be used to reinforce the selling argument.

- *Quadrant 2: Feeling/High Importance.* Also called the affective model, this approach views the consumer as an individual who relies less on specific information and more on attitudes and feelings about the product because the purchase decision is related to one's self-esteem. Products for which this strategy works include jewelry, cosmetics, fashion apparel, and motorcycles. Image advertising, which communicates with dramatic visuals and emotional statements as opposed to logic, is the rule of thumb here.

- *Quadrant 3: Thinking/Low Importance.* Also called the habit-formation model, this approach views the consumer as one who makes purchasing decisions with minimal thought. Simply inducing a trial purchase, as with a coupon, may generate subsequent purchases more readily than pounding home undifferentiated points in the copy. Campaigns for food and household cleaning products often use this approach; the messages always remind the consumer to choose the brand.

- *Quadrant 4: Feeling/Low Importance.* Also called the self-satisfaction model, this approach sees the consumer as a reactor. It is reserved for products that satisfy personal tastes, such as smoking and consumption of alcoholic beverages, and that make the user feel "special" when using the brand in front of his or her peers. Messages are designed primarily to draw attention to the brand.

Note that, because consumers buy a variety of goods and services, they may fit any of the four quadrant profiles, depending on the specific purchasing decision.

Think ROI

Before you finalize your strategy, think about the return on investment (ROI) that your client will receive from advertising by answering the question "Why is advertising the best answer?" After all, in this age of integrated marketing communications, a variety of other approaches might bring about similar—or even better—results than an advertising campaign. For example, if research shows that people aren't shopping at a store because they don't like the service they receive, an ad campaign probably won't help as much as improving employee morale at the store—something human resources or public relations could do far better than an ad agency. (See Chapter 12 for examples of Integrated Marketing Communications.)

There's another ROI that's important in testing your strategy. Doug Walker defines it as "relevance, originality, and impact." Is your strategy relevant to the target audience? Is it original or is it too similar to that of the other brands in your product category? Does it have an impact? Will it bring results?

Checklist for Strategy

- ✓ Does your strategy have the potential for relevant and unexpected connections that can build a relationship between the brand and the prospect?
- ✓ Did you place the brand at the appropriate point on the thinking/feeling and high/low-importance scales?
- ✓ Does your strategy address one or more of the basic human needs?
- ✓ Did you include emotional benefits as well as rational ones? Can the product and its advertising support these benefits?
- ✓ Did you consider what strategies the competition is using, as well as what they may have missed?

STRATEGY STATEMENT FORMAT

STRATEGY STATEMENT FOR [NAME OF PRODUCT, SERVICE, AND SO ON]

Give a brief description of the product or service to put the strategy in context—no more than one or two paragraphs, but enough to help the reader understand what is to be advertised.

1. *Who is our target?* Give brief lifestyle/attitudinal descriptions. Include some demographics, but this is not as important for most products. Users, heavy users, nonusers, users of competitive brands? Relationship to other product/service usage?

2. *Where are we now in the mind of this person?* They don't know us. They know us, but don't use us. They prefer another brand because. . . . They don't understand what we can do. They don't use us for enough things. And so on.

3. *Where is our competition in the mind of this person?* Use the same approach as above but focus on the competing brands.

4. *Where would we like to be in the mind of this person?* Product is positioned as. . . . Product is the best choice because. . . . Now they know product will. . . .

5. *What is the consumer promise, the "big idea"?* State the major focus of your campaign. Not a slogan or tag line at this stage, but an idea in simple language that will serve as the basis for a tag line—a brief statement that sums up what the campaign is about.

6. *What is the supporting evidence?* Draw on consumer benefits to strengthen and elaborate on what you chose in item 5. Build benefit after benefit in support of your big idea.

7. *What is the tone of voice for the advertising?* Decide on the appropriate tone—warm, family values, startling, hi-tech, sobering fact, mild guilt, humor, and so on.

✓ Does your strategy address the target market in a tone appropriate to this market?

✓ Does your strategy contain enough information to give the creative team direction, but not so much information that it overwhelms them?

✓ Does your strategy address both types of ROI?

Suggested Activities

1. Using the strategy statement format as shown in the box above, write a strategy for a product, service, or organization of your choosing or as assigned by your instructor.

2. Collect several advertisements for a single product, service, or organization. How much of the original strategy can you infer from what the ads say and how they say it? Is the target audience evident? What is the problem, and what is the ad's approach to solving it? Which basic human needs are addressed? If you were in the target market for this ad, would you believe what it says? Why or why not? Strategically speaking, what might be another way to approach the problem?

3. Using this same campaign or another, do an Internet search for the product or service. What differences do you note in the strategic approach? For example, you might do a search for Bell Helmets and determine if their Web strategy is in keeping with the "Courage for your head" campaign.

Search Online! Discovering More About Strategy

Use InfoTrac College Edition to discover more about strategy. Try these phrases and others for Key Words and Subject Guide searches: *strategy, strategic planning, advertising strategy, creative strategy, target market, consumer as gatekeeper, basic human needs, Bell Helmets, brand image, positioning.*

For more information about branding and account planning, go to:

brandchannel.com: www.brandchannel.com

Account Planning Group: www.apg.org.uk

BRIEFCASE

Eat Mor Chikin or These Cows Are Goners!

Chick-fil-A is a quick-service restaurant chain with more than 1000 units and over $1.2 billion in sales. From 1963 to the 1980s, Chick-fil-A grew to become America's dominant mall-based restaurant chain on the strength of their signature chicken sandwich. As mass merchandisers began to erode mall traffic in the 1980s, Chick-fil-A management moved the chain's expansion strategy out of the mall and onto the street with freestanding units.

Chick-fil-A now competes in one of the economy's largest and most competitive segments—fast-food restaurants. Chick-fil-A is outnumbered in store count by up to 15 to 1 and is outspent in the media by up to 20 to 1 by the likes of McDonald's, Burger King, and Wendy's. Industrywide, flat pricing and rapid store growth have held average same-store sales increases to a modest 1 to 2 percent for several years. Also, deep discount has been the dominant marketing message in the fast-food industry.

In 1995 Chick-fil-A hired The Richards Group to develop a campaign that would clearly position Chick-fil-A as the preferred alternative to hamburgers in the fast-food restaurant marketplace. To arrive at the best approach, The Richards Group used their Spherical branding process, where they define the client's business, the brand's positioning, personality, and the desired affiliation.

The Spherical branding process revealed significant differences between the Chick-fil-A customer and traditional fast-food customers. Chick-fil-A customers were older, better educated, wealthier, more white collar, and skewed female. They came to Chick-fil-A for a unique, better-tasting chicken sandwich.

Research confirmed that Chick-fil-A was rich with positive associations. Great-tasting chicken sandwiches was the strongest association. Also, customers associated Chick-fil-A with a clean, comfortable restaurant environment, well-run operations; accurate service; friendly, clean-cut employees; and strong values. Customers described the brand's personality as upscale, successful, healthy, intelligent, clean-cut, and wholesome. Sounds perfect, right?

Courtesy of Chick-fil-A

"Calling All Cows" :60 radio

SFX:	OPEN ON SFX [sound effect] OF DIAL TONE. THEN WE HEAR NUMBERS BEING DIALED, BUT THE TONE IS SLIGHTLY OFF AS IF THE NUMBERS AREN'T BEING PRESSED PROPERLY. THIS GOES ON FOR A FEW SECONDS AND IS FOLLOWED BY AN OFF-THE-HOOK SFX.
ANNCR:	The cows are calling . . .
SFX:	WE HEAR A SORT OF COW GRUMBLING/MOO AND THEN MORE EFFORT IN MISDIALING THE PHONE.
ANNCR:	The cows are trying to call you on the phone to tell you to eat more chicken.
SFX:	DISGRUNTLED MOO. MISDIAL, MISDIAL, MISDIAL.
ANNCR:	Unfortunately, cows have hooves. So not only is the receiver hard to pick up, but the little numbers are nearly impossible to dial.
SFX:	POORLY DIALED NUMBERS AND COW SFX CONTINUE UNDER.
ANNCR:	Oh, how stubborn cows can be. You see, they want you to know about Chick-fil-A. Chick-fil-A invented the chicken sandwich over 30 years ago. Made a special way, it's more tender, juicier, better. The cows want you to eat more chicken.
SFX:	DIAL TONE.
ANNCR:	The cows also want to tell you to quit puttin' bells around their necks, but that's a whole other story. Chick-fil-A. We didn't invent the chicken, just the chicken sandwich.
SFX:	ROTARY DIAL SOUND FOLLOWED BY A MORE SATISFIED MOO SOUND.

Well actually, a bit too perfect. The Richards Group discovered other personality traits included status driven, finicky, uptight, self-absorbed, and boring.

Clearly, Chick-fil-A was seen as the premium chicken sandwich in the quick-service restaurant category. The Richards Group, however, understood that talking about "quality" products was not unique or motivating. In fact, it might even add to the negative characteristics of being uptight and finicky.

After thorough consumer research and an extensive review of the fast-food restaurant category, The Richards Group developed the following brand positioning for Chick-fil-A:

To choosy people in a hurry, Chick-fil-A is the premium fast-food restaurant brand that consistently serves America's best-loved chicken sandwiches.

"The B-Word" :60 radio

ANNCR: And now the Chick-fil-A update. The BCC—the Bovine Communications Committee, sister agency of the FCC—has banned the use of a number of words on commercial airwaves. First and foremost is (BEEP). The cows call it the "B" word—ends in "F," two "E's" in the middle. This particular word, the cows claim, is corrupting the minds and bodies of America. Phrases like (BEEP) jerky, (BEEP)-cake, (BEEP) stroganoff, "Where's the (BEEP)," "One-hundred percent, pure, Grade-A Angus (BEEP)" are now punishable with time in a pig trough and random electric cattle prodding. An acceptable substitute is the "C" word, a.k.a. Chicken. Saying (BEEP) in private is still legal, but the cows don't recommend it. Should you find yourself saying (BEEP), thinking about (BEEP), or craving (BEEP), head to Chick-fil-A. There you can purge your wrongdoings by thinking wholesome thoughts and eating wholesome things. Like the Chick-fil-A Original Chicken Sandwich. It features a tender, all-white breast of chicken cooked a special way to seal in the juices, then placed atop a hot, buttered bun with two crucial pickles. I've got no (BEEP) with that. Chick-fil-A. We didn't invent the chicken. Just the chicken sandwich.

The target of choosy people in a hurry encompasses those who, regardless of their demographics, are a little more choosy about the food they eat, the restaurant they eat in, the employees who serve them, and the healthfulness of the food. In fact, they are choosier people about most aspects of their lives.

From the consumer perspective, Chick-fil-A is first and foremost fast food. The frame of reference as a premium fast-food restaurant acknowledges the fact that consumers consider Chick-fil-A among the most respected, highest-quality fast-food restaurants.

Chicken sandwiches are the dominant signature products and the most compelling reason for choosing Chick-fil-A. "Consistently serves America's best-loved chicken sandwiches" is a specific and vivid reason to choose Chick-fil-A.

Chick-fil-A's brand personality had to be easy to connect to emotionally. The Richards Group determined that Chick-fil-A's brand personality should be:

Caring. Genuine. Clean-cut. Dependable. Unexpectedly fun.

Caring to capture the community and people orientation of the company and its principled and giving culture. *Genuine* to capture the sense of an organization that is authentic, classic, and comfortable with itself and that puts substance over style. *Clean-cut* to capture the wholesome and healthy quality of the nature of the people. *Dependable* to characterize people who have their act together and have some stability in their lives. They are people who you would consider good neighbors. *Unexpectedly fun* to leave room for the company to not take itself too seriously, to be lighthearted and creative.

The Richards Group wanted people to feel the following brand affiliation when they choose to eat at Chick-fil-A:

> People who eat at Chick-fil-A see themselves as a little more discerning. "Chick-fil-A is a little more expensive, but it's worth it." They also see Chick-fil-A as a place for active, family-focused folks who appreciate Chick-fil-A's strong values.

With the Spherical branding process complete, The Richards Group realized they needed to create a campaign that would leverage the premium product and enhance the personality of the brand. The creative solution, "Eat Mor Chikin," features cows trying to persuade consumers to eat more Chick-fil-A chicken.

The campaign rolled out initially in 1995 as a three-dimensional billboard in which cows appear to be writing "EAT MOR CHIKIN" on the sign. This board is used when Chick-fil-A opens in a new market to welcome new customers. As a market matures, the cows begin to rotate other boards into the mix. Sometimes the cows are used outdoors to promote specific items

like breakfast with boards such as "EAT MOR CHIKIN OR WEER TOAST."
They aren't really particular, however, about how humans eat chicken, just
that we do. So sometimes they encourage the general consumption of
chicken by tying their message to current events with boards like the "VOTE
CHIKIN" board that ran during an election year. A fully integrated campaign

was added in 1996, which included outdoor billboards, TV, radio, freestanding inserts, direct mail, costumed mascots, and apparel/novelty items.

The campaign has won numerous awards in the Cannes, ADDY, OBIE, EFFIE, and other competitions. As an added bonus, the campaign, particularly the outdoor billboards, has generated significant attention on national/local news wires and in restaurant trade publications. The media value of the public relations coverage is more than $5 million.

In the process, the traffic-stopping cows have convinced a lot of people to Eat Mor Chikin. Since 1996 Chick-fil-A's unaided brand awareness has grown 81 percent. During that same period, sales have increased 120 percent. That's a lot "mor chikin" than before the cows and The Richards Group came on the scene. Now if only we can get the cows to use Spell Check.

IDEAS:
THE CURRENCY OF THE 21ST CENTURY

5

"We're in the idea business, because ideas will be the currency of the 21st century," Roy Spence, founder of Austin-based GSD&M, explained to *USA Today.* But Spence also observed, "The market is ad rich and idea poor."[1] The key question becomes, How do you come up with the big idea?

How Do You Come Up with the Big Idea?

Some writers and artists say their ideas come to them while they're taking a hot bath or a long walk. Others get ideas in the shower or while driving. And still others get ideas through free association with a colleague. Terence Poltrack describes the process of coming up with the big idea as

> *one man, one style. For every idea out there, there's a way to get to it. Ask advertising's creative thinkers about their personal road maps to The Answer, and you confront a mix of fear and bravado, chilly logic and warm emotion. The process is one part reason, one part heart, and one (big) part pure, simple intuition.*[2]

[1] Bill Meyers, "He's in the Idea Business," *USA Today,* 29 April 1999, p. B1.
[2] Terence Poltrack, "Stalking the Big Idea," *Agency,* May/June 1991, p. 26.

James Webb Young, a former creative vice president at J. Walter Thompson, described a five-step process in his book *A Technique for Producing Ideas:*[3]

- **Step 1:** *Immersion.* Totally immerse yourself in background research. Even the pros don't write the magic line the first time. Before Goodby, Silverstein & Partners arrived at "Courage for your head" for client Bell Helmets (see the BriefCase in Chapter 3), they visited the client, viewed the manufacturing process, and absorbed hours of information, which led to a group-think session in which the tag line finally emerged.

- **Step 2:** *Digestion.* Play with the information. Look at it from different angles. Make lists of features. Draw doodles. Write down phrases. Exercise your mind. This chapter will give you some creative exercises that may help spark an idea.

- **Step 3:** *Incubation.* Put the advertising assignment aside. Go for a walk. See a movie. Shoot some hoops. Do whatever will relax your mind. Young likened this step to the way Sherlock Holmes solved mysteries. In the middle of a case, Holmes would drag Watson off to a concert. This habit was very irritating to the literal-minded Watson, but it always helped Holmes crack the case.

- **Step 4:** *Illumination.* Once your brain has been allowed to relax after being loaded with information, it will spurt out an idea. It can happen anywhere, any time. Be ready to write the idea down because, as quickly as an idea pops into your head, it can pop out of it. Forever. It doesn't matter if the idea is captured on a scrap of paper, a cocktail napkin, or in the dust on your car's dashboard, just as long as you record it somehow.

  Creative director Ann Hayden was having a difficult time coming up with the right approach for a Roche commercial. She knew the commercial needed to convince patients to discuss their weight with their doctors. But every idea she came up with seemed trite. Finally, the big idea came to her when she was having dinner at a restaurant and noticed the couple at the next table had a baby with them. That's it! Babies. One of the first things that happens when a baby is born is that he or she is weighed. This inspired a commercial that opens on a baby and dissolves into a grown woman who is overweight. The announcer says, "We're all born into this world small, within three to four pounds of each other. Then life happens. And we can end up weighing more than is healthy for us. Fortunately, today there are some truly different prescription options that can help. Doctors have been weighing you since you were born. Isn't it time you talked about it?"[4]

- **Step 5:** *Reality testing.* Ask yourself, Is the idea really good? Does it solve the problem? Is it on strategy? As you gather ideas, put them inside an envelope or folder and don't look at them right away. If you evaluate

---

[3] James Webb Young, *A Technique for Producing Ideas,* 3rd ed. (Chicago: Crain Books, 1975).
[4] Adapted from a lecture given by Ann Hayden at the University of South Carolina, 13 May 2000.

Luke Sullivan, chief creative officer at WestWayne Advertising, is also author of a book on advertising, *Hey Whipple, Squeeze This.* Be sure to read the other ads in the feature Tips & Tactics in Chapters 1, 4, 6, and 7.

Courtesy of the Newspaper Association of America.

HOW TO WRITE A NEWSPAPER AD.

BY LUKE SULLIVAN

I DRAW A LITTLE BLANK WHITE SQUARE. ABOUT ONE INCH WIDE, TWO INCHES DEEP. I FIGURE IF I CAN'T GET MY IDEA INSIDE OF THAT SMALL SPACE, IT MUST NOT BE A VERY BIG IDEA AND IT'S ONLY GOING TO LOOK WORSE FILLING UP A 13" x 21" NEWSPAPER PAGE.

THEN I STARE AT THAT LITTLE WHITE SPACE. I JUST STARE. AND I TRY TO FILL IT WITH SOMETHING INTERESTING. UNFAILINGLY, THE FIRST 100 IDEAS THAT I DRAW INSIDE THAT LITTLE WHITE SQUARE ARE AWFUL LITTLE THINGS.

THAT'S WHEN IT STARTS: A SPECIAL SORT OF CHEST-SPLITTING PANIC KNOWN ONLY TO PEOPLE WHOSE WORK IS PRODUCED ON A DEADLINE AND APPEARS IN FORUMS AS PUBLIC AS THE NEWSPAPER.

THE CREEPING HORROR

TO DEAL WITH THIS "HORROR", MATURE WRITERS POUR ANOTHER CUP OF COFFEE AND BUCKLE IN. I, HOWEVER, REMEMBER THAT THE MOVIE MEMENTO JUST OPENED AND SNEAK OUT OF THE AGENCY LEAVING A POST-IT® NOTE ("AT FOCUS GROUP, HAVE CELL PHONE") STUCK ON THE DESK, NEXT TO MY CELL PHONE.

DAVIS

AFTER I COME BACK FROM THE MOVIE IDEA #101 COMES ALONG. IT'S NOT GREAT, BUT IT'S "PRETTY GOOD." BRACED WITH THIS SMALL VICTORY, I CHANGE GEARS. IF I'VE BEEN THINKING VERBALLY, I SWITCH TO VISUAL.

FINALLY, MY PEN STARTS MOVING. BUT UPON REVIEW, IDEAS #102 THROUGH #130 ALL STINK AND I GO HOME IN DESPAIR.

THE NEXT DAY OR MAYBE THE NEXT WEEK I DISCOVER IDEA #101 CLICKS LIKE A LEGO® INTO IDEA #131.

"WOW," I THINK. "IT'S NOT BAD." AND THE ANVIL THAT HAS BEEN ON MY CHEST SINCE THE DAY I STARTED WRITING, SLIDES OFF.

Luke Sullivan is chief creative officer of WestWayne, headquartered in Atlanta. He's the author of HEY, WHIPPLE, SQUEEZE THIS, a book widely used in ad schools. He counts among his awards an ATHENA, representing the best newspaper advertising in the country. To see examples of his work and other great newspaper ads, visit www.naa.org.

The Newspaper

This message is brought to you by the Newspaper Association of America and the publishing newspaper. Drawing: Paul Davis.

early on, you may settle for an idea that's just so-so, or you may never allow a gem of an idea to develop.

Be sure to test your idea on others. You may be so close to the idea that you don't see potential problems, so show it to others and get their feedback. Ogilvy & Mather tells its account people to ask the following questions when evaluating creative work: Is it on strategy? What did you get from the advertising? Was that net impression a good or bad one? Why? Did you remember to react to this ad as a consumer, not as an advertising person? Does the ad address the right group of people? Is the tone consistent with the strategy? Is it a good execution? Is the promise visualized effectively? How? Is the brand name up front enough? Is the core selling idea clear? Does the execution lend itself to a total campaign? If so, what might be some other executions? Does something make you stop, look, listen quickly? What is it?

Creative Exercises

Apply the following questions to your advertising problem, and you'll likely come up with some creative answers. One of them might lead to the big idea.

Is There an Idea in the Strategy Statement?

The strategy statement you learned to write in the last chapter serves as a road map for your idea-generation process. Try taking key words from this statement and use them as a springboard for other words, phrases, and images. For instance, the strategy for Kellogg's NutriGrain breakfast bars told the creative team that consumers want to eat the right thing. They know healthy food will make them look and feel good, but they're tempted by junk food that goes straight to their hips and thighs. By jotting down words, phrases, and images from this consumer insight, the creative team came up with the imagery of a humongous donut wrapped around someone's waist and giant sticky buns stuck on a woman's rear end. The benefit of eating NutriGrain, self-respect, led to the line, "Respect yourself in the morning."[5]

Where Will Your Ad Run?

NutriGrain ran billboards next to donut shops and fast-food restaurants to reinforce their message. DiGiorno Rising Crust Pizza reinforced their message "It's not delivery. It's DiGiorno." by placing ads in yellow-page directories next to ads from take-out pizza restaurants. The headline asked, "Looking for a pizza that bakes up fresh like pizzeria pizza? Look in your

---

[5] Adapted from a lecture given by Dr. Lauren Tucker at the University of South Carolina, 16 October 2001.

Figure 5-1
What's that giant spot doing on this newspaper ad?! If you're a dog owner, you know. Good boy! And good use of media to generate a creative idea!

Good Boy!

freezer." The copy led users to an 800 number for a coupon worth $1.50 off the consumer's next purchase.

Minute Maid bought the back page of each section of the *New York Times* to introduce its Premium Choice juice. The ad in the Business section included a coupon along with some financial advice: "This might be the only sure thing you'll ever find in the business section." The ad in the Metropolitan section played off of the fact that so many New Yorkers become snowbirds when they retire: "Today, the Metropolitan section also has important news from New York's sixth borough, Florida."

Students from The Creative Circus showed how newspaper ads are the perfect medium to reach dog owners (see Figure 5-1).

Don't just stick to traditional media to run your message. Think creatively as Kirshenbaum Bond & Partners did when it stenciled the sidewalks of New York with the message "From here, it looks like you could use some new underwear. Bamboo Lingerie."

Crispin & Porter Advertising also used unconventional media to describe what it's like to be homeless. Ads for the Miami Rescue Mission ran on shopping carts, bus shelters, park benches, and trash dumpsters. Each had the following copy: "When you're homeless, you see the world differently. To help call 571-2273." What made the ads so powerful was how the headlines and media choices related to the overall message: The ad on the park benches was headlined "Bed." The message on the dumpsters read "Kitchen." The poster inside the bus shelter was labeled "House." The sign on the grocery carts described it as a "Closet."

What's the Context of Your Message?

What will the members of your target audience be doing when they see or hear your ad? For example, several television stations in the Philippines run "insomnia ads" in place of the standard color bar sign-off signals. An Advil ad reads, "If you're reading this instead of sleeping, you'll probably have a headache later." Bayan Tel's message has a twist on a popular movie title: "Sleepless in Manila? Call Seattle or any place in the U.S. for only 40¢/min." Mr. Donut asks, "Already thinking of breakfast? Suggestion: Mr. Donut."

Noxema bought ad space in women's restrooms throughout Manhattan. The ads grabbed your attention because they were printed in reverse—you needed a mirror to read them. Appropriately, the ads were hung in frames on the walls across the mirrors so that, when a woman checked her makeup in the mirror, she was greeted with messages such as these:

"Look as good as the woman your date is hitting on."

"Did someone miss her beauty sleep?"

"He must really love you for your inner beauty."

Here are other clever messages that make a relevant connection to what consumers are doing when they see the message:

"Ref, you need glasses."
   (Outdoor board for an optician, placed at a sports stadium)

"Hello to all our readers in high office."
   (Message for *The Economist* magazine, painted on the roof of a bus)

"20 ounce soda. 6 inch pothole"
   (Message for Tide, placed on the exterior of a bus)

What's the Timing of Your Ads?

When will your ad run? Is the timing significant to your target audience? For example, Pepto-Bismol ran an ad in April issues of magazines. How does the month of April relate to queasy stomachs? April 15 is tax day, a day that can make some taxpayers sick to their stomachs. That's why Pepto-Bismol ran a full-page copy of a 1040 form, with a corner rolled up to reveal a bottle of Pepto-Bismol.

Wild Turkey Kentucky Straight Bourbon Whiskey made an unexpected but relevant suggestion for people who were expecting company for the holidays: "This Thanksgiving serve Turkey before dinner." Vick's NyQuil ran an ad during the holiday season, when many people seem to catch colds, with this message: "Silent night." And Saatchi & Saatchi used holidays as a source of inspiration for Tide laundry detergent ads:

> "The only way to wear white after Labor Day."
>   (Ran on Labor Day)

> "It takes a wee bit more than luck to get green beer out of your clothes."
>   (Ran on St. Patrick's Day)

> "Removes alien goo, fake blood and, oh yeah, chocolate."
>   (Ran on Halloween)

What's in the News?

Did something major just happen? Is something about to happen? Ads that tap into current events reflect what's on people's minds and make your brand seem timely. This approach is great if you have the resources to constantly change your ads.

America's Dairy Farmers and Milk Processors frequently tap into major events such as sporting events, elections, and television shows. For instance, on Super Bowl Monday, you'll see the winning quarterback sporting a milk mustache. Two versions of the ad are shot in advance, just in case the outcome isn't what everyone expects.

Can You Borrow from the Pages of History?

McCann–Erickson, Singapore, studied old ads from the Simmons Bed Company and discovered an old brochure from the 1930s that featured a testimonial from Eleanor Roosevelt. This inspired an idea that won gold at the One Show. The headline read:

> FOR PRESIDENT ROOSEVELT,
> A DAY AT THE OFFICE
> INVOLVED SENDING 750,000
> MEN INTO A MINEFIELD.
> EVER WONDERED HOW HE
> SLEPT AT NIGHT?

What Are the Negatives About Your Brand?

What negative thoughts do your potential customers have about your client? What negative thoughts do you have about your client? Don't try to cover up a negative—embrace it. After all, what's negative to one person can be positive to another. A copywriter at Macy's was faced with the challenge of selling orange luggage. It was just plain ugly. What could she do? She could omit the fact that it was orange. After all, she wasn't taking mail and phone orders, so she didn't have to mention color at all. And, because the ad was going to run in black and white, no one would know the difference, right? Wrong. Customers would know the minute they came to the store. They would be furious, and the store could lose valued customers. So she wrote something along these lines: "Does your luggage get lost at the airline terminals? We've got the perfect luggage for you!" The luggage sold out because she turned a negative into a selling advantage, and she told the truth.

What if Your Product Were Something Else?

Make an analogy. If your product were a person, would it be young? Old? Carefree? Uptight? If it were a tree, would it be a giant redwood or a bonsai? How about if it were a dog or cat? Crate & Barrel described its "Sonoma" collection of furniture as if it were a fashion model: "Shapely legs. French looks. Mildly distressed. Available for dinner." *Good Housekeeping* magazine touted the virtues of its Seal of Approval to advertisers: "The seal is like your therapist: It assures you everything will be alright."

An MTV campaign promoted the use of condoms by using an analogy to other types of safety equipment. In one spot, a roller coaster attendant tries to put a safety belt on the young man who protests, "I want to be free. I want to feel everything. I just want to make this time special." The attendant reluctantly agrees, "All right, just this once." The roller coaster takes off, a scream is heard, and the young man's seat is empty when the roller coaster returns. Another spot shows a young man swimming in shark-infested waters without a shark cage, and a third shows him climbing a mountain without a harness. The spots end with the message "Stop making excuses. Always use protection"; viewers are directed to a toll-free number and Web site for more information about AIDS prevention.

What Is Your Target Audience Reading and Watching?

Books, movies, plays, and television programs can serve as inspiration. It can be the highbrow variety or the pop culture variety. Just make sure it's relevant to your target audience.

Federal Express did its own version of the movie *Cast Away* in a commercial that shows a FedEx employee delivering a package that he has protected the entire time he was marooned on a deserted island. He asks the grateful recipient what's in the package and discovers it contains a satellite phone, GPS locator, fishing rod, water purifier, and some seeds. "Silly things" to the recipient, but the very things that could have helped get him off the island or at least made his stay more enjoyable.

A scene from the film *When Harry Met Sally* inspired the idea behind the Clairol Herbal Essences campaign. In the movie, Meg Ryan fakes an orgasm in the middle of a restaurant. She moans, "It's so gooooood. Ohhhhh. Ohhhhh. Yes! Yes! YES!!!!" The movie camera pans to a middle-aged woman who tells the waiter, "I'll have what she's having." This scene inspired the idea of the totally organic experience offered to people who wash their hair with Clairol Herbal Essences shampoo.

British Airways exchanged partners of famous couples in literature to communicate that companions fly free. One ad read, "Romeo & Delilah"; another, "Jekyll & Gretel"; and another, "Hansel & Juliet." All ran with the tag line "Who you bring is up to you."

What Does the Product Look Like?

Try dipping a french fry in some ketchup. See anything special? Saatchi & Saatchi, Singapore, saw a matchstick that led to an ad for Burger King's "Fiery fries." Meanwhile, fast-food rival McDonald's golden arches have appeared in ads as the straps on a backpack, ears on an Easter bunny, and the body of a car.

In an effort to influence behavior, Allstate Insurance illustrated how drinking and driving don't mix. No, they didn't show a car wreck. Instead, they invented a "killer cocktail"—a martini with a car key jabbing the olive as if it were a toothpick. To make their brand welcome in any home, American Standard put a friendly face on its bathroom fixtures (Figure 5-2).

Where Is the Product Made? Where Is It Sold?

Pace Picante Sauce promoted its authentic Tex-Mex heritage by poking fun of other brands that were "made in New York City!" Meanwhile, a billboard for Zamboli's Italian restaurant (located in South Carolina) told drivers the mileage to the closest great Italian food:

> Great Italian Food Ahead
>
> Rome 4,574 Mi.   Venice 4,634 Mi.   Zamboli's Next Right

What regions of the country (or the world) will see your ad? Can you customize it in any way? Some ads have fun with regional accents. An ad promoting a concert by a southern choir read, "Hallaluy'all." An ad in a tourist magazine invited people to visit "The Boston Museum of Fine Ahht."

Can You Say It with Just Pictures or Just Words?

Think of a solution with just pictures. Then think of a solution with just words. For example, Target wanted to communicate that their stores sell a wide variety of merchandise in a hip and unexpected way. Billboards listed

IT'S SEEN YOU
NAKED
IT'S HEARD YOU
SING

Your bathroom probably knows more about you than your own mother. So it's only fitting you make it the most wonderful room in the house. Call us and we'll send you a free guidebook overflowing with products, ideas and inspiration. 1-800-524-9797. *American Standard*

Figure 5-2
What does your product look like? Is there an idea in the shape of your product? In this case, the bathroom fixture looks like a friendly face.

series of three things you could find at their store. Here are some of our favorites:

"Twinkies. Cheetos. Wide Aisles."

"VCRs. Barney Tapes. Aspirin."

"Aquariums. Fish Food. Toilet Plungers."

Target used a visual approach in its magazine campaign. One ad shows a woman jumping in the air as she twirls a lug wrench as if she were a cheerleader. Another shows a woman wearing a black top and what looks like curlers—only on closer examination they turn out to be paint rollers. Still another shows a woman wearing a car's air filter as a necklace. Another shows a woman wearing a backpack and a lampshade as a skirt.

Is There an Ideal Spokesperson?

As Chapter 1 states, the right spokesperson can help you break through the clutter and make a relevant connection with your target audience. Bob Dole made older, conservative men realize it was okay to use Viagra. *Crocodile Dundee* star Paul Hogan helped turn Outback Steakhouses into a fun destination. For more than 50 years, Smokey Bear has convinced children not to play with matches.

Sometimes a mistake in the celebrity's past can trigger an idea. Willie Nelson's troubles with the IRS inspired a commercial for H&R Block. In real life, Nelson had to release a double album to raise the money he owed to the IRS. In the commercial, Nelson learns he owes $30 million in back taxes. To become solvent, Nelson agrees to shave his beard for a shaving cream commercial. The message? Don't get bad advice. Let H&R Block double-check your taxes.

Is There an Idea in the Brand's Name?

Insurance is one of life's necessities that few people understand. Consider life insurance, for example. Young & Rubicam found that many people thought of it as a premium that's paid only after someone dies. So how could they get people to think of Metropolitan Life in terms of life, not death? Part of the answer was in the name of the company, Met Life. A series of ads show people enjoying life's simple pleasures and the tag line "Have You Met Life Today?" sums up the idea. One commercial shows a little girl kissing her mother as a female voice-over says, "Today, one of our advisors showed this single mother that when her daughter is ready for college she'll be ready to send her. Financially at least." Another shows a man playing with his children on a swing set. The voice-over says, "This afternoon one of our advisors showed this dad how to protect his family and still retire at 55."

If life insurance is difficult to understand, imagine what supplemental insurance is like. Most people never heard of it until the spunky AFLAC duck came along. As people search for the name of the company, the duck quacks, "Af-laccck!" Brand-name recognition rose from 13 to 91 percent, and the company experienced double-digit percentage gains in 2000 and 2001. The commercials are so popular that fans routinely shout, "Af-laccck!" when they see actor Ben Affleck.[6]

What's the Opposite of What You're Trying to Say?

If you're trying to say that something's comfortable, show something that's uncomfortable (Figure 5-3). If you're trying to sell something big, show a tiny detail. Likewise, if you want to sell peace, show the tragic outcome of war. A famous political commercial featured an adorable girl counting the petals on a daisy. When her count is about to reach ten, the visual motion freezes, and you hear a countdown in a man's voice. As the countdown proceeds, the

---

[6] Stuart Elliott, "This Duck Means Business," *New York Times,* 11 February 2003, nytimes.com.

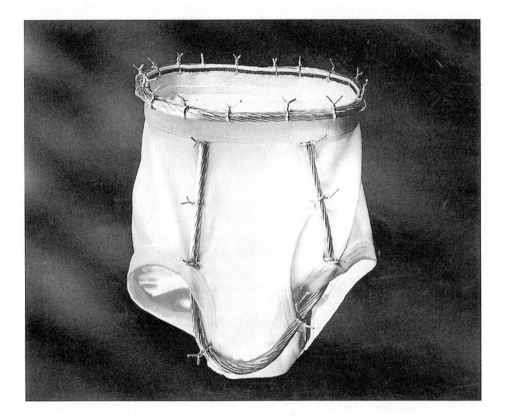

GUYS SAY WE'RE MOODY AND EMOTIONAL. LET'S SEE HOW THEY FEEL AFTER 8 HOURS IN AN UNDERWIRE.

Chances are, few men would choose to wear a device that pokes, pinches and rides up into their delicate parts. So why should we? Introducing Magic Ring, the first true wireless support bra by Lovable. With unique

Magic Ring™

Wearing is believing.™

Comfort Panels™ stitched into the garment running from cup to shoulder, it cradles you in soft fabric. Instead of hard steel. Giving you the same shape and support as a wire. Without radically altering your state of mind.

by LOVABLE ♡

To find the Magic Ring bra in the store nearest you, call 1-800-822-9113. Original Magic Ring • Lace • Sports Bra • Body Briefers

Figure 5-3
One way to come up with an idea is to ask "what if"? This clever ad asks, "What if men wore an underwire?"

camera zooms in on the girl's face until you're looking into the pupil of her eye. You see black for a tiny fraction of a second. When the countdown reaches zero, a nuclear mushroom cloud appears in the girl's black pupil and you hear Lyndon Johnson: "These are the stakes, to make a world in which all God's children can live, or to go into the darkness. Either we must love each other or we must die." The screen goes to black with white type, "on November 3rd, Vote for President Johnson." The commercial ran only once, but some say it demolished Barry Goldwater's chances of winning the 1964 election. A spin-off of the commercial ran in 2000 by MoveOn, an advocacy group that suggested Al Gore's dealings with China were a threat to national security.[7]

Can You Combine Creative Exercises?

Combine your client's brand name with timing, media, location, or pop culture. What do you get? Absolut vodka got an award-winning campaign that turned an obscure brand into the leading imported vodka. Here are a few examples:

> ABSOLUT PSYCHO
> *Visual:* Shower curtain with slash marks that form the shape of an Absolut bottle
>
> ABSOLUT CHICAGO
> *Visual:* Bottle of Absolut with letters being blown off of it
>
> ABSOLUT SCROOGE
> *Visual*: Mini bottle of Absolut, ran before Christmas
>
> ABSOLUT CENTERFOLD
> *Visual:* Absolut bottle without any lettering on it. Ran in *Playboy*

Guidelines for Brainstorming

1. *Don't think you must come up with the big idea all by yourself.* Steve Hayden, one of the creators of the famous 1984 commercial for Apple Computers, puts it all in perspective: "It's better to own 20% of a great idea than 100% of a so-so idea."[8]

   A great visual idea can come from a writer. The perfect headline can come from an artist. And, as we saw earlier, creative solutions can come from media experts. You may want to work independently at first and

---

[7] Although we do not condone negative political advertising, the original commercial, produced by Tony Schwartz, is an excellent example of production techniques and may be viewed at a variety of historical advertising archives and Web sites including www.ammi.org.

[8] Laurence Minsky and Emily Thornton Calvo, *How to Succeed in Advertising When All You Have Is Talent* (Lincolnwood, IL: NTC Business Books, 1995), p. 99.

then bounce ideas off your creative partner. You may want to start out by doing free association with one or two colleagues. Perhaps you want to brainstorm with a group of six to twelve people. When you brainstorm in a group, be sure to designate a leader who will keep the session going and record the ideas. Also, be sure that every person participates and that no idea is considered stupid. After the session, there will be time to sort quality from quantity.

2. *Start a swipe file.* Fill a folder or file cabinet or wallpaper an entire room with work you consider outstanding. You shouldn't "swipe" ideas, but you can use them as a springboard. The legendary Leo Burnett used to rip out ads that struck him as being effective communications. About twice a year, he'd riffle through that file—not with the idea of copying anything, but in the hope that it would trigger an idea that could apply to something else he was doing. Burnett also kept a folder of phrases he liked.

> *Whenever I hear a phrase in conversation or any place which strikes me as being particularly apt in expressing an idea or bringing it to life or accentuating the smell of it, the looks of it or anything else— or expressing any kind of an idea—I scribble it down and stick it in there.*[9]

Burnett made that comment back in the 1960s, but the advice is still appropriate today.

3. *Exercise your creative mind regularly.* Hang out with creative people, whether in your field or a totally different one. Go to the zoo. Visit a museum. See a play. Do something you've never done before. And be sure to pay attention to the nuances of everyday life. Creative director Jim Riswold admits,

> *I have never had an original thought in my career. Everything I have ever done has been borrowed, reformulated, regurgitated, turned upside down or inside out, played back at a different speed, and sometimes just plain stolen from either popular culture, music, history, art, literature, the back of cereal boxes, Hegelianism, an athlete's life, a bedtime story my grandmother once read me—whatever. Anything and everything is fair game when it comes to stimulus.*[10]

4. *Give yourself some down time.* You need to give your mind a break otherwise you'll overload on stimuli. Try spending some time alone. Try turning off the TV, radio, and email for a week. You'll find that removing the extra "noise" is the equivalent of meditation. Also, write in a journal every day to keep your ideas flowing. Don't think of it as creative writing;

[9] Denis Higgins, *Conversations with William Bernbach, Leo Burnett, George Gribbin, David Ogilvy, Rosser Reeves* (Lincolnwood, IL: NTC Business Books, 1989), p. 47.
[10] Warren Berger, *Advertising Today* (London: Phaidon Press Limited, 2001), p. 157.

think of it as "brain dumping." The idea is to get two to three pages of your thoughts on paper daily.

5. *Come up with a lot of ideas.* The more ideas, the better. Luke Sullivan, an award-winning copywriter, warns, "As a creative person, you will discover your brain has a built-in tendency to want to reach closure, even rush to it. . . . But in order to get to a great idea, which is usually about the 500th one to come along, you'll need to resist the temptation to give in to the anxiety and sign off on the first passable idea that shows up."[11] (For more inspiration from Sullivan, read the ad he wrote on page 95.)

Consider these two sets of instructions:

Instruction 1: "Come up with a good idea that will solve the problem of declining student enrollment at XYZ University. Your name and idea will be forwarded to the president of the university."

Instruction 2: "Come up with as many ideas as possible to help solve the problem of declining student enrollment at XYZ University. Jot down as many ideas as possible. Try to come up with at least 25 ideas. Don't judge the merits of your ideas. Write every idea you have."

What would happen if you got the first set of instructions? You'd probably freeze up because you'd place unnecessary pressure on yourself. You'd second-guess the thoughts that came into your head and would automatically dismiss any that you felt weren't good. The idea you finally put on paper would most likely be a safe approach because you knew others—including the president of the university—would be evaluating it.

Now what would happen if you got the second set of instructions? Well, you'd probably come up with some pretty dumb ideas. But you'd also probably come up with some pretty good ones. In fact, you might even come up with a great idea. Idea 23 might be the winner. But if you only came up with one idea, idea 23 would never occur to you. And who knows what would happen if you came up with 100 ideas or more!

Keep the second set of instructions in mind in the idea-generation stage. Give yourself total freedom to come up with bad ideas. Who knows? Those bad ideas may spark great ideas when someone else hears them. And if the idea is a real dud, you can always drop it later in the process.

Turn an Idea into a Campaign Theme

It's very rare that you will be asked to come up with an idea for a single ad. Most often, you'll be asked to come up with an idea that has "legs"—one that can run over time as a campaign. Some of the most famous and successful

---

[11] Luke Sullivan, *Hey Whipple, Squeeze This: A Guide to Creating Great Ads* (New York: Wiley, 1998), p. 72.

campaigns have been running for decades. So before you settle on an idea for a single ad, ask yourself, what will the next ad be like? And the one after that? And the one a year from now? And five or ten years from now? Does the idea stand the test of time? That is, is it campaignable?

A campaign is a series of ads that reflect the same big idea and have a similar theme and attitude. Often the individual ads will have the same look, in which the art director specifies the size and location of the visual and logo, the size and font of the type, and so on. Also, often the copy in each ad follows the same structure, from the length of the headline, right down to the last line of copy. But it doesn't have to be this structured. For instance, look at the ads for Bell Helmet found in the BriefCase in Chapter 3. Some of Bell Helmets' headlines ask questions whereas others give statements. Headlines range from three words to seventeen. Some ads show the product in use whereas others show what happens if you don't wear a Bell Helmet. There are similarities, however. The type font is the same, as is the tag line, "Courage for your head." So is the attitude and writing style of the ads. The ads may not look the same, but they're definitely part of the same campaign.

Campaign ideas transcend different media. Take a peak back at the Chick-fil-A BriefCase found in Chapter 4, and you'll see how the big idea— cows pleading for people to "eat mor chikin"—works for outdoor billboards, television, and radio. In each case, the cows appear to be creating the ads. The brand personality is very evident in each of the ads.

At times you'll be asked to develop multiple campaigns to reach different target audiences. For example, Loeffler Ketchum Mountjoy created numerous campaigns to convince a wide variety of people to vacation in North Carolina. Their research showed some people want to "veg out" and leave their worries behind them when they go on vacation. Others prefer to commune with nature and want to know the name of every wildflower and bird they encounter on their journey. The more adventuresome want to test their endurance by going head-to-head with nature. History buffs want to explore old sites and learn from yesterday's past. These wonderful campaigns for North Carolina are scattered throughout this book. The BriefCase in this chapter looks at how Loeffler Ketchum Mountjoy targeted filmmakers and producers to convince them to film in North Carolina.

Using Criticism to Improve Your Ideas

A critical part of the creative process involves working in teams and checking your work by asking others to react to it. The other person can see your idea with a clear and unbiased mind. Second, if your evaluator knows advertising, chances are that he or she can judge your work both as a consumer and as a professional. The key to a good critique is objectivity. This means you critique the work, not the person. Look for positive things and then question things that may not seem clear or strong or that simply don't work for you.

Here are some additional pointers to help you make criticism palatable:[12]

1. *Make "I" statements.* Own your criticism by saying "I'm confused by this sentence" not "You confused me."

2. *Be clear and specific, commenting on the work, not the person.* Instead of "Why do you always make the same mistake?" try "This should be written as two separate sentences. Do you remember doing that before?"

3. *Never say, "This is great, BUT . . ."* Eliminate the threatening *but* and get to the point: "I think the opening is fine. Here in the middle, I don't know if you're stressing the right benefits."

4. *Control your emotions and speak in a normal tone of voice.*

5. *Show some empathy and understanding.* "I wonder if you didn't hear me when I gave directions for this assignment."

6. *Offer practical suggestions.* Without suggestions on how the work might be improved, criticism is generally useless. Surprisingly, students seem to have a greater knack for offering suggestions to their peers than for figuring out how to fix their own work. Try it; pair up with someone in your class and trade suggestions for improvement.

7. *Be honest.* If you don't like something, explain why. But begin with a positive comment, end on a positive note, and sandwich the negative comment in-between. This helps the recipient be more accepting of what you have to say.

Here are some guidelines for nonverbal behaviors:

1. *Make eye contact with the person.* Looking away diminishes the power of the communication.

2. *Show your interest through a warm and expressive tone of voice.*

3. *Use facial expressions that are consistent with your message.* Don't grin as you address deficiencies and don't frown as you offer compliments.

4. *Don't slouch or slump.* This is important because these postures suggest that either you're uncomfortable with what you have to say or you're not honoring the evaluator's effort.

5. *Stand or sit an appropriate distance from the other person.* Either both of you stand or both sit.

6. *Choose an appropriate time and place for this discussion.* As the recipient of the critique, you have both rights and obligations in this process. First, you have the right to ask for a later meeting if the time or place chosen is inconvenient or uncomfortable. And you have the right to terminate the critique if it is delivered in an offensive manner.

---

[12] Compliments of Dr. Serge Piccinin, director of the Teaching Centre at the University of Ottawa.

Suggested Activities

1. Think of unconventional media to convince people to stop smoking, to drink responsibly, and to recycle. Now develop messages for each of these issues.

2. Create an ad that uses a headline and visual to communicate a selling point in an unexpected way. Next, create an ad that uses just a headline. Finally, create an ad that lets the visual stand on its own. Which approach works best? Why?

3. Develop twenty advertising ideas for a pawnshop. Here's some background information:

   • Pawn shops date back to ancient times.

   • Queen Isabella of Spain pawned her jewelry to finance Columbus on his voyage to America.

   • The three gold balls in front of a pawnshop are derived from symbols used by Italian merchants.

   • Pawnshops are the forerunner of modern banks. The pawnbroker loans money on personal property that his customers give him. The customer is issued a ticket, which is a contract stating the amount of the loan, the service charge, and the specific time the pawnbroker will hold the property. The process takes only a few minutes.

   • All pawnbrokers are regulated by law, so the customers know they're not being "taken."

   • Pawn shops offer values. Because pawnbrokers deal with people from all walks of life, they can offer for sale a vast array of merchandise: TVs, diamond rings, power tools, exercise equipment, and much more, at lower prices than just about any other place.

   • All classes of people borrow and buy from pawnbrokers.

4. Let your imagination run rampant, relax, and write a whimsical paper on any or all of the following fantasy situations:

   If it rained all day, how would my life be different?

   If I had unlimited income, how would my life be different?

   If I lived on an island in the Pacific, how would my life be different?

   If the sun never set, how would my life be different?

   If 50 degrees were the temperature constantly and forever, how would my life be different?

5. Using the scenarios listed in the previous activity, develop ideas for new products that will make the most of the situations.

6. Create a game to see how creative you and your friends are. On one set of index cards list various products and services (for example, cough medicine, facial tissues, soft drinks, canned soup, sports car, bath towels, dental floss, bottled water, luggage, lamp). On another set of cards,

Figure 5-4
You probably heard of reading messages in tea leaves. Now you can read social messages in alphabet soup. Public donations to the Food Bank of Central New York increased 70 percent as a result of this campaign.

BREAKFAST IS THE MOST IMPORTANT MEAL OF THE DAY. ESPECIALLY WHEN IT'S THE ONLY ONE.

That's the harsh reality for thousands of families right here in Central New York. But every $1 you donate helps us put $14 worth of nutritious food in their bowls. So please help us help them.

FOOD BANK
OF CENTRAL NEW YORK
437-1899

describe various sounds on paper (man snoring, buzz, creak, cricket chirp, scream, siren, running water, and so on). Without looking, draw one card from each stack. Use the sound you have drawn as the basis for a radio commercial to sell the product or service you have drawn. Act it out.

7. Look at the two campaigns for food banks shown in Figures 5-4 and 5-5. Which campaign do you think is stronger? Why? Now come up with new ideas that will motivate people to donate to food banks.

Figure 5-4 (continued)

SOUP IS GOOD FOOD. WHEN YOU HAVE SOME.

The harsh reality is, thousands of families right here in Central New York don't. But every $1 you donate helps us put $14 worth of nutritious food in their bowls. So please help us help them.

FOOD BANK OF CENTRAL NEW YORK 437-1899

8. Make an inventory of your "creative resources" and seek new worlds to conquer. First, make a list of your favorite films, entertainers, music, fiction and nonfiction books, magazines, live plays and musicals, live concert performances, television programs, and leisure activities. Share these with classmates and your professor. Now make a concerted effort to add something different to that list. If you watch TV sitcoms, spend an hour or more watching a nature program, a ballet performance, or a historical documentary. If you like country music, try a symphony. What did you learn about yourself as a result of this exercise?

Figure 5-5
All too often people think
bad things happen else-
where. Henderson Adver-
tising woke up residents
of Greenville to the reality
that hunger is right in
their backyards.

Figure 5-5 (continued)

Search Online! Discovering More About Finding the Big Idea

Use InfoTrac College Edition to discover more ways to find the big idea. Try these phrases and others for Key Words and Subject Guide searches: *advertising ideas, exploring possibilities, lateral thinking, finding answers, finding solutions, brainstorming, visualization, analogies, metaphors, idea generation, criticism.*

The following Web sites will inspire ideas:

GoCreate.com: www.gocreate.com

CreativeThink: www.creativethink.com

North Carolina Plays a Starring Role

*F*orrest Gump was filmed in North Carolina. So was *Last of the Mohicans, The Hunt for Red October, Divine Secrets of the Ya-Ya Sisterhood, Teenage Nina Turtles, Dawson's Creek,* and hundreds of other movies and TV shows. In fact, North Carolina is one of the top film-making states in the United States, ranked behind only California and New York.

Since 1980, North Carolina's Film Office has recruited more than 600 movies, nine television series, and thousands of national TV commercials, generating more than $6 billion in production revenue. In 2002 alone, the film industry spent more than $230 million in North Carolina while making movies, television shows, and commercials.

Why are filmmakers interested in North Carolina? For starters, it offers an impressive array of locations from pristine beaches to tropical swamps to panoramic vistas from atop the Blue Ridge Mountains. More than a million acres of national and state forestlands provide vast unspoiled areas for filming wilderness scenes. Locations in the state's cities and towns feature authentic Colonial, antebellum, modern high-tech, and middle-American architecture.

Another plus is that North Carolina has a generally mild climate, plus the advantage of distinctive spring, summer, fall, and winter seasons. It also has a well-established production infrastructure that includes a world-class crew base of more than 1500 seasoned film professionals, eight full-service studio complexes, more than 30 soundstages, 400 support-service companies, and five regional film commissions. And there's some truth to the legendary southern hospitality—the crews are very friendly and accommodating. Over-all, there are fewer day-to-day hassles than what filmmakers may experience elsewhere.

The advertising campaign created by Loeffler Ketchum Mountjoy speaks the language of filmmakers and producers and offers convincing reasons to shoot on location in North Carolina. The body copy for the ads follows:

Information from www.nc.film.com. Ads courtesy of Loeffler Ketchum Mountjoy.

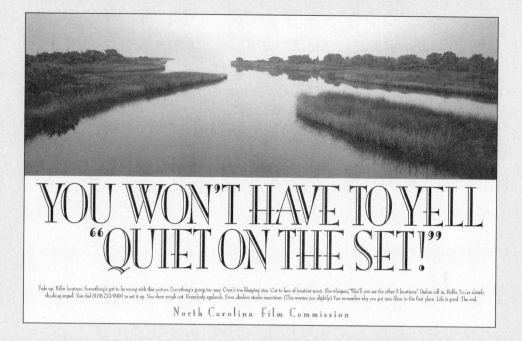

YOU WON'T HAVE TO YELL "QUIET ON THE SET!"

"QUIET ON THE SET!"

Fade up. Killer location. Something's got to be wrong with this picture. Everything's going too easy. Crew's too bleeping nice. Cut to face of location scout. She whispers, "Wait'll you see the other five locations." Dailies roll in. Boffo. You're already thinking sequel. You dial (919)733-9900 to set it up. You show rough cut. Everybody applauds. Even clueless studio executives. (This worries you slightly.) You remember why you got into films in the first place. Life is good. The end.

THERE'S ONLY ONE PROBLEM WITH SHOOTING IN THOSE FAMOUS BIG CITIES. SOMEBODY MIGHT SHOOT BACK.

Fade up. Gritty urban location. You'd swear by the look that you're somewhere in Brooklyn. Southside Chicago. L.A. But the feel is entirely different. People are friendly. Cooperative. Even government officials. No traffic nightmares. No sea of red tape to wade through. You're having a blast on the shoot. You're getting really good craft service. When you yell "Cut" nobody knifes you. It's the way things should be. You're able to concentrate on your art instead of a lot of moronic distractions. Get your acceptance speech ready. The end.

IF THE SCRIPT ISN'T EXACTLY OSCAR BAIT, AT LEAST THE CINEMATOGRAPHY CAN BE.

Fade up. Location to die for. Cameraman needs a cigarette after every shot. Dissolve to scene of your footage arriving in Hollywood. Small crowds gather to marvel over it. Execs are suddenly calling you "that

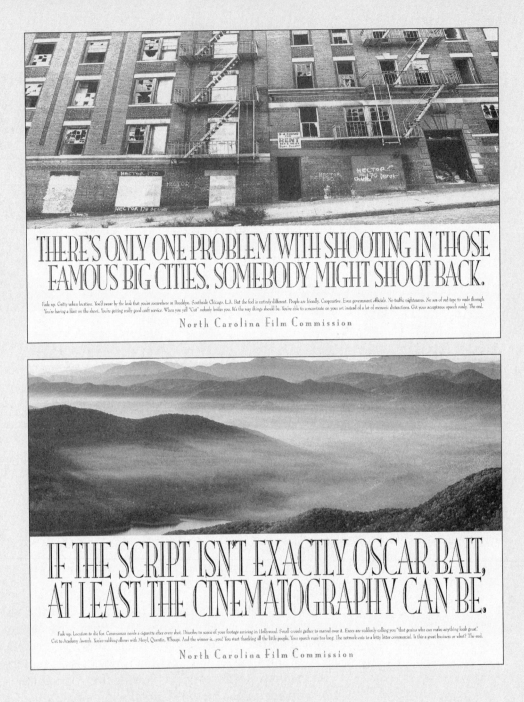

THERE'S ONLY ONE PROBLEM WITH SHOOTING IN THOSE FAMOUS BIG CITIES. SOMEBODY MIGHT SHOOT BACK.

Fade up. Gritty urban location. You'd swear by the look that you're somewhere in Brooklyn. Southside Chicago. LA. But the feel is entirely different. People are friendly. Cooperative. Even government officials. No traffic nightmares. No sea of red tape to wade through. You're having a blast on the shoot. You're getting really good craft service. When you yell "Cut" nobody insults you. It's the way things should be. You're able to concentrate on your art instead of a lot of moronic distractions. Get your acceptance speech ready. The end.

North Carolina Film Commission

IF THE SCRIPT ISN'T EXACTLY OSCAR BAIT, AT LEAST THE CINEMATOGRAPHY CAN BE.

Fade up. Location to die for. Cameraman needs a cigarette after every shot. Dissolve to scene of your footage arriving in Hollywood. Small crowds gather to marvel over it. Execs are suddenly calling you "that genius who can make anything look great." Cut to Academy Awards. You're rubbing elbows with Meryl, Quentin, Whoopi. And the winner is...you! You start thanking all the little people. Your speech runs too long. The network cuts to a kitty litter commercial. Is this a great business or what? The end.

North Carolina Film Commission

genius who can make anything look great." Cut to Academy Awards. You're rubbing elbows with Meryl, Quentin, Whoopi. And the winner is . . . you! You start thanking all the little people. Your speech runs too long. The network cuts to a kitty litter commercial. Is this a great business or what? The end.

WORDS ON PAPER:
CONNECTING TO CONSUMERS' HEARTS AND MINDS

Stephen King admits he doesn't so much create his stories as he does unearth them. Likewise, mystery writer James Lee Burke never sees more than two or perhaps three scenes ahead in a story. For him, the creative process is more one of discovery than creation. Ernie Schenck, columnist for *Communication Arts*, thinks that there's a lesson in this for advertising copywriters:

> *I've got a theory on why we don't see as many long copy print ads anymore. And it's got nothing to do with shrinking attention spans or MTV or video games. I think it's because we've lost touch with our inner storyteller. We think the concept is the story. Nail the big idea. Funky headline. Hip layout. Few lines of mandatories at the bottom and thank you, thank you very much.*[1]

Schenck suggests that advertising copywriters spend less effort manufacturing a brand and more helping it to simply reveal itself:

> *Yes, there are points we have to make. Information we need to impart. But how we get there, how we weave the story, this is something you can't plot out. You just start writing, conscious of the stuff that needs to*

---

[1] Ernie Schenck, "Mummies, Lost Arks and Long Copy Ads," *Communication Arts*, March/April 2003, pp. 134–136.

Courtesy of Loeffler Ketchum Mountjoy.

Figure 6-1

Copy reads: Why sugarcoat it? There is an undertone—the slightest whiff—of danger about the place. Of course, that's what gives the Outer Banks its seductive, otherworldly appeal. These islands were, after all, the favorite hideaways of some of history's most feared pirates: Blackbeard and Stede Bonnet. Today, the same qualities that drew those fugitives from justice attract a different breed of runaways: vacationers. Qualities like its remoteness. Its unapologetic plainness and simplicity. Its stark contrast to the bland tranquility of the cities. It's an edge of the world type of place. A place where the sand dunes grow taller than four-story buildings. Where dignified old lighthouses shine beacons atop the restless waters. And over 2,000 shipwrecks lie below them. The Outer Banks. Spare. Romantic. Unhip. Stunning. Part beauty. Part beast. We'll be expecting you.

find its way into the copy, but letting it form on the page almost on its own. Instead of consciously writing, you are unconsciously writing. The story tells itself.[2]

Let's look at an advertising campaign for North Carolina tourism for an example of great writing (Figure 6-1). Notice how the writer was able to weave information about North Carolina's history and topography into the ads? But you didn't sense that you were reading a fact sheet. Instead, you were reading a story about a destination that now beckons you. The copy in each ad is more than 150 words long, but you probably didn't even notice the length because it was so engaging.

[2] Ibid.

Figure 6-1 (continued)
Copy reads: In the beginning, they were both part of the prehistoric continent called Pangaea. Today, a living link still remains: the North Carolina Zoo in Asheboro, America's first natural habitat zoo. Here, during the course of a day, you and your children can watch antelopes and birds gather as they do on the African veldt. Observe endangered white rhinos feeding in a natural grassland habitat. Laugh at the antics of a family of lowland gorillas. And the age-old bond between the two lands continues to flourish in other ways. For example, a rare female wattled crane born in captivity here was recently flown back to her native South Africa to breed and help replenish their dwindling population. Strolling the grounds, you get a sense of the fragile interrelatedness of things. But that's as it should be. You see, long ago, we learned a valuable lesson: It's not just animals who benefit from staying connected with the past. Human beings do, too.

Your goal is to write in such an engaging way that the readers will give you their undivided attention. The message you write may be a line or two, or hundreds of words long. In some cases, the right visual can do most of the talking. We'll address the design process in the next chapter, but for now what's important to remember is that *how* an ad looks and *what* an ad says can contribute equally to the effectiveness of the message.

Headlines Help Form Good First Impressions

Be honest. You don't usually pick up a magazine or newspaper and say, "I can't wait to see the ads." In fact, you probably just skim the ads unless something stands out from the clutter and captures your attention. It's the

N eil French, world-wide creative director at Ogilvy & Mather, is a typical writer. He changed the original headline of the ad series, didn't want an illustration, refused to allow a logo from the newspaper sponsoring the ad, and had difficulty sticking to the 300 words of copy maximum. Heck, he couldn't keep to 1000 words. But every word is worth it. Be sure to read the other ads in the feature Tips & Tactics in Chapters 1, 4, 5, and 7.

Courtesy of the Newspaper Association of America.

Nobody reads long copy any more. Here's why.

Americans either don't read, won't read, or can't read. Somebody famous said that, so it must be true.

More importantly, absolutely no-one reads *newspapers* any more. That is a well-known fact.

And yet, blissfully ignorant of this, thousands of journalists and reporters spend their lives, pointlessly gathering information, news, and opinions, and writing about it. Day in, day out. Day after wasted day.

Sadder still, many more thousands of lost souls are glumly occupied in setting the result in type, designing the pages, and printing the damned things.

And strangely enough, millions of otherwise seemingly-sane people go out and buy... yes, buy... newspapers, every day. This is presumably, one imagines, because they need a cheap substitute for an umbrella, drawer-liners, or an inexhaustible supply of kitty-litter, for a herd of terminally incontinent 'cats'.

But nobody actually *reads* the newspaper. Dearie me, no.

By the way, Elvis was abducted by aliens, but has returned and is now working as a singing coconut for a time-share in Boca Raton.

So there *is* a God.

Oh, and I'm a little teapot.

Go away!

You're not still reading this drivel are you? Why, for heaven's sake? Believe me, it's not going to get any better. Go and do something useful. Count your socks.

Run along now. Shoo!

(Have they gone?)

Right then. Sorry about that, but you've got to get rid of the riff-raff. That's the only problem with writing for newspapers. All sorts of people pick them up. Beastly people, a lot of them, probably. Probably clip their toe-nails in bed. That sort of thing.

Where were we?

Erm... nobody reads newspapers, that was it. Well, I suppose we might admit that the people who *write* the newspapers read their own stuff. So do their Mums, unless there's wrestling on the tele.

For example, this particular exercise in futility was intended to be one in a series of ads headlined "How I write a newspaper ad; by (in this case) Neil French". Surely a headline so mind-numbingly dull as to rival the marvellous all-time great, "Small earthquake in Peru. Nobody hurt", as the most boring ever.

It was, God 'elp us, going to feature an illustration of *me*. My mother would have liked that, except she's dead, and one assumes, no longer collects my bits.

The fact is that the vast majority of the folks that bought this rag are never, ever, going to write an ad, and still less give a rat's bottom who Neil French is. And there are no words to describe how very little they care what a bloke they've never heard of *looks* like.

So, we changed the look of the ad, to somewhat disguise the fact that it is, on the one hand, insanely incestuous, and on the other, seems to contradict the very point it hopes to make.

Now, anyone still with us will be the anally-retentive sort of loser who has to deconstruct everything, and will have recognised the first bit of this epic as a rather plodding attempt at heavy irony. A useful tool for debunking, is the old irony-ploy.

But did you know that there's a myth that Americans don't understand irony? Since they apparently don't read either, it's probably academic, but, well, we're all-friends here, so for what it's worth, and to give us all a break, here's my favourite irony-story.

An American chap goes on holiday to England. On his return, he's telling his pal all about it:

'I was coming out of a shop, one day, and it was raining outside, so I took shelter in the doorway.'

'Another feller was sheltering, too, and he turned to me, and he said, "Nice weather."

'Well, of course, it wasn't nice weather at all. In fact it was terrible weather... and then I got it! This was the famous British irony. I loved it!

'And I've been using irony ever since. Like the other day, I was having this barbecue for the family and a bunch of neighbours, and I burned the burgers.

'And Joe, from next door, was standing there. And I turned to him, and I looked at the burgers, and I said, "Nice weather."'

(Pause for... bewilderment, I suppose... and back to business.)

Can we acknowledge, then, that the hundreds of thousands of words printed in this newspaper aren't put there *just* to make your fingers dirty?

Irony aside, people buy newspapers so that they can *read* them.

And since this is obvious to anyone with the intellect of a soap-dish, why is the newspaper not chock-full of ads for big, sexy, Brands?

The short, honest answer is, stupidity.

And the combined stupidity of agencies, researchers, (yes, *there's* a surprise), and one hates to say it, but clients, is a terrible thing to behold.

Basically, remember, you can prove just about anything: And if you want to prove that people don't read long copy in ads, you start by proving that people read only a small proportion of all the editorial articles in a newspaper.

(Television viewers, however, watch every show, every night, without ever switching channels. Note: In future, all irony will be in italics. But not all of the subsequent italicised words are ironic. Everybody clear on this?)

The fuzzy logic then goes like this: People don't read all the words in a newspaper. Therefore, people don't like to read.

Therefore, we must avoid all ads that depend on words.

Newspapers are full of words, so we must not advertise in them.

In the end, you know, you really cannot fight determined stupidity.

I once produced a campaign for a client who published newspapers, that proved beyond doubt that you could launch a beer brand, using newspapers only, more successfully than you could on T.V., and at a fraction of the cost.

The big-brand brewers were unmoved. Having been panicked for weeks by a press campaign that widdled all over their T.V. commercials, they ignored the evidence once the campaign was over.

So I somehow doubt that the opinions of the copywriters engaged in this little exercise are going to sway the prejudices of the sort of client who always knows best.

Still, we can but try.

Rule One of advertising is "Decide who you're talking to". It's also Rule Two. There is no rule three or four.

So, why talk to them in a newspaper? Because, simply put, a newspaper is not a mass medium. It's personal.

You can watch T.V. in a group. Posters are public. Radio is wallpaper.

But hold up a newspaper, and you have an effective barrier against the rest of the world. It is private.

Newspapers are portable. No-one tells you when or where to read them.

T.V. is, on the face of it, free. Radio is free. Posters are free. The internet is free. And advertising on all of them is regarded as an irritation, and rudest of all, an interruption.

People buy newspapers. You think they don't value them? Think again.

If you can't get people to read your ad in a newspaper, it's nobody's fault but your own.

(You recall that the original brief was to write an ad about how I write an ad? Well, I do it like this).

[signature]

They wanted to put a big, newspaper logo down here, so you'd know who paid for the space, but I thought that'd be obvious. I didn't get paid for writing it. I truly believe in newspapers.

job of the copywriter and art director to create headlines that turn skimmers into readers.

Functions of Headlines

1. *Capture the attention of your target audience.* Imagine that you're reading a food magazine filled with delicious recipes. You have a ravenous appetite when suddenly you read, "Start your next meal with Clorox bleach." The advertisement shows a fish with an eerie stare. It's disgusting. You don't want to look, but you can't help yourself. You read on and learn that Clorox bleach can sanitize your kitchen and prevent salmonella. You've lost your appetite, and you want to start cleaning. The ad has done its job.

2. *Select your audience.* You need to make certain the right people are reading your ads. Leo Burnett, founder of one of the most famous ad agencies in the world, had this to say:

   > *Best attention comes from the entirely natural interests of the reader, built around the results of the product advertised. Being different from others is not an asset if the others are right. An ad may get attention and fail completely in getting anything else. An able show window designer once said, "The thing to avoid is drawing a crowd. The hard thing is to catch the eye of every possible customer and keep the others walking past." It is better to attract the serious attention of possible buyers than, through an exaggerated and clever headline, to attract other possible readers who won't be interested in the message anyway.*[3]

   Notice how the headlines for Pro Dent (Figure 6-2) speak directly to drivers who baby their cars. These ads were placed on the sides of buses to reach car enthusiasts while they're driving.

3. *Lure readers into the body copy.* A good headline will make you think, "This is interesting. I want to know more." For example, who could resist wanting to know "What not to do in bed"? By the way, just in case you're interested, read on to find the answer later in this chapter.

4. *Communicate a benefit.* Tell readers what your product will do for them. Will it make them look better? Help them get ahead in their jobs? Make their children smarter? Protect their home? Your job as a writer is to

---

[3] Leo Burnett, from a memorandum to his creative staff, 13 November 1947. Reprinted in *Communications of an Advertising Man—Selections from Speeches, Articles, and Miscellaneous Writings of Leo Burnett,* Copyright 1961 by Leo Burnett Company, Inc., Chicago. For private distribution only. Used with permission.

Figure 6-2
Among people who drive expensive cars, a ding is a threat to identity. In four words, "I am my car." These busboard ads reach drivers while they're in their cars.

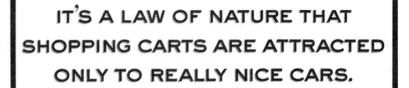

IT'S A LAW OF NATURE THAT SHOPPING CARTS ARE ATTRACTED ONLY TO REALLY NICE CARS.

Pro Dent
paintless dent removal
867.9324

HAIL HAPPENS.

Pro Dent
paintless dent removal
867.9324

FOR ALL YOU GUYS IN FANCY SPORTS CARS, REMEMBER: NO MATTER HOW LITTLE YOUR DING IS, WE CAN FIX IT.

Pro Dent
paintless dent removal
867.9324

take the benefit and bring it to life. Here's how Chevrolet told customers that their S-10 model could go really fast:

WITH 190 HORSEPOWER, THERE'S A REASON WE PUT SCOTCHGARD™ ON THE SEATS.

5. *Reinforce the brand name.* Have you ever loved an ad but been unable to remember the name of the product? While it's fine to entertain readers, don't sacrifice getting the product name across for the sake of creativity. The award-winning campaign for Absolut vodka is a wonderful example of how a brand name can be used creatively. Here are two examples:

ABSOLUT L.A.

(Visual of a swimming pool in the shape of an Absolut bottle)

ABSOLUT NANTUCKET

(Visual of a boardwalk in the shape of an Absolut bottle)

6. *Make an emotional connection to the customer.* Most people are suspicious of advertising claims. Therefore, you must make your message believable. Avis won a spot in people's hearts with the line "We're #2. We try harder." This is much more convincing than boasting, "We're one of the nation's leading car rental companies."

7. *Enhance a visual.* If a picture is worth a thousand words, a picture and a headline are worth thousands more. Together, a headline and a visual create synergy, whereby the whole is greater than the sum of its parts. For example, how do you show that a portable vacuum cleaner is really powerful? One solution is to run the warning "Be careful where you point it." This is a rather boring statement until you see the picture of a man's toupee flying toward the nozzle of the vacuum. Now that's picking up a rug!

Types of Headlines

Direct benefit   This type of headline offers readers a reason to use the product. For example, Shore's Fishing Lures boasts:

IT'S LIKE TOSSING A TWINKIE
INTO A WEIGHT WATCHER'S MEETING.

Reverse benefit   This type of headline implies that consumers will be worse off without the advertised product or service. Some also imply, "You'll be sorry if you go with the competition." If you use a reverse benefit, make sure you don't give your competition free advertising. Also, be careful that you don't make any remarks about your competition that aren't true.

The ads for Icelandair's BWI flights, shown in the BriefCase in Chapter 1, are great examples of a reverse benefit. Here are some other examples:

No wonder they call it high fashion.
To dream up some of those prices you'd have to be high.

(Ad for Daffy's clothing discounter)

I NEVER READ THE ECONOMIST.
—MANAGEMENT TRAINEE. AGED 42.

(Ad for *The Economist* magazine)

Factual   People love to read interesting pieces of trivia. The following head-line gives an interesting fact:

It takes 12 miles of cotton to
make a Lands' End® pinpoint oxford.
And that's just the beginning

The Lands' End copy goes on to explain that the shirt is tailored with 69 different sewing steps and the buttonholes are edged with 120 lock stitches. How much will readers remember? If they recall only that Lands' End really cares about the quality of its clothing, they got the message.

Selective   To attract a specific audience, address them in the headline. Sometimes, the audience is directly identified. For example, a headline for Allstate Insurance asks, "Do you own a small business?" Other times, the tone and choice of the words and visual will identify your audience:

Michelin. Because so much is riding on your tires.

(Ad shows a baby sitting next to a tire.)

Curiosity   Tempt your readers with just enough information to make them want to read more. "Ever wonder why most people make love in the dark?" entices readers to continue, especially when the only visual is a black rectan-gle where the picture should be. The ad, for a workout program, talks about getting in shape.

Although curiosity headlines can pull readers into the copy, they should be designed to arouse interest, not to confuse. An impatient reader who turns the page after reading an incomplete thought will miss your message.

News   Just as you want to know what's new with friends and family, you want to know what's new to eat, to wear, and to see. In fact, many advertis-ing experts believe that the word *new* is one of the most powerful in a copy-writer's vocabulary. Other powerful words include *introducing, now, finally, at last, today, presenting,* and *first.* Here's an example:

LIFE IN THE SOUTH
JUST GOT A LITTLE SWEETER.

(Ad for Kellogg's Raisin Bran in *Southern Living* magazine)

Command   Order the reader to do something. For years, Nike told sports fans, "Just do it." In the process, this simple phrase convinced people to just buy it (Nike, that is). Other persuasive command headlines include:

*Hire us to paint your house
and you won't need this newspaper.*

(Ad with paint blotches on it for Merriam Park Painting)

Rekindle your love affair with New York.

(Ad for New York City)

Imagine filling out a job application
and running out of room
where it says "Experience."

(Ad for U.S. Army ran in college newspapers)

Question   A question piques your curiosity and involves you in the ad. A question headline should make readers want to stop, think, and read your ad for the answer, so be careful not to make the answer too obvious. Here are questions that grab your attention and make you think:

IF YOU WERE TWO YEARS OLD,
COULD YOU TELL THE DIFFERENCE?

(Visual of a plastic jug of milk and a gallon of bleach)

Test climb, anyone?

(Ad for Land Rover)

Shortly after the introduction
of the first underwire bra,
Valium® was invented. Coincidence?

(Ad for Magic Ring wireless support bra by Lovable)

Repetition   Some lines are worth repeating to hammer home the message. An ad for McGraw-Hill magazines uses repetition to communicate the power of advertising:

I DON'T KNOW WHO YOU ARE.
I DON'T KNOW YOUR COMPANY.
I DON'T KNOW WHAT YOUR COMPANY STANDS FOR.
I DON'T KNOW YOUR COMPANY'S CUSTOMERS.
I DON'T KNOW YOUR COMPANY'S RECORD.
I DON'T KNOW YOUR COMPANY'S REPUTATION.
NOW—WHAT WAS IT YOU WANTED TO SELL ME?

Figure 6-3
The idea for this campaign came straight from the mouths of consumers who want to get back in shape and lose their big rear ends and potbellies.

Word play   Writers love to play with words, twisting them in a way that gives special meaning. Done right, word play can attract readers' attention and make them pause a few moments to process the message. For instance, the word play in the Gold's Gym ads (Figure 6-3) is unexpected, relevant, and communicates a selling idea. This regional campaign, created by Henderson Advertising, was named "Best Gold's Gym Advertising Worldwide."

Figure 6-3 (continued)

Be careful not to get so caught up in the play that you forget that you're selling a product. Make sure the word play helps further your message and isn't clever for the sake of entertainment. Beware, also, of overdosing on puns. Your readers won't appreciate it, nor will creative directors when you're showing your portfolio.

Metaphors, similes, and analogies   One way to describe your product is to make a connection to another commonly known image. A *metaphor* takes the characteristics of one thing and associates it with something entirely different. An ad for Books-A-Million tells book lovers

Think of us as an amusement park for readers.

A *simile* states that one thing is "like" something else. For example, to dramatize the odor problem of litter boxes, an ad for Kitty Litter Brand shows a skunk in a litter box. The headline reads

SOMETIMES YOUR CAT CAN SEEM
LIKE A WHOLE DIFFERENT ANIMAL.

An *analogy* compares two things on the basis of a similar feature. For example, an ad for Lubriderm lotion shows an alligator to communicate rough, scaly skin. The headline implies the lotion will smooth and soften dry, flaky skin. It reads

SEE YOU LATER, ALLIGATOR.

Parallel Construction   This headline repeats the structure of a phrase or sentence to emphasize a point. As Figure 6-4 shows, Target uses the technique to promote its practical Bridal Registry.

Rhyme   Rhyme headlines use the repetition of sound to make a point. Avoid the temptation to make a rhyme unless it helps to stress a selling point, as in this example:

SAIL BY MAIL.

(Ad for Royal Caribbean inviting the reader to write for a brochure)

Body Copy Tells the Rest of the Story

Whereas the headline piques the readers' attention, the body copy completes the story. Remember the headline "What not to do in bed"? As promised, here's the answer:

You can read.

You can rest.

You can sleep.

You can make phone calls.

You can eat breakfast.

You can watch television.

You can listen to music.

You can exercise.

You can snore.

You can even eat crackers—provided you're alone.

And, yes, you can snuggle.

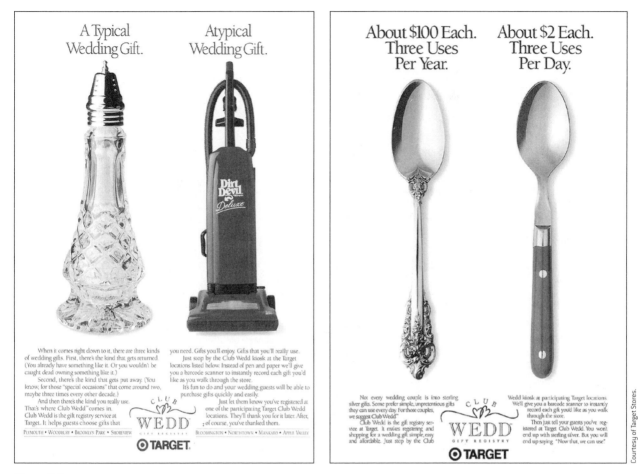

Figure 6-4
Too many wedding gifts become dust collectors. Target's Club Wedd uses parallel construction to tell couples how they can get gifts they will actually use.

But don't ever light up a cigarette when you're in bed.

Because if you doze off just once, all your dreams can go up in smoke.

Although R. J. Reynolds could have run a public service ad with the simple headline "Don't smoke in bed," the combination of an intriguing headline and interesting copy gets readers involved and makes it more likely that they'll remember the message.

Approaches to Writing Body Copy

The Standard Approach   Most ads start with a lead-in paragraph that bridges the headline and the rest of the copy. Like the headline, this paragraph should pique readers' curiosity and make them want to continue reading. The interior paragraphs stress benefits as they elaborate on the selling

Figure 6-5
Truly there is nothing standard about this ad. The headline certainly might make you curious, but nothing about it will confuse you, mainly because the headline bears a direct relationship to the product. Remember the difference; it's an important one.

premise. The closing paragraph ties the ad together and often invites the reader to consider the product.

The ad for Columbia Sportswear Company (Figure 6-5) follows a standard approach, although there's nothing standard about the ad—or the company or its chairman, for that matter. The headline grabs your attention: "She snaps necks and hacks off arms." You read on and learn in the first paragraph that "My Mother, Columbia Sportswear's chairman, will stop at nothing to get what she wants—superior outerwear." In the next few sentences, you learn about the demands of "Mother," the vociferous chairman; in the process, you learn about the construction of a Columbia Sportswear parka. The copy closes with "All in all, it's easy to see why not just any parka can survive Mother's rather pointed demands."

Copy as story   Narrative copy reads like a piece of fiction because it sets a scene and presents characters who get involved in some action.

Dialog copy   You know the routine "I said. She said." Although you usually find this format in radio and television, it works in print, too. However, make certain that your dialog sounds realistic by reading your copy out loud. The

Figure 6-6
This innovative ad uses personification to convince readers that it's okay to eat eggs again.

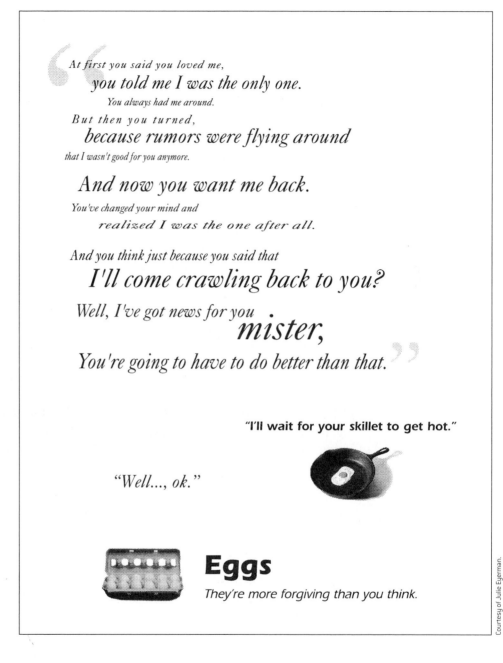

"At first you said you loved me,
you told me I was the only one.
You always had me around.
But then you turned,
because rumors were flying around
that I wasn't good for you anymore.

And now you want me back.
You've changed your mind and
realized I was the one after all.

And you think just because you said that
I'll come crawling back to you?
Well, I've got news for you .
mister,
You're going to have to do better than that."

"I'll wait for your skillet to get hot."

"Well..., ok."

Eggs
They're more forgiving than you think.

ad for eggs (Figure 6-6) is a fun example, even if the conversation is a bit one-sided.

Bulleted copy/listings   An ad for the Massachusetts Society for the Prevention of Cruelty to Animals was headlined "Get the best of everything. Adopt a mutt." The picture shows an adorable mutt looking straight into the reader's eyes, and bulleted copy addresses the advantages of adopting a mutt: "The smarts of a Lassie. The spots of a Dalmatian. The bark of a Shepherd. The friendliness of a Beagle. The heart of a St. Bernard. The paws of a Great Dane."

Poetic copy   Norwegian Cruise Lines used poetic images to sell its fantasy adventures:

> It's different out here.
>
> I will put first things last.
>
> I will study a sunset.
>
> I will be naked more.
>
> I will discover a color.
>
> I will memorize clouds.
>
> I will be amphibious.
>
> I will eat a mango.
>
> I will get a really good tan.

Mandatories: Writing the Small Print

Mandatories are statements that are required to appear in your ads and are usually found in the small print along the bottom or side of an ad. Sometimes law requires these statements. For example: The Windsor Jewelers ads (Figure 4-3) include the line "Licensed by Consumer Affairs #0817887." The DuPont ads (Figure 4-1) state "Read and follow the label." The South Carolina National ad (Figure 2-3) states "Equal Opportunity Lender. Member FDIC." Other times the statements are something the client insists on including. Motel 6 ads, for example, include the statement, "Motel 6. An Accor Hotel." It's your job as a writer to ensure that your copy contains these small but very important words.

Answers to Common Questions About Writing Copy

Is It Okay to Break the Rules?

Some people believe advertising has destroyed the dignity of our language. They are appalled when they read sentences such as "Winston tastes good like a cigarette should." Cringe when they read incomplete sentences (like this one). And they wince when a sentence starts with a conjunction. Others argue that advertising must sound like people talking, so it's okay to break the rules. However, most people agree that, before you break the rules, you'd better know them. See the box on the next page for some copy mistakes.

Here are some headlines that break the rules intentionally:

I QUIT SKOOL WHEN I WERE SIXTEEN.

(A convincing message to stay in school)

i HAS A DREAM

(Ad sponsored by Atlanta's Black Professionals asking people to speak out against Ebonics)

COPY MISTAKES

You must proofread your copy. Spell Check is a big help, but it can't find every type of error. Here are some mistakes from the classifieds:

"For sale: an antique desk suitable for lady with thick legs and large drawers."

"Four-poster bed, 101 years old. Perfect for antique lover."

"Now is your chance to have your ears pierced and get an extra pair to take home, too."

"Wanted: 50 girls for stripping machine operators in factory."

"Tired of cleaning yourself? Let me do it."

"Used cars: Why go elsewhere to be cheated? Come here first!"

Church bulletins have their share of gaffes. Here are a few of our favorites:

"Thursday, at 5 p.m., there will be a meeting of the Little Mothers Club. All those wishing to become little mothers, please meet the pastor in his study."

"The ladies of the church have cast off clothing of every kind and they may be seen in the basement on Friday afternoon."

"This being Easter Sunday, we will ask Mrs. Johnson to come forward and lay an egg on the altar."

But don't think it's just small-town classifieds and church bulletins that make mistakes. Consider the following:

A Mercedes-Benz accessories ad begins, "Her trademark has always been making art out of the everyday. First, she was taken with fruits and vegetables. Next, she was inspired by popcorn, footballs and sharks. Then one day, Nicole Miller was struck by a Mercedes-Benz."

Bruce Hardwood Floors insulted a few grandmothers with the line "Solid oak, just like your grandmothers."

What's the Best Headline Length?

Unless you're writing to a specific layout with a predetermined character count, there is no "best" length. One of the most famous headlines for a car was one simple word, "Lemon." This unexpected headline for Volkswagen motivated people to read the copy, which explained the auto manufacturer's rigorous quality standards. In contrast, another famous headline for a car contained eighteen words: "At 60 miles an hour, the loudest noise in the new Rolls Royce comes from the electric clock." Sometimes you'll find you don't need a headline at all—the visual can stand alone.

Which Is Better, Long or Short Copy?

Certain product categories, such as perfume and fashion, are sold primarily on the basis of image, so brief copy, along with a striking visual, is probably the best answer. Other products, such as cars and computers, require quite a bit of thought before the buyer takes the plunge; therefore, they warrant longer copy with specific details about the various features. However, even these rules are successfully broken from time to time. Volkswagen ads often contain only a few lines of copy. Lands' End fills the page with details about its clothing.

The best advice is to write as much as you need to accomplish your advertising objectives. You may find you don't need any copy at all. The right visual and logo may be all you need. The North Carolina tourism ads shown in this chapter use long copy to capture the interest of nature lovers, but there's almost no copy in the North Carolina tourism ads that targets those who need a vacation to escape from the pressures of work (see Figure 4-2).

Do You Need a Slogan?

A good slogan captures the essence of your brand in a few words. Here are a few that work:

"It's not delivery. It's DiGiorno."
(For DiGiorno frozen pizza)

"Have you Met Life Today?"
(For MetLife Insurance)

"Hey. You Never Know."
(For New York State Lottery)

Unfortunately, many slogans say very little and are indistinguishable from those used by other brands. For years Macy's slogan said, "We're a part of your life." Meanwhile, Sears boasted, "There's more for your life at Sears." And General Electric claimed, "We bring good things to life." Each of these slogans could have worked for a hospital, a real estate agent, a bank, a health food store, a veterinarian, or any number of products and services.

Like the previous examples, too many slogans do little more than add clutter to an ad. Still, many clients will insist on having a slogan, almost as if they're not getting their money's worth from their ad agency if they don't have one. As a writer, you can do two things. Talk the client out of one or write one that means something to your customer.

How Should Copy Be Formatted?

Figure 6-7 shows a suggested copy format for print ads. "Slug" the ad in the upper-left corner with the name of the company, size, and medium (full page, magazine) and a working title in quotes. Identify the visual idea, headline, copy, logo, and baseline, plus other elements when used. Double-space so that it's easy to read, easy to revise, and easy to sell. Figure 6-8 shows how the finished ad looks.

Guidelines for Writing Effective Copy

The following guidelines will help improve your copy, whether you're writing for print, broadcast, direct mail, or news media. Keep these rules in mind as you read future chapters.

1. *Love your product.* Have you ever dreaded taking a required course and then loved it because the professor was so interesting? The professor's love of the subject made you want to go to class and learn more about the topic. It's your job to have a similar passion about your product so that your target audience will want to learn about your brand and then go out and buy it.

Figure 6-7
In this sample copy draft, note the use of a working title, double-spacing, and adequate margins on all sides. To see how this translates into an ad, see Figure 6-8.

COLONIAL SUPPLMENTAL INSURANCE

Two-page spread

"Adorable kids."

VISUAL: Close-up of two adorable kids in the back seat of a car

HEADLINE: On Tuesday, she'll begin ballet and he'll begin chemotherapy.

COPY:

How will you pay for what your health insurance won't? How will you pay the deductibles? The travel expenses to see specialists? The everyday life things? Especially if you're forced to miss work and miss paychecks. Colonial Supplemental Insurance offers affordable cancer, critical illness, disability, accident, and life coverage that can help ease the burden of unforeseen expenses. And, most importantly, provide you with peace of mind. Find out more at www.coloniallife.com.

LOGO: COLONIAL SUPPLEMENTAL INSURANCE

BASELINE: for what happens next

MANDATORIES: (none)

Figure 6-8
This moving ad makes it clear why you need supplemental insurance. Sales of Colonial Supplemental Insurance increased 40 percent in advertised markets. To read the text of the ad, see Figure 6-7.

Courtesy of Colonial Supplemental Insurance.

Before you begin writing copy, it's important to put advertising in perspective. You're not writing a letter to your mom who will still love you even if you run on a bit. You're not writing an essay for a professor who is paid to read your work or, conversely, a textbook that students are required to read. You're not even writing a story for readers who have bought a newspaper or magazine to catch up on the news. You're writing for people who view advertising as an intrusion. Therefore, you've got to be interesting. Perhaps David Ogilvy said it best when he wrote that there are no dull products, just dull writers.

2. *Don't try to do everything in one ad.* You should develop one theme and follow it through. To illustrate the point, creative director Stavros Cosmopulos slams a piece of cardboard against 100 sharp nails. The cardboard remains intact because the nails have formed a solid mass, preventing them from penetrating the cardboard. He then slams a piece of cardboard against a single nail and bam! It breaks through, proving that one single point is more powerful than several.

3. *Write to one individual.* Have you ever noticed how annoyed some people get when you start reading over their shoulders? That's because reading is a very intimate activity, one that exists between the writer and reader.

   When people read your copy, they should feel as if you're talking directly to them, not to a vague demographic profile. Use the word *you* liberally and stick to singular nouns and verbs when possible.

4. *Translate business-speak into human-speak.* Many clients know their products so well that they begin to talk in jargon, which will be lost on the average reader. Your job is to listen, ask questions, and translate the jargon into tangible benefits that your readers will understand. Edward T. Thompson of *Reader's Digest* poked fun at a scientist who wrote "The biota exhibited a one hundred percent mortality response," instead of simply saying "All the fish died."

5. *Avoid catchall phrases.* If a dress is "perfect for any occasion," does that mean you'd wear it to the opera after you've worn it while gardening or cleaning the house?

6. *Be specific.* Avoid vague generalities, such as "Save on a vast collection of beautiful tops in a variety of colors." What does this mean? Are they T-shirts? Turtlenecks? Scoop necks? Do they have long sleeves? Short sleeves? Cap sleeves? Are they tailored? Frilly? Sporty? Are they pastels? Brights? Neutrals? And, just what is a "vast" collection?

7. *Don't brag.* Few people are going to care how proud you are of your product or how long you've been in business unless you can translate that information into a specific consumer benefit. Instead of bragging about your product's features, tell your readers what your product will do for them. For example, compare the following sentences:

   "We are proud to announce our new flight schedule to New York."

   "Now you can fly to New York five times a day."

Did you notice how the second sentence turns the airline's feature (the new schedule) into a traveler's advantage? The second sentence also gives more information in fewer words. That's good writing.

8. *Use the present tense and active voice whenever possible.* The present tense communicates a sense of immediacy, and the active voice enlivens your copy. For example, "We try harder" sounds better than "We have tried harder."

9. *Use transitions to connect different thoughts and establish a relationship between them.* Here are some words that bridge thoughts:

So	On the other hand
Therefore	Furthermore
However	First
Additionally	Second
In fact	But

10. *Avoid vague descriptions.* The right choice of words will allow your readers to see, hear, feel, smell, and taste things that seem real but exist only in their imaginations. If you've ever been disappointed in a movie after having read the book, you know what we mean. So choose your words carefully. Give details. Avoid saying things like *quality craftsmanship* or *caring service* or *inspired design.* Refer to Figure 1-4 and read the ads for Taylor guitars. Notice how they convinced you that the guitars were expertly crafted without ever saying "expertly crafted"?

11. *Avoid clichés.* Describe your product in a new, refreshing way; don't resort to overused clichés such as these:

Age-old secret	Out of this world
Bright eyed and bushy tailed	Sharp as a tack
Early birds	Sleep like a baby (or log)
For all seasons	State of the art
Hustle and bustle	Talk of the town
It's not rocket science (or brain surgery)	Whose time has come
Knock your socks off	World class

Radio copywriter Steven Lang created the following spoof to demonstrate how ridiculous clichés and vague generalities can be:

> *Spring has sprung at the Cliché Factory. They've got all the names you know and love at everyday low, low prices for all your needs. There's a huge selection of savings throughout the store. Their friendly qualified factory-trained technicians will meet or beat any offer. But wait there's more. Prices have been slashed to the bone. So next time you're in the mood for fantastic unbelievable super savings, check out the friendly folks down at the Cliché Factory. And of course, don't miss out because they service what they sell. Conveniently located for your shopping convenience. Check them out.*

12. *Vary the length and structure of sentences.* To highlight the importance of this, the International Newspaper Promotion Association printed the following statement in its Copy Service Newsletter: "The simple sentence starts with a subject. Then the simple sentence has an object. The simple sentence ends with a period. The simple sentence gets boring as hell after you've read three or four of them. And you just did!"

Doug Williams demonstrates this by writing the same message two different ways. Read the following paragraphs. Which one do you think is more engaging?

> *The ear demands variety, so listen as I vary the sentence length, and create music that sings with a pleasant rhythm and harmony. I use short sentences, medium sentences and sometimes when I am certain the reader is rested, I will engage him in sentences of considerable length. These sentences burn with energy and build with the impetus of a crescendo. They have a roll of the drums and a crash of a cymbal. They have the kind of sound that urge a reader to listen because this is important.*

> *The ear demands variety. Now listen: I vary the sentence length, and create music. Music. The writing sings. It has a pleasant rhythm, a harmony. I use short sentences. And I use sentences of medium length. And sometimes when I am certain the reader is rested, I will engage him in sentences of considerable length—a sentence that burns with energy and builds with all the fire and impetus of a crescendo, the roll of the drums, the crash of a cymbal. Sounds that say, Listen to this. It's important.*[4]

13. *Make the strange familiar, the familiar strange.* Explain something complex in simple terms. Or take something simple and describe it in colorful language. Here's how the writer described the size of the Biltmore Estate:

THE DRIVEWAY IS MEASURED IN MILES.

THE FLOORPLAN IS MEASURED IN ACRES.

14. *Write "out loud."* Use spoken language, not the written language you use in the typical term paper. Imagine your customer is sitting in front of you and you're talking to her. If you're having a hard time doing this, try recording your conversation. Zap the "uhs," "ums," and "ya knows," and you should have some convincing copy.

15. *Use contractions.* Don't be afraid of using words like *don't* or *couldn't* or *haven't* or *it's.*[5] After all, it's the way people speak.

---

[4] From a lecture entitled "Mass Media Writing," given at the University of South Carolina, March 1998.
[5] Be careful not to make the common mistake of confusing "its," a possessive, and "it's," a contraction for "it is" or "it has."

16. *Pay attention to every word you write.* In his book *The Pursuit of Wow!*, Tom Peters tells how thrilled he was when he noticed that the expiration date on a fresh fruit drink read "Enjoy by March 12." He wrote, "Why fuss over 'Enjoy by' instead of the normal 'Expires on'? Simple. It's the very essence of humanness, of connecting with the customer—and a strong indicator of superior service and quality. 'Enjoy by' brought a smile to my face and an 'ahhh' to my lips."[6]

17. *Test your copy.* Be sure to read it out loud. If you find yourself cringing or saying "That sounds stupid," ditch it and start again. Once you have copy you like, test it again on someone who represents your target audience.

18. *Revise your work.* Edit. Edit. Edit. Author Truman Capote once said of the revision process, "I know my book is done when the publisher grabs it out of my hands."

Checklist for Writing Copy

✓ Does your message reflect the strategy?

✓ Does your message make an emotional connection to the reader?

✓ Is the tone of the ad appropriate for the product and target?

✓ Does your headline stop, intrigue, and involve the reader?

✓ Does your headline encourage readership of body copy?

✓ Does your headline offer a promise or benefit relevant to the selling idea?

✓ Does your headline work with the visual to create synergy?

✓ Does your body copy contain readable paragraphs, conversational language?

✓ Does your copy sound like a conversation between the writer and reader?

✓ Do you present selling points in a nonboastful way?

✓ Does your message end with an urge to action, a summary of the main idea, or an open-ended statement designed to provoke readers to complete the thought?

✓ Will customers connect your message to the brand name?

Suggested Activities

1. Go through several recent magazines and cut out advertisements that contain headlines and visuals that fall into at least six of the thirteen types listed in this chapter (news, benefit, selective, factual, metaphor,

[6] Tom Peters, *The Pursuit of Wow!* (New York: Vintage Books, 1994), p. 10.

and so on). If the same headline accomplishes several things, list them all. As you complete your search, also note why some ads attract you and others do not. To accompany your ad collection, write a brief paper on their positive and negative qualities.

2. Using the strategy statement that you developed in Chapter 4, write two pieces of print copy with headlines. Describe any visuals you plan to use and include a rough layout of the ad along with your copy. *Note:* To do the layout, draw a rectangle on a standard sheet of paper, roughly letter in your headline in the size you think it should be, sketch your visual (stick figures are okay), use lines to indicate where copy goes, and place a logo somewhere near the bottom. Don't spend more than a few minutes on the layout. Instead, focus on the idea for the visual and the copy that will accompany it.

3. Present the ad you created in number 2 above to the class as if you were presenting it to the client. How will you explain your strategy or your ad concept?

4. Find a national ad that has what you think is effective copy. State why you chose it and what you believe to be outstanding about it. How does it meet the criteria for creativity presented in Chapter 1?

5. With a classmate, work out a series of ads for a local business. Begin by gathering information about your "client" and then brainstorm before you try your ideas on each other. Once you've agreed on a solution, develop and present a series of at least three ads.

Search Online! Discovering More About Print Advertising

Use InfoTrac College Edition to discover more about print advertising. Try these phrases and others for Key Words and Subject Guide searches: *newspaper advertising, magazine advertising, advertising concept, advertising headline, advertising copy, advertising clutter, breaking grammar rules, product benefit.*

To view award-winning newspaper ads, go to the Newspaper Association of America's Web site at www.naa.org and click on Athena Awards.

To view award-winning magazine ads, go to the Magazine Publishers of America's Web site at www.mpa.org and click on Kelly Awards.

These Lost Dogs Belong in the Inhumane Society

The state of Alabama has a tremendous problem with deadbeat parents—parents who don't meet their obligation of paying for child support—with the cumulative, long-term unpaid debt reaching more than $1 billion. The dependent children who do not receive regular child support payments face a reduced standard of living, and some families are forced to resort to welfare. Alabama's Department of Human Resources (DHR) handles about 314,000 child cases per year. However, the sheer lack of human resources has made it very difficult for caseworkers to track down many of these deadbeat parents. In 2000 the Alabama legislature passed a law requiring DHR to publish lists in Alabama newspapers of the Top-10 delinquent child support obligors.

Lewis Communications was hired to develop a public relations and advertising campaign to help combat the problem. Their main objective was to increase child support payments by targeting the Top-10 deadbeat parents and their families and friends. A second objective was to raise awareness throughout the state on the seriousness of the issue. A final objective was to generate as much media coverage as possible to help reinforce the advertising campaign.

To determine who should be included on the list, each of the 67 counties was asked to rank their worst offenders. Each person on the list owes substantial child support and has demonstrated a long-term lack of cooperation with the Child Support Program. The Top 10 in the state were then picked for the ad. This research revealed that child support is a problem encompassing the entire spectrum of the population, regardless of gender, race, or income.

Lewis developed a no-holds-barred approach to this problem. After all, for responsible parents, it is unfathomable to think of abandoning a child. DHR had originally wanted to picture the Top 10 like a FBI most-wanted list. Lewis decided the problem needed a tough headline, so the "Lost Dogs" idea was born. From a production standpoint, the copy and visuals have the look and feel of actual lost dog posters pinned on neighborhood telephone poles.

Reprinted with permission of Lewis Communications.

Name: Donald R. Thomas Sr.
County: Baldwin
Amount Owed: $129,501
Children: 4

Name: Bonnie S. Third
County: Blount
Amount Owed: $15,659
Children: 2

Name: Eural Ray Allen
County: Butler
Amount Owed: $155,968
Children: 3

Name: Richard M. Goodson
County: Cleburne
Amount Owed: $41,182
Children: 2

Name: Bennie Bradley
County: Coffee
Amount Owed: $44,327
Children: 2

LOST DOGS

HAVE YOU SEEN US?

Neither have our kids. But we can't help it if it's in our nature to run off without paying child support. After all, we're dogs. So if you should happen to see us wandering the streets, do everyone a favor and call the Alabama Department of Human Resources. They'll know exactly how to handle us.

Call toll free: 1-877-774-9512

Name: Elbert J. Crawford
County: Hale
Amount Owed: $18,158
Children: 1

Name: Robert Chapman
County: Madison
Amount Owed: $220,739
Children: 3

Name: Paul E. Tucker
County: Marshall
Amount Owed: $93,055
Children: 1

Name: Albert J. Velarde
County: Shelby
Amount Owed: $31,054
Children: 1

Name: James Carr Sanders
County: Talladega
Amount Owed: $131,177
Children: 3

Alabama's 10 Most Wanted is sponsored by Governor Don Siegelman.

For greater impact, the ad pictures each offender, the amount owed, number of children, and the county of last-known residence. The copy reads "Have you seen us? Neither have our kids. It's in our nature to run off without paying child support. After all, we're dogs. So if you see us wandering the streets, do everyone a favor and call the Alabama Department of Human Resources. They'll know exactly how to handle us."

After initial resistance toward the concept, DHR grew to love the idea. With a budget of only $90,000 for public relations, ad development, and ad placement in more than 20 newspapers, finances were a major obstacle that had to be overcome. The public relations staff at Lewis worked with the governor's office to develop media strategies and materials for a briefing held at the state capitol to launch the campaign. The Lost Dogs ad ran in every daily newspaper in the state two days after the media briefing. The ad and press conference generated more than 150 television stories across the state, 25 print articles, and dozens of radio interviews. Within the first week, the DHR Web site had 3000 hits, and the department received more than 300 phone calls, leading to positive leads for at least five of the offenders.

In the three months following the launch of the campaign, the amount of child support paid in Alabama rose by $1.7 million from missing deadbeat parents. Five months after the first ad ran, the number of Web hits on the DHR child support section exceeded 12,000, and nearly 900 phone calls were received on the hotline. Tips were for the Top 10 and other deadbeat parents.

"Lost Dogs" was a hit not only with Alabama citizens and media but also with the communications trade publications. *PR Week* and *Adweek* both did feature stories on this truly integrated and persuasive campaign.

LAYOUTS:
DESIGNING TO COMMUNICATE
By Ronald J. Allman II

Advertising is a team sport. The copywriter and art director begin by exchanging ideas on content and approach, and then proceed to work out the problems. The design idea may come from the writer, and the headline may come from the art director. Such teamwork implies that each partner has some understanding of and appreciation for the other's talent. We may not all be great artists, but we should certainly be able to understand the principles involved in arriving at a graphic solution.

In fact, designing is like writing. You have to put your imagination to work to produce vibrant headlines and powerful text, just as you do when you come up with a traffic-stopping visual. You're thinking visually, whether you know it or not, when you attempt to find the right words to explain product benefits. So when you start to think about how you want the campaign to look, imagine that someone else will be doing the finished artwork and dig in—just start sketching. It's okay if it's rough. As you will see, the processes for these two endeavors are also similar. Each consists of finding a solution to a problem, and each begins with ideas. And the toughest part of each process is the beginning, when you've got to do some serious thinking.

Functions of Design

In designing your advertisement, keep its purpose foremost in your mind. Remember that an ad must communicate quickly and effectively (see Figure 7-1). The prettiest ad is worthless unless what you want to convey to your

Figure 7-1
Why waste unnecessary words describing a product's attributes? Sometimes a picture is worth a thousand words.

audience is clear, understandable, and useful to them. Good design makes your message easier to understand. In other words, your design needs to get as much information as possible to the audience in the shortest time possible. A thoughtful design helps you accomplish this.

Your design must attract your target audience. Thousands of media messages are competing for consumers' attention. A well-designed ad grabs their attention, at least momentarily. Since you have their attention only briefly, your design must help them remember the message. Good design not

Figure 7-2
These knots capture the Outward Bound experience: butterfly knot, fisherman's knot, your stomach.

only commands attention but also holds it. If your audience is quickly bored with your ad, you're not going to communicate much of anything. Figure 7-2 is a great example of a campaign that speaks directly to its target audience.

Design enables you to organize ideas. Information carefully placed breaks the facts into digestible messages—some visual, others textual; some large, others small. This helps product facts stick in consumers' minds. Good design makes information easier to remember.

Good design emphasizes the most compelling information. Where you place information in the ad, how large you make that information, and how you display it in relation to other elements in the ad can strengthen or diminish its importance.

Basics of Design

Before you organize information visually, it helps to know something about the basics. Do you know what negative, or "white," space is? What do *gestalt, balance, contrast, harmony, proportion, rhythm,* and *movement* mean in terms of design?

Figure 7-2 (continued)
Single-ply, 2-ply, quilted, extra strength. Now that's roughing it!

Negative, or "White," Space

You can think of your layout as the "package" for your idea. How you use white space in your layout can determine how effective your package will be. By white space, we mean blank, or negative, space. Always leave some white space on the outside of your layout. Allow white space to invade the center of your layout, and you are guaranteed to have a scattered, incohesive design. However, there is more to white space than simply including it on the outside of an ad. Use lots of white space, a great expanse of white space, and what's the result? Often, it's a feeling of exclusivity. This can be great for an upscale target audience but probably isn't appropriate for bargain hunters.

Gestalt

Put simply, gestalt is the idea that the whole is greater than the sum of its parts. Although the parts can be—and should be—observed and analyzed on their own, the whole of a design should strike you first. When you first see a painting, you take it in as a whole. Only later do you look at the individual parts. Similarly, a designer uses to advantage the mind's tendency to group things together and see them as a whole. (See Figure 7-3.)

Figure 7-3
Gestalt principles remind us that elements of design should be integrated so that the design, not the elements, is the first thing the viewer observes. The design principles of contrast, harmony, rhythm, and proportion are other ways to focus attention, hold various elements together, and present elements in ways that please the eye.

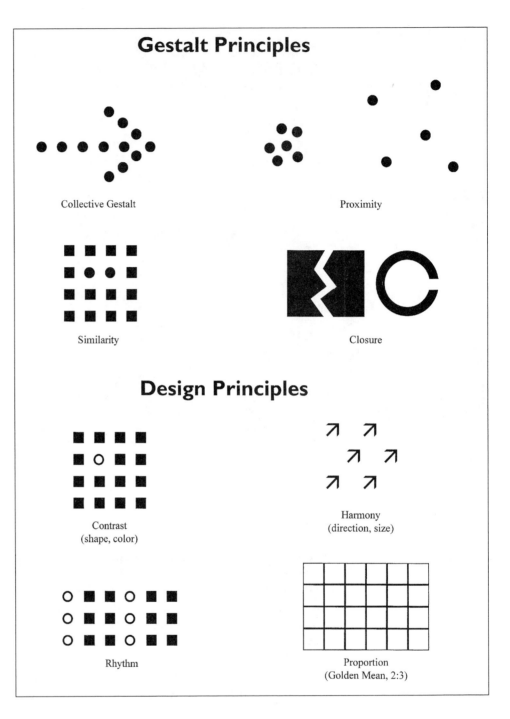

If two objects are similar and are near each other, we mentally close the distance between them and see them as whole. Imagine a flock of geese flying overhead—we first see the wedge shape they form rather than the individual birds. When flowers are arranged a certain way, they can spell out words—we see the words, not the individual flowers. Our eyes are drawn more to groups than to things spaced widely apart. Because we are drawn to such patterns, we respond to them in predictable ways.

Figure 7-4
Asymmetrical balance is the dominant choice in advertising because it allows one point of the design to "take over" and attract the eye to the rest of the ad. To achieve asymmetrical balance, just be certain that there's a difference top to bottom or right to left in the ad, all the while arranging elements so that the ad doesn't appear lopsided. Symmetrical balance suggests a static quality; asymmetrical balance suggests dynamism. Which is appropriate for your ad?

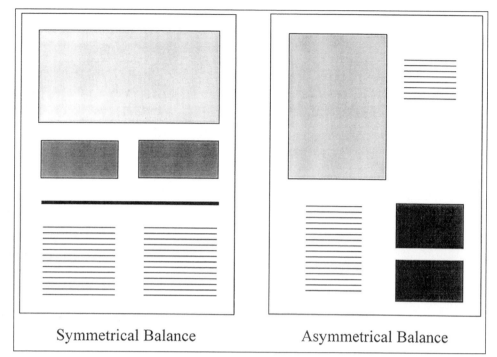

Symmetrical Balance   Asymmetrical Balance

Conversely, when an item is dissimilar to the objects around it, it commands attention. At a baseball game, the person in a rainbow-colored wig is definitely going to stand out. When a car is going the wrong way on a one-way street, we notice it at once. (Thank goodness!) People notice and react to items that stand out.

Balance

Balance can be symmetrical or asymmetrical (Figure 7-4). When both sides of an advertisement are equal, the design is symmetrical. So, if there is a picture on the left, symmetrical balance requires that there be a picture on the right that is similar in size, shape, and placement. Think of two children on a seesaw—if they are the same size and you place them the same distance apart, they will balance each other.

Asymmetrical balance depends on the weight of the items on a page. Imagine our seesaw again, only this time with a large child on one end and a much smaller child on the other end. To balance the seesaw, the larger child moves closer to the center, the smaller child moves farther away from the center, or more small children join the smaller child. Although symmetrical balance is fine, it can also be static—something advertisers usually wish to avoid. So we see more ads with asymmetrical balance because the advertisers are striving for a dynamic look.

Knowing what is "heavier" or "lighter" in a layout takes some practice, but you probably already have an intuitive feel for the concept of weight. A

Lee Clow, chairman/creative director at TBWA Worldwide, changed the title of the series from "how to write" to "how to create." Read the ad and you'll learn why. Be sure to read the other ads in the feature Tips & Tactics in Chapters 1, 4–6.

Courtesy of the Newspaper Association of America.

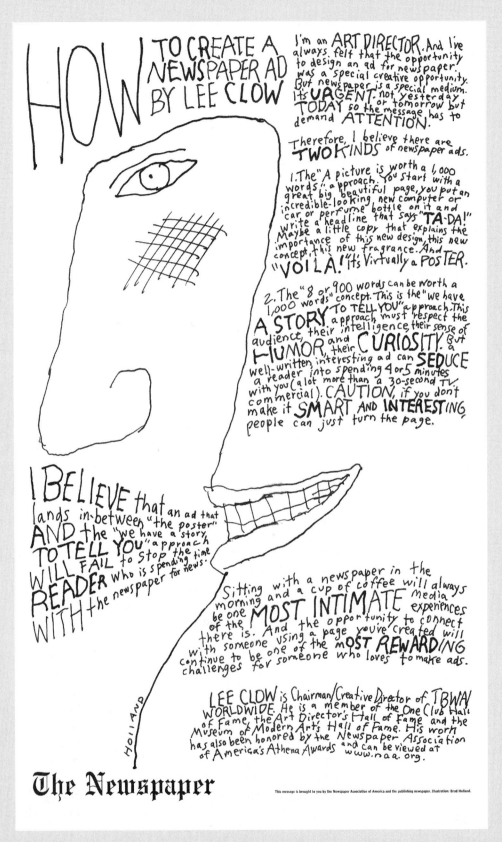

HOW TO CREATE A NEWSPAPER AD BY LEE CLOW

I'm an ART DIRECTOR. And I've always felt that the opportunity to design an ad for newspaper was a special creative opportunity. But newspaper is a special medium. It's URGENT. not yesterday or tomorrow but TODAY so the message has to demand ATTENTION.

Therefore, I believe there are TWO KINDS of newspaper ads.

1. The "A picture is worth a 1,000 words" approach. You start with a great big beautiful page, you put an incredible-looking new computer or car or perfume bottle on it and write a headline that says "TA-DA!" Maybe a little copy that explains the importance of this new design, this new concept, this new fragrance. And "VOILA!" It's virtually a POSTER.

2. The "8 or 900 words can be worth a 1,000 words" concept. This is the "we have A STORY TO TELL YOU" approach. This approach must respect the audience, their intelligence, their sense of HUMOR, and their CURIOSITY. But a well-written interesting ad can SEDUCE a reader into spending 4 or 5 minutes with you (a lot more than a 30-second TV commercial). CAUTION, if you don't make it SMART AND INTERESTING, people can just turn the page.

I BELIEVE that an ad that lands in-between "the poster" AND the "we have a story, TO TELL YOU" approach WILL FAIL to stop the time READER who is spending time WITH the newspaper for news.

Sitting with a newspaper in the morning and a cup of coffee will always be one of the MOST INTIMATE media experiences there is. And the opportunity to connect with someone using a page you've created will continue to be one of the MOST REWARDING challenges for someone who loves to make ads.

LEE CLOW is Chairman/Creative Director of TBWA/ WORLDWIDE. He is a member of the One Club Hall of Fame, the Art Director's Hall of Fame, and the Museum of Modern Art's Hall of Fame. His work has also been honored by the Newspaper Association of America's Athena Awards and can be viewed at www.naa.org.

HOLLAND

The Newspaper

This message is brought to you by the Newspaper Association of America and the publishing newspaper. Illustration: Brad Holland.

darker item is heavier than a lighter item. A bigger item is heavier than a smaller item. Thick is heavier than thin. It is when you combine layout elements that their weights become less clear. Photos and headlines are usually seen as heavier than text or logos. Text usually is the lightest item on a page.

Imagine the pieces of your design as little weights on a page. To balance this design asymmetrically, you must arrange the pieces in such a way that the balance is in the center of the page. You need to balance not only left with right but also top with bottom. A bottom-heavy design will tempt the reader to turn the page. A top-heavy design will discourage the reader from reading the rest of the ad.

Contrast

We encounter contrast everywhere. A white circle stands out among black squares and thus attracts and keeps our attention. But contrast is not limited to color or shape. Contrast can be effectively used in type size, slant, font, and weight. Texture—in both images and text—is another way to use contrast. A feather on a piece of sandpaper will stand out even if the feather and sandpaper are similar colors. Too much contrast, however, and your design can lose its cohesiveness.

Harmony

Harmony is the opposite of contrast. Using text that is all one font, even if the sizes are different, produces a harmonious layout. Harmony lets the viewer know that all elements are related. Using harmonious shades of one color brings a design together. Harmony, like contrast, can also be found in texture, direction, and weight. But remember, if things get too harmonious, people tend to fall asleep.

Proportion

We like things to be in proportion. We get a feeling of discomfort when one side of an item cannot be equally divided into the other side. We sense discordance—something is wrong even if we can't explain it. Our minds reject these items. If your layout violates the rules of proportion, your consumer may reject the whole advertisement. The "perfect" proportion is a 2-to-3 proportion, known as a *golden mean*. Most photographs are designed to adhere to the golden mean. The Greeks used this proportion when they built the Parthenon.

Rhythm

Repetition creates rhythm. A layout in which photo is followed by text is followed by photo is followed by text creates rhythm. Rhythm lets us know when to expect text in this layout. We get used to the pattern. When you use repetition to create direction, you create a sense of movement in your design. Dots placed horizontally across the page move the viewer's eyes across the page. But make sure that you place important information at the end of this movement.

Movement

We have a natural tendency to start at the upper-left corner of the page and move in a diagonal Z motion to the lower-right corner of the page. With this Z movement in mind, try not to place important elements, such as your logo, in the lower-left corner.

The eyes and hands of the models shown in your ads can also direct the reader's eye movement. The dog in Figure 7-5 beckons the reader to pay attention.

The Four Rs of Design

You're ready to start designing an ad. How do you begin? Where do you go from there? All designers use the same process. They may have different names for it, but they all use it. We like to call this process the four Rs: research, roughs, revise, and ready.

Research

You've been asked to design an ad for Acme Flakes. So where do you start? Remember Chapter 3. That's right—you start with research! You first need to know what Acme Flakes are. Are they soap flakes, instant potato flakes, or corn flakes? Or is it simply a cute name for an advertising design company? You find out all you can about the product, company, or service. Would you approach the design of an ad for Ben & Jerry's Ice Cream differently than you would for Breyer's Ice Cream? They both sell the same product—premium ice cream—but everything about the two companies and their products is different. They offer different flavors, have different public images, attract different buyers, and are packaged in different ways. The more you know about your client, the more appropriate your design will be.

Not only do you need to research the product, company, or service, but you must also know your target audience and your competition. How do your competitors advertise? What do their ads look like? What do you offer that they don't? How can you design an ad that will lure consumers away from their product to yours? What is your target audience like? What do they read? What kind of design catches their attention? Once again, the more research you do, the easier your designing job will be.

Another type of research is less project specific but still vital. This involves your *swipe file,* a collection of advertisements and visuals (photos, illustrations, and the like) that you think are interesting, attractive, or just

Figure 7-5
Show a cute dog in an ad, and you've got people's attention. Show a cute dog that needs help, and you've got people's undivided attention. This ad for FlexCheck gives a compelling reason why you may need their cash advance service.

Vet bill
$379.56

Checking balance
$197.37

Life doesn't always fit into your budget.

Or your pay schedule. That's where we can help.

By providing a cash advance of $100 - $300.

Just write us a personal check. We'll give you cash on

the spot, then hold your check until your next payday.

It's quick. It's confidential. It's respectful.

Because financial jams aren't your fault.

They're just something you've got to get through.

FlexCheck
C A S H   A D V A N C E
Life. It takes money.

2828 Main Street,
Newberry, SC 29108, (803) 276-3456

plain different. Ideas are not copyrighted. Good designers appreciate good design, so make a copy of a good idea for later reference. Who knows? It may be just the stimulus you need next week. What's important is to borrow the idea, not the ad itself. A swipe file is a great place to start when you need ideas. It's also a good way to see what sorts of designs, typefaces, and visuals are being used; what they look like; and how they work in layouts.

Roughs

Once you've completed your research, you're ready to start sketching. These early sketches are just rough versions. The important thing is to get your ideas on paper. There are as many ways to do roughs as there are people doing them. Whichever way works best for you, the idea behind the rough is the same. You want to put down on paper every idea you have about what your finished ad might look like. Don't be afraid—some of these ideas will be goofy. The best designs often start this way. What is important is that you get your ideas on paper before you forget them.

Many designers like to create little roughs called *thumbnails.* Thumbnails are useful because you can sketch an idea quickly, without much detail, and you've got your concept in miniature form. There is no need for great artistic skill here. You just want to give yourself a lot of options. How do you create a thumbnail? Like this: Using a soft-lead pencil or a fine-to-medium black marker or roller-ball pen, draw a number of small horizontal rectangles (about 2 inches wide by 3 inches deep) to represent the general shape of a magazine page. Don't try to draw a straight line, just freehand. Place your ideas for headlines and visuals within each rectangle. Scribble the words of the headline in the space and use shapes and simple stick figures to represent the visuals. Indicate body copy with a series of lines and place a rough logo at the bottom, probably in the right-hand corner. Congratulations! You have just done your first thumbnail rough, the beginning stage of every print layout. As you place other headlines in other rectangles, you'll probably think of still more ideas for words and pictures. Good! Don't stop until you've exhausted your topic, even if some of the ideas seem bizarre or ridiculous.

Revise

Once you've got your roughs, take a look at your ideas and pick the ones you like best. Let your knowledge of your client and of your target consumer guide you in deciding which ideas will work. Don't become too attached to one idea yet. Develop several ideas. Start making more elaborate sketches and then revise them. And remember that revising is never a one-way street. You can always go back and do more roughs or more research. You may get lucky and have a couple of ideas that you can develop, but don't be afraid to backtrack if you get stuck.

The revision stage is often a good time to get some initial feedback from your client. But remember: Although your client is in business, his or her business isn't design. The client may not have the background to visualize your big idea from a thumbnail rough, so make certain your ideas are finished enough for him or her to visualize the end product. Also, listen carefully to the client's feedback because he or she has to be happy with your efforts thus far. Get feedback from other designers, too. They might see ideas or mistakes that you've missed. Just remember that this is your design, not theirs. Keep revising until you create a couple of versions you're happy with. Then choose one and base your campaign on it.

Ready

Once you've got an ad with the copy and design elements in place, it's time to prepare a finished layout for your client's approval. Using a computer, you can produce a presentation ad that is nearly as finished as what will be submitted for publication.

After doing scores of thumbnails and choosing the one that best solves the advertising problem, it's time to use the rough to create the final layout. This layout should be actual size. Because a majority of magazines use the following dimensions, this is a good size to start with:

Trim size: 8 inches by 11 inches

Nonbleed and type area: 7 inches by 10¼ inches

Bleed: 8¼ inches by 11¼ inches

The trim size represents the finished size of the page after the magazine has been printed, bound, and trimmed. Your layout should be drawn to this size if you're designing a full-page ad. Be aware, however, that magazine sizes do vary, so always check the mechanical specifications for each magazine you plan to use. A bleed ad is one that runs all the way to the trim on at least one side. A nonbleed ad is contained within the nonbleed page limits, with a margin surrounding it on all sides. Whether your ad is designed for bleed or not, you should keep all type within the nonbleed limits. In setting type too close to the trim, you run the risk of having a letter or two trimmed off. You might want to draw the nonbleed limit as a second frame within the frame you draw to establish the trim. This will remind you to keep all type within the inner frame, or nonbleed area.

Selecting Type

If you spend any time around designers, you'll hear them talk about type in descriptive, affectionate terms and with good reason. Different fonts have totally different personalities. Zapf Chancery is an elegant but still a very legible font. Helvetica is a workhorse as far as fonts go, but it's rather boring and plain. Gill Sans has the flair that Helvetica is missing. As Paul Silverman put it, "These days, even the Shakespeare of Madison Avenue would be

Type Categories

Serif Type	Sans Serif Type	Script	Novelty
Times Roman	Helvetica	Brush Script	Comic Sans
Garamond	Gill Sans	Lucia	CRACKLING
Goudy	**Impact**	Elegant	CRYPT
Bodoni	Eras		Saint Francis

Cursive

Coronet

Zapf Chancery

Text Letter

Old English

Lombardic

Figure 7-6
Literally thousands of type fonts are at your disposal on computers. Unless you're a type expert, however, be wary of using most of them. Generally, stick to the serif and sans serif fonts, which contrast with each other nicely. Or use one font for all type in your ad, using a larger size for the headline and other display lines, and perhaps a bolder face than for the body copy. Script and cursive, although lovely on invitations, should be used cautiously because they're harder to read. For the same reason, avoid novelty and text letter fonts unless the concept calls for something unconventional. The body copy for this book is Centennial.

defeated by lousy typography. Typography supplies color and mood, much as the voice does in spoken language."[1]

Type can be divided into six groups: serif, sans serif, script, cursive, text letter, and novelty (Figure 7-6). Letters in a serif font have little horizontal strokes at the tops and bottoms of the letter. These serifs help draw the eye along a line of type. Most body text is in a serif font for this reason. The most common serif font is Times Roman. Other serif fonts are Palatino, Goudy, Bookman, Caslon, Bodoni, and Garamond. Serif fonts are sometimes called roman fonts.

Letters without serifs are called sans serif fonts. Sans serif fonts have a more modern and geometric look than serif fonts. Sans serif fonts can be distinctive in headlines and logos. They are clean-looking fonts that communicate a sense of simplicity. Some common sans serif fonts are Helvetica, Futura, Gill Sans, Avant Garde, and Optima.

Fonts designed to look like handwriting are either script or cursive fonts. The difference between script and cursive fonts depends on whether the letters connect. If they connect, it's a script font; if they don't, it's a cursive font.

[1] The Designers and Art Directors Association of the United Kingdom *The Copywriter's Bible* (Switzerland: Roto Vision SA, 1995), p. 151.

These fonts add a sense of formality and elegance and so are popular for invitations and announcements. But their use in advertising is limited, perhaps because of their delicacy and the fact that they can be difficult to read. Park Avenue, Mistral, and Brush Script are common script fonts; Zapf Chancery, Freestyle Script, and Reporter No. 2 are popular cursive fonts.

If the font was created to look like the hand-drawn letters of monks and scribes, it's a text letter font. These fonts, also known as black letter fonts, are usually found in newspaper nameplates and church logos. They are very hard to read and usable only in certain situations. The most common text letter font is Old English.

Novelty fonts are those that don't easily fit into the other categories because they are unusual or unconventional. Fonts that make type look like stenciled letters or Old West "wanted" posters are novelty fonts. Novelty fonts are good for display headlines and logos when you need a certain flair. Some of the more commonly used novelty fonts are Hobo, American Typewriter, and Stencil. Text letter fonts are sometimes considered to be novelty fonts.

When choosing a font, keep in mind the message you want to convey. A headline that says "Welcome to the Electronic Age" in a script font sends a mixed message. A long paragraph in Old English would be tedious to read.

You may want to set your headline in a customized font that reflects the theme of your ad. For instance, the Food Bank of Central New York made a powerful statement by writing headlines using letters from cereal and alphabet soup to remind readers of the need to help others (Figure 5-4). To reach symphony lovers, the Food Bank set the word "food" in music notes (see Figure 7-7). Creative approaches such as these work great in headlines with a few words, but would be difficult to read if they were set in a long paragraph of body copy. Keep in mind that readability must always come first.

Type is measured in points. There are 72 points to an inch. Body text is usually between 10 and 12 points. Type larger than 18 points is considered display type and is usually used for headlines. For advertisements, it's wise to consider 10 as the minimal point size, and 12-point type may be more legible in some fonts.

The space between lines of type is known as leading and is also measured in points. If you have 10-point type and want 2 points of space between the lines, you will specify 12 points of leading. In this case, to tell a designer what size type and leading you are using, you would say, "10 on 12." When you want the same font size and leading, specify "set solid." For legibility, however, it's usually wise to have at least 2 points of leading between lines.

The space between letters is known as letter spacing. If you adjust the spacing between two letters, you are kerning the letters. For display lines such as headlines, subheads, and baselines, this is useful with certain letters that can be moved closer together because of their shapes, such as AV, To, AW, and Te. If you adjust the spacing between all letters, you are adjusting the type's tracking.

Figure 7-7
This ad ran in a program for the Syracuse Symphony and reminded concert goers to help the less fortunate.

When you're hungry, it's hard to think of anything else.

Think about this: Every night thousands of families right here in Central New York go to bed hungry. But every $1 you donate helps us get $14 worth of nutritious food on their plates. Which is sure to put a song in their hearts. Please help us help them.

(315) 437-1899   www.foodbankcny.org

FOOD BANK
OF CENTRAL NEW YORK

WE WORK FOR FOOD

You can line up paragraphs of type in four different ways (Figure 7-8). If you want all your text lined up vertically on the left side, specify flush left. If you want it lined up only on the right side, specify flush right. If both sides are lined up, your text is justified. Of course, you can always center your type. Most advertisements are set flush left, ragged right. This is easier on the reader because the eye goes back to a consistent starting point and the

Type Alignment

Flush Left	*Centered*	*Flush Right*	*Justified*

Dolor in hendrerit in vulputate velit esse molestie consequat, vel illum dolore eu feugiat nulla facilisis at vero eros et accumsan et iusto odio dignissim qui blandit praesent luptatum zzril delenit augue duis dolore te feugait nulla facilisi. Soluta nobis eleifend option congue nihil imperdiet doming id quod mazim placerat facer possim assum. Lorem ipsum dolor sit amet, consectetuer adipiscing elit, sed diam nonummy nibh euismod tincidunt ut laoreet.
Soluta nobis eleifend option congue nihil

imperdiet doming id quod mazim placerat facer possim assum. Lorem ipsum dolor sit. Sit amet, consectetuer hendrerit in vulputate velit.
Hendrereit in vulputate velit aliquip exea lorem ipsum minim. Ut hendrerit in vulputate velit aliquip ex ea commodo minim hendrerit i vulputate velit veniam: Sed diam nonummy nibh tincidunt ut laoreet. Dolor in hendrerit in vulputate velit esse molestie consequat, vel illum dolore eu feugiat nulla facilisis at vero eros et accumsan et iusto odio dignissim qui blandit

praesent luptatum zzril delenit augue duis dolore te feugait nulla facilisi. Soluta nobis eleifend option congue nihil imperdiet doming id quod mazim placerat facer possim assum. Lorem ipsum dolor sit amet, consectetuer adipiscing elit, sed diam nonummy nibh euismod tincidunt ut laoreet. Soluta nobis eleifend option congue nihil imperdiet doming id quod mazim placerat facer possim assum. Lorem ipsum dolor sit. Sit amet, consectetuer hendrerit in vulputate velit:

Hendrereit in vulputate velit aliquip exea lorem ipsum minim.
Ut hendrerit in vulputate velit aliquip ex ea commodo minim hendrerit i vulputate velit veniam: Sed diam nonummy nibh tincidunt ut laoreet.
Dolor in hendrerit in vulputate velit esse molestie consequat, vel illum dolore eu feugiat nulla.
Facilisis at vero eros et accumsan et iusto odio dignissim qui blandit praesent luptatum zzril delenit augue duis dolore te feugait nulla facilisi.
Soluta nobis eleifend option congue nihil imperdiet

Figure 7-8
The majority of ads today have body copy set flush left, ragged right, as in the first column here. The ragged-right column provides "breathing space" between columns of type. Centered type must fit logically into the rest of the layout. Flush right might be used to offset a visual silhouette to the left of the type column. Justified type, while common in books, creates a formal look that also allows little white space between columns.

ragged right allows for some "air" in the text, especially between columns if you use more than one column.

At times you will want to wrap your type around an object or have it form a design to help further your message (see Figure 7-9).

Basic Ad Layouts

If you can't decide how to lay out your ad and your swipe file is no help, try some of these basic advertising layouts: Mondrian, grid, picture window, copy heavy, frame, silhouette, type specimen, color field, band, axial, or circus. (Figure 7-10 gives examples and descriptions of each.) Bear in mind that your ad concept affects the design choice, not the other way around.

Figure 7-9
Notice how the ad copy is placed in a way that mimics a motorist shifting from first gear to overdrive.

Figure 7-10
These thumbnail sketches show eleven approaches to selling wineglasses.

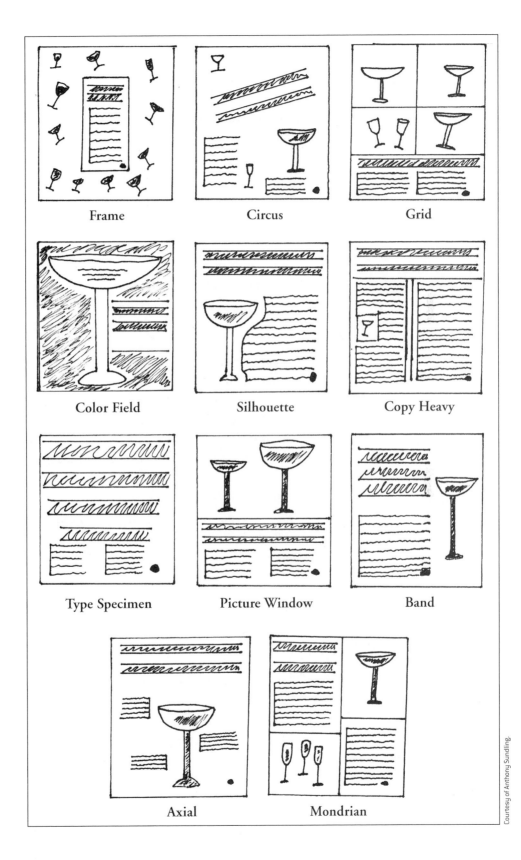

Frame

Circus

Grid

Color Field

Silhouette

Copy Heavy

Type Specimen

Picture Window

Band

Axial

Mondrian

Inviting Readership

You have many options at your disposal for luring readers, including the following:

1. *Don't set type wider than 39 characters.* Any wider and you discourage readership. Instead, break the space into two or more columns of equal width. The larger the type, of course, the wider it can be set.

2. *Avoid setting copy in less than 10-point type.* Smaller type is hard to read.

3. *Break up long copy blocks with subheads.* Careful paragraphing will also help you avoid the "gray-mass" look.

4. *Avoid setting body copy in reverse (white on black).* This tends to cut down readership. Headlines may be reversed for impact, provided the type is large and bold enough.

5. *Take care when you print copy over tonal matter, such as photographs.* If you must do this, be certain there is enough contrast to make the type legible.

6. *Use lowercase when possible.* It tends to be more legible than all-capital letters, especially in smaller type sizes.

7. *Either capitalize the entire headline or capitalize only the first word of a sentence and any proper noun.*

8. *End the headline with punctuation.* Use a period or a question mark. Save the exclamation point for the rare occasion when it is warranted.

9. *Align all copy elements to avoid a jumbled look.* This is easily done in an axial layout by aligning them on a common axis.

10. *Use normal punctuation throughout.* Avoid leaders (. . .), which look sloppy and uninviting.

11. *Use italics sparingly.* They are good for occasional emphasis, but too many italics make copy look pale and weak, just the opposite of what is intended.

Creating the Finished Ad: Computers and Design

An advertising designer might use four types of computer applications:

- *Photo manipulation software.* Software such as Adobe Photoshop is mainly used for making changes to photographs and other images on the computer, but it can also be used to create images and text. Because these applications can manipulate images, you can create interesting, eye-catching text and visuals.

- *Presentation software.* Software such as Lotus Freelance Graphics is mainly used for business presentations, but it is also useful in creating quick and easy advertisements. The idea behind business presentations and advertisements is basically the same—to present information in the most useful and interesting way.

- *Illustration software.* If you are looking for more control over image creation and special effects with text, an illustration program might be your design tool of choice. Software such as Adobe Illustrator and Macromedia Freehand allows you to create any type of image or text you can imagine. These applications are less friendly to images already created, such as scanned images, but if you are creating directly from your imagination, this type of software is best suited to your needs.

- *Desktop publishing software.* Perhaps the most useful application for advertising design is desktop publishing software such as QuarkXPress or Adobe PageMaker. These programs were written specifically for designers who create pages for publication. Most newspapers and magazines use desktop publishing software in creating their pages.

Designing Outdoor and Transit Ads

Outdoor advertising is a true test of creativity because you need to communicate your entire selling message in an instant. This is one time when the rule "write as much as you need" doesn't apply. It's also not the time to experiment with complicated layouts. Your message must be bold and clear because people will have mere seconds to read and understand the billboard when they're cruising down the interstate and little more on a city thoroughfare. Here's how to achieve an optimal reaction to your outdoor messages:

1. *Keep the graphics simple.* One large headline with one major visual is the rule. Some boards are all type, with no visual. Others are all visual, with just a logo.
2. *Make the type bold and big.* Remember, it must be read quickly.
3. *Keep the word count to no more than six to eight words, fewer if possible.*
4. *Make the brand or company name prominent.* If it's not in the main headline, use a logo big enough to get noticed.
5. *Consider using your campaign theme/tag line as the headline.* This way, your outdoor ad also reminds viewers of the rest of your campaign.

In preparing your outdoor layout, follow the same procedures as for other print layouts. Standard outdoor posters (paper pasted to existing structures) are scaled to a proportion of 1 to 2¼. Outdoor bulletins, painted on boards, are usually scaled to a proportion of 1 to 3½. This translates to a 4- by 3- by 9-inch layout for the poster and a 4- by 3- by 14-inch layout for the painted bulletin.

Transit advertising appears on the inside and outside of public transportation vehicles, as well as in bus, rail, subway, and air terminals. Like outdoor advertising, it works best when the message is short. It differs from outdoor ads in that the audience can spend more time with the message. For this reason, many transit ads include "take-one" cards or other literature attached to the ad.

Answers to Common Questions About Design

Must You Show the Product?

Many clients want to have their product shown in their ads. However, as Guido Heffels says, "We are not paid to put a product in an ad, but in the consumer's mind."[2] It's not necessary to show a product that's been around for years because consumers know what it looks like. However, if the packaging changes, you'll not only want to show it, but you'll also want to make a big deal about it in your ads. The same is true with new products.

Must You Show a Logo?

In most cases, you'll want to include a logo, but there are exceptions even to this rule. For instance, there's no need to show a logo if you show the product that has a clear logo on the package.

Must Every Ad in the Campaign Look the Same?

No. As mentioned in Chapter 5, ads in a campaign should have a common attitude, but there's no need for them to look as if they came from the same mold. Still, most ads in a campaign will share a similar typeface, color scheme, and logo treatment.

Is Color More Effective Than Black and White?

According to Andy Grunberg who writes on photography for *The New York Times,*

> *Color has become transparent. It represents reality so well that it sometimes seems to be reality itself. We take color advertising for granted. Black-and-white photography, on the other hand, suggests the realm of the imagination. Once the essence of documentary believability, black and white has become the color of fantasy.*[3]

Still, Grunberg acknowledges that most customers still want to see fashion, food, and home furnishings in their true colors.

---

[2] Jim Aitchison, *Cutting Edge Advertising* (Singapore: Prentice Hall, 1999) p. 65.
[3] Andy Grunberg, "Selling You on Black and White," *Metropolitan Home,* June 1989, p. 42.

What About Photography Versus Illustrations?

Like color images, photographs seem more real and are more widely used in advertising. Illustrations, on the other hand, lend themselves to the imagination of the viewer. Figure 7-11 uses a combination of illustration and photography.

Should You Study the Look of Your Competitors' Ads?

Absolutely! Line a wall with your competitors' ads. Study them. And then do something entirely different to stand out and make a memorable statement about your brand. For instance, the ads for Icelandair shown in Chapter 1 look nothing like other airline ads. Likewise, the ads for Chick-fil-A shown in Chapter 4 look nothing like ads from other fast-food restaurants. Both campaigns break through the clutter and make consumers take notice.

Suggested Activities

1. Find a black-and-white ad that presents strong possibilities for re-arrangement; perhaps it can even be improved. Don't choose an ad with a simple picture window, in which the only possible change will be to transpose the picture and the headline. Challenge yourself! After looking long and hard at the original ad, sketch some thumbnails. How many different ways can you rearrange this ad? Choose your best arrangement. Now, tape the original ad to your drawing board. Draw the border on your layout paper, making certain it corresponds to the size of the original ad. Using your thumbnail as a guide, start moving your layout paper around to trace the various components from the original. Shade in dark values with the side of your no. 2 pencil. Compare the new ad to the original. What do you think?

2. Find a gestalt-type print ad or one with a silhouette design. With tracing paper, draw the positive shape and shade in the negative shape. This will produce a silhouette of the positive shape (the headline, copy, and illustration) while sharply emphasizing the negative space. The result will be quite abstract; this will force you to see the negative and positive shapes in the original design.

3. Collect several ads that you think are effective and set the headlines in three other typefaces from samples you've collected. Lay the new type over the old. What effect does the change in type style have on the advertisement?

4. Take one of your ads and enlarge and reduce elements to form a new design. Compare your design to the original.

5. Find eight ads with different typefaces and defend or criticize the choices. Does the personality of the type fit the image of the ad? Does it

Figure 7-11
Copy reads: He never worried about the effects of smoking. The thought of lung cancer never even entered his mind. Then the easy things started to get harder. Climbing stairs. Dancing with his wife. Breathing. That's when he came to us. The Institute for Regional Cancer Care at St. Joseph's/Candler offers complete cancer care including prevention, education, diagnosis, treatment, and rehabilitation. The most advanced care a patient can receive in the region. He never worried about the effects of smoking. And with our help, he may never have to.

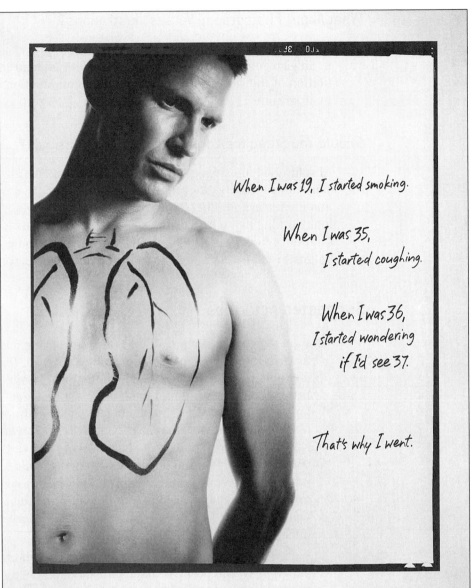

Figure 7-11 (continued)
Copy reads: He wanted to protect his most precious possession. His mind. Home to his memories. His dreams. His wisdom. The things a stroke or other neurological disorders can suddenly take from you. So he came to us. The Institute for neurosciences at St. Joseph's/Candler is the area's leader in stroke prevention, treatment, rehabilitation, and management. Under the care of the region's most experienced stroke team, we also provide advanced neurological services including neurosurgery and neuro intensive care. He wanted to protect his most precious possession. So we gave him the care he would never forget.

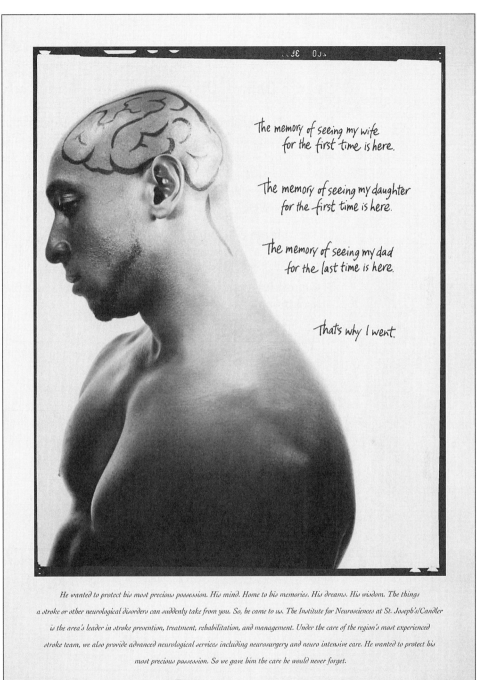

work with the visuals? Does the type overpower everything else and undermine the effectiveness of the ad?

Search Online! Discovering More About Advertising Design

Use InfoTrac College Edition to discover more about advertising design. Try these phrases and others for Key Words and Subject Guide searches: *copywriter + art + director, visual thinking, advertising design, negative space + design, gestalt + design, balance + design, contrast + design, typography, type fonts, reverse type + design, computer design, desktop publishing, outdoor advertising.*

To see a large collection of print advertisements, go to:

www.adsgallery.com

For more information on outdoor advertising, visit the Outdoor Advertising Association of America's Web site:

www.oaaa.org

National Geographic Traveler Magazine
Sends Their Minds—Media Buyers Soon Follow

By Brett Robbs, University of Colorado

When Arnold Advertising of McLean, Virginia, won *National Geographic Traveler*'s trade advertising account, the agency's challenge was clear. Its advertising would have to establish a strong image for the magazine and change the target's perception of *Traveler* readers. With a target consisting of hard-nosed media buyers seeking the best vehicles for their clients' ad monies, the campaign had to get it right.

In the publishing industry, a primary goal of trade advertising is to convince media buyers to place their clients' advertising in particular periodicals. Obviously, a publication's readership is one of its key sales points. Reports from the *National Geographic Traveler* sales force indicated that, although research showed the magazine's readers to be relatively affluent, college-educated professionals who led active lives and who liked to travel, media buyers had quite a different view of these readers.

Media buyers saw *National Geographic Traveler* readers as older, armchair travelers who were more likely to get in a car and visit a state park than to hop on a plane and fly to an international resort. For the magazine to meet its new advertising sales objectives, that perception would have to change—no easy task, given the magazine's relatively modest ad budget and the firmly established positions of its main competitors, *Travel and Leisure* and *Conde Nast Traveler.*

But according to Julie Leidy Bradsher, account supervisor at Arnold, the agency was confident it could meet the challenge because *National Geographic Traveler* has a number of unique assets. One of the most important is the heritage and credibility of the National Geographic Society itself. The Society's name is closely associated with international travel. Its reputation gives *Traveler* strong credibility, and that credibility is one of the primary reasons readers rely on the magazine's stories and maps to plan trips.

The agency realized that this heritage and the readers' subsequent belief in the magazine were the keys. The advertising would need to employ these keys to convince its target market, consisting of potential advertisers, that *Traveler* inspires its readers to travel abroad. If it could do that, the

Photographer: Jonathan Blair

Ah, the inimitable dolce vita of Positano—sunshine, warm spirits, cool wine, and the fruits of local orchards and the sea. Who would not linger on the celebrated Amalfi coast

WE SEND THEIR MINDS.

THEIR BODIES SOON FOLLOW.

NATIONAL GEOGRAPHIC
Traveler

For more than a century, the National Geographic Society has inspired people to see the world. For more than a decade, National Geographic Traveler has shown them how.

THE ISLAND IS ONLY a few miles in diameter, but after eight days I hadn't seen it all and wasn't ready to leave. Like a kaleidoscope, Mackinac can re-create itself in an endless array of dramatic designs.

WE SEND THEIR MINDS.

THEIR BODIES SOON FOLLOW.

NATIONAL GEOGRAPHIC
Traveler

For more than a century, the National Geographic Society has inspired people to see the world. For more than a decade, National Geographic Traveler has shown them how.

Photographer: Declan Haun

...etc...
Jurassic desert some
years ago—now lie etched by wind
and water into delicate swirls of
geologic time. Rococo formations
and cool, deep, narrow slot canyons
characterize the Paria Canyon
...an Cli...

WE SEND THEIR MINDS.

THEIR BODIES SOON FOLLOW.

NATIONAL
GEOGRAPHIC
Traveler

For more than a century, the National Geographic Society has inspired people to see the world.
For more than a decade, National Geographic Traveler has shown them how.

advertising would get *Traveler* on the media buyers' short list and open the door so that the magazine's sales force could complete the sale.

Knowing what to say is one thing. Giving the message impact is something else. As Francis Sullivan, a creative director at Arnold, noted, "One of the things most people immediately associate with the National Geographic Society is beautiful photography. Since we wanted to play on the Society's heritage and also suggest the quality of the magazine, we knew great photography would be a dominant element in the campaign." But, as Sullivan pointed out, *Traveler* is also extremely well written, and the stories have a special flair. So he wanted the advertising to include a passage from an actual story to give the target a better sense of the magazine's editorial flavor.

Sullivan and the art director, Nora Jaster, knew some of the elements they wanted to include in the advertising, but they needed a memorable idea that would cut through the clutter and remind the target that *Traveler* inspires its readers to travel abroad. They tried a variety of approaches. Some ideas focused on the magazine's value to its advertisers. Other ideas attempted to project a more contemporary image for the magazine.

Sullivan and Jaster knew they'd found the solution when they came up with the line "We send their minds. Their bodies soon follow." From there, it was simply a matter of developing the visuals. Placing a passage "torn" from the magazine near the headline "We send their minds" and a striking color photograph showing people in exotic locales next to "Their bodies soon follow" visually reinforced the message and suggested the very process that *Traveler* readers go through: They read a story in the magazine; then they decide to travel to see the place for themselves. Jaster subtly enhanced this message, Sullivan says, by taking a color from the photograph and adding it to the type. "It's a way of visually saying that the words transport you there."

The body copy cements the magazine's image to the National Geographic Society's proud travel heritage. Interestingly, to create the copy, Sullivan drew on a headline idea he had developed for another *Traveler* campaign.

Because the campaign had to deliver its message with a limited number of media insertions, consistency of theme and design was of special importance. To firmly establish *Traveler*'s position, the theme line became the headline for every ad. Theme and look were carried over to the magazine's collateral pieces and sales presentation materials aimed at prospective advertisers.

The target is definitely getting the message, says Pandora Todd, the magazine's director of promotions. The campaign has helped the sales force attract not only new advertisers but also new categories of advertisers. The ad series has also been recognized for its creative excellence—two Gold Clios and a first place in the London International Advertising Awards.

RADIO:
CAN YOU SEE WHAT I'M SAYING?

Radio is everywhere—at home, in cars, at places of business. Radio reaches everyone, from teens to seniors. There's a format for every listener and for every advertiser: country, adult contemporary, news, talk, sports, business, oldies, religion, Spanish, alternative rock, classic rock, hip hop, ethnic, classical, jazz, and new age. You name it; radio has it.

Why Advertise on Radio?

Advertisers love radio because it's a great way to take a small budget and do big things with it. Exciting things. Creative things. Funny things. Production budgets are tiny compared to television, as is the cost of airtime. Radio is a great stand-alone medium and a great support for other media. Airing commercials for its Bubble Jet printer on radio allowed Canon USA to create awareness among a specific audience, the ones ready to buy a printer. Spots were aired in thirteen large markets on news, talk, sports, and classical music formats. In each market, radio ads were supported by newspaper ads on the "best computer day," including a Tuesday "Science Times" section in one market and a Monday business section in another.

And what do writers love about this medium? One calls writing for radio a unique adventure that transcends the limitations and the costliness of the camera lens and the shooting schedule. Another likes the fact that the writer is involved in every stage—writing, casting, selecting sound effects, directing, and editing. Others say radio is "a lot sexier than sex" and must touch our hearts to work effectively. And seasoned radio writers will remind you that radio is a visual medium, in which the audience sees whatever the writer makes them see. The better the writer knows radio, the more the audience will see.

The Theater of the Mind

Radio has been called, appropriately, "the theater of the mind" because, without pictures, radio writers have to deliver visual impressions through their choice of words, voices, sounds, and music. For example, a commercial for Aztec suntan lotion uses a character called the Aztec Sun God, who speaks as if he's just earned an Ivy League degree. (Nothing like unexpected connections to hold interest, remember?) As he converses with a store manager, he mentions that most customers won't recognize him in his suit and wingtip shoes. Then he begins to strip down to his bronzed body as the store manager expresses understandable anxiety. That's not only funny and involving, but it also reinforces the point of the spot: Aztec suntan lotion can make your body look like a sun god's body.

Guidelines for Writing Effective Radio Spots

1. *Write for the ear, not the eye.* Remember, radio is unique. Your eyes don't see the message; your mind does. Don't just run the soundtrack from a TV commercial on the radio. Don't read a print ad into a microphone and expect it to work as a radio commercial. Some copy that works in print sounds absolutely dreadful when read aloud. For example, a radio commercial sent a powerful message about the problem of child abuse. The sound of an abused child's blood-curdling scream sent chills down listeners' spines. But the mood was blown when the announcer read the tag line in an upbeat voice; "Kids. You can't beat them." While the line may have worked as part of the logo in a print ad, it was far too cute when read out loud.

   As you start to write your commercial, think of the voice or voices that will work best for your message. Imagine sounds and music or no sounds and no music. Begin with something relevant yet unexpected to gain the listener's attention. End with something as memorable to drive home your point.

2. *Keep it simple.* Radio is a wonderful medium for building brand awareness. But it's not so good for spewing out a long list of benefits or making complex arguments. In 60 or 30 seconds, you can't expect listeners to remember a series of facts. They can't go back and reread what interests them as they can in a print ad or on the Internet. As you start to conceive your radio commercial, think about the one big idea you need to commu-

nicate and then take this idea and play it for all it's worth for the length of the commercial.

3. *Use sound effects to paint scenery in your listeners' minds.* Consider how you would "show" the ad's location on a radio spot. You could simply have a voice say, "Here on the streets of Manhattan . . ." or you could use sounds to present the location: stalled traffic in New York City with a few well-chosen taxi driver groans or muffled car horns thrown in for good measure.

   Sound effects (SFX) should further the message, not be the ends in themselves. They shouldn't attempt to duplicate reality; calling for footstep sounds serves little purpose unless it helps make the point. Unexpected sounds may be more compelling. One public service announcement on child abuse uses the violent sound of doors slamming as the narrator talks about how some people hide such abuse behind closed doors. A spot urging older people to remain active uses a constant background sound of rocking chairs squeaking on a wooden porch as the narrator tells listeners to do quite the opposite. Here's a spot that uses unexpected sound effects very effectively:

ANNCR:	Some of the fastest automobiles in the world take their names from some of the fastest animals in the world. Ford Mustang. 0 to 45 . . .
SFX:	CAR SPEEDS BY
ANNCR:	6.9 seconds. Volkswagen Rabbit. 0 to 45 . . .
SFX:	CAR SPEEDS BY
ANNCR:	6.4 seconds. Jaguar XKE. 0 to 45 . . .
SFX:	CAR SPEEDS BY
ANNCR:	4.3 seconds. But even the fastest animals on four wheels can't catch the fastest animal on four feet. The African cheetah. 0 to 45 miles per hour in 2.0 seconds.
SFX:	THE ROAR OF A JET
ANNCR:	Catch the cheetahs if you can. Now through Labor Day at the Minnesota Zoo.

This clever spot, which encouraged fathers to take their children to the zoo, probably wouldn't have been as effective with the target audience if it had used the more expected sounds of animals growling, chirping, and snorting.

4. *Identify your sound effects.* Unless you do, you may confuse listeners. For example, what does "s-s-s-s-s-s-s" sound like to you? To some, it may sound like bacon sizzling in a pan. To others, it may remind them of rain falling in a tropical forest. Others may think it's the hissing of a snake or the sound of air being let out of a balloon. Let the context of the spot remind listeners of what they're hearing or even have someone voice an explanation. ("Another day in the rain forest, where the waters feed lush tropical plants.")

5. *Avoid annoying sound effects.* A loud siren may grab your listeners' attention, but it'll likely distract them from your message. If they're driving, they may lower the volume of their radio and look around to learn where the sound is coming from. Once they realize it's "just" a commercial, they'll become annoyed, which is the last thing you want. Also avoid other offensive sounds, such as a dripping faucet, a fly buzzing in your ear, or fingernails scratching a chalkboard. After all, you want to keep the audience listening to you, not searching for another station.

6. *Use music as a sound effect.* Music can enhance a mood or take your mind to exotic destinations. A brokerage house created an image of financial power with the same sounds of kettledrums Prokofiev used in his classic symphony *Peter and the Wolf* to conjure up hunters. Another commercial depicted a German neighborhood by playing a few bars of oompah band music.

   Be certain that the music you select adds to your message. Never plug music in for its own sake. If the tune has a life of its own, it may detract from what you're trying to say. And remember not all music is readily available for advertising purposes. Even a recording of a classic such as the *1812 Overture* must be cleared because the performing orchestra will own a copyright to its rendition. Obtaining commercial rights to copyrighted music and music performances can be extremely costly, and such rights usually have to be renewed annually. The Internet company Excite paid $7 million for the rights to use Jimi Hendrix's song "Are You Experienced," and Microsoft paid about $12 million for "Start Me Up."[1] Some music isn't available at any price because some musicians refuse to allow their art to be part of a commercial endeavor.

   Consider finding music in the public domain or using original music that you have commissioned especially for your campaign. Several music companies offer public domain (PD) music for a small fee, and most radio stations have libraries of PD selections for the convenience of their advertisers.

7. *Consider using no sound effects.* A distinctive voice, a powerful message straightforwardly delivered, can be extremely powerful. People love a good story. If it can stand alone, be conservative in your use of other sounds. The following commercial for Ant-Stop Orthene Fire-Ant Killer from Ortho used an announcer with a serious voice to deliver a hilarious message:

ANNCR: Fire ants are not loveable. People do not want fire ant plush toys.

         They aren't cuddly; they don't do little tricks. They just bite you and leave red, stinging welts that make you want to cry.

---

[1] Michael Miller, "Even Out of Context, the Beat Goes On (and On)," *Pittsburgh Business Times,* 27 November 1998, p. 12.

That's why they have to die.

And they have to die right now.

You don't want them to have a long, lingering illness. You want death. A quick, excruciating, see-you-in-hell kind of death.

You don't want to lug a bag of chemicals and a garden hose around the yard; it takes too long. And baits can take up to a week.

No, my friend, what you want is Ant-Stop Orthene Fire-Ant Killer from Ortho.

You put two teaspoons of Ant-Stop around the house and you're done. You don't even water it in. The scout ants bring it back into the mound.

And this is the really good part. Everybody dies. Even the queen; it's that fast.

And that's good. Because killing fire ants shouldn't be a full-time job—even if it is pretty fun.

Ant-Stop Orthene Fire-Ant Killer from Ortho. Kick fire ant butt!

8. *Describe the voice or voices that can best command the attention of your audience.* Help cast the spot by describing the type of person who should say your words: skeptical young woman, trustworthy older woman, genius child, conservative Vermonter, gushy southern belle, or thick-headed caveman. Be sure to offer directions on the script in parentheses as to delivery: for example, angry, sarcastic, dopey, heavy British accent, or snobbish.

9. *Tailor your commercial to time, place, and a specific audience.* If it's running in morning drive time, remember that most people tuned in may be on their way to work. If it runs in Milwaukee, tailor it for Milwaukee. Talk breakfast at 8 a.m. or offer a commuter taxi service during rush hour.

10. *Repeat the name of your client.* You can't show the product's package or product logo as you can in print and television. Instead, you need to incorporate it into your overall message. As a general rule, try to state your client's name at least three times. The trick, of course, is to do it without being obnoxious. Mnemonic devices, such as a unique voice, music, or sound effect, are great ways to put the brand's name in the listener's mind. An award-winning campaign for Bud Light opens the same way each time:

SFX:	Music up.
ANNCR:	Bud Light Presents . . . Real. American. Heroes.
SINGER:	Real American Heroes.
ANNCR:	Today we salute you . . . Mr. _____

The music, announcer's voice, and the phrase "Real American Heroes" serve as cues that this is another commercial for Bud Light. Likewise, every time you hear "Hi, Tom Bodett here" or "We'll leave the light on for you" you know it's a commercial for Motel 6.

11. *Avoid numbers.* Very few people (if any) are sitting next to the radio with a pen and pad in hand, just waiting for you to give them an important number. So avoid numbers if you can. If you have to give a phone number, spell it out as a word. It's much easier to remember the American Red Cross's phone number as "1-800-HELP-NOW" than it is to remember a bunch of numbers. And if you need to include a street address, put it in terms your listeners can visualize. Instead of "17349 Main Street," say, "On the corner of Main and Green Street" or "On Main Street, across from City Hall."

Sometimes there's no getting around mentioning a number. If you absolutely must include a number, then you'll need to find a clever way to repeat it to make it memorable. The public radio station in Albany, New York sets its phone number (1-800-323-9262) to the tune of Stephen Foster's "Camp Town Races" so that listeners will remember the number when they go to the phone to make a pledge during the fund drive.

One eight hundred three two three

Nine two. Six two.

One eight hundred three two three . . .

Nine two six two.

Nine two six twooooo . . .

Nine two six two . . .

One eight hundred three two three,

Nine two six two.

Notice how many times the number sequence 9-2-6-2 is mentioned? That's because the area code and first three digits of a phone number are easier to remember and therefore don't need to be repeated as often as the last four digits.

12. *Be aware of time considerations.* Too much copy works against you by forcing performers to rush through your lines with little time for those pauses and special inflections that add color, clarity, and depth to the spoken word. And too little copy will give dead airspace. As a general rule, about two words per second is a good place to start when writing your script. But the best way to time a commercial is to set a stopwatch and read your spot aloud, pacing it the way you want it recorded and acting out the sound effects and music. Also be sure to time your spot for the personality of your brand. A spot for a used-car dealer will likely be read fast to instill a sense of urgency, whereas a spot for an expensive restaurant will be read more slowly to reflect the elegant dining experience.

13. *Make your copy easy to read.* Specify pronunciations in parentheses after the word appears. For example, "Nutella (NEW-TELL-AH)" will ensure that the announcer won't mispronounce the brand as "NUT-ELL-A." Do the same with local pronunciations. Huger Street is pronounced "YOU-GEE" in Columbia, South Carolina, not "HUE-GER" or "HUG-ER" as outsiders are prone to say.

    Also avoid tongue twisters and stilted language. Alliterative phrases—red roosters rarely run recklessly—may look fine in print but can cause even a pro to stumble over the words.

14. *Present your commercial idea to the client on a CD if possible.* Dialog, timing, vocal quirks, and sound effects come alive when you can hear them. And most recording studios will produce a "demo" at a reduced cost if you promise to let them produce the approved script. If you can't get it on a CD for presentation, have a person or persons on hand who can act out voices and sounds and indicate music.

Approaches to Radio Commercials

However you structure your radio script, remember to begin with an attention-getting opening. The lead-in must lure the listener into hearing what follows. Generally, it's a good idea to have an announcer drive home the key selling idea at the end. Think of the announcer as the voice of the advertiser, while character voices in the rest of the spot should sound like genuine people or exaggerations of them.

One Voice

Make the voice interesting and relevant. Make the words exceptional. You might add music or sounds, or you might choose to let the voice "speak for itself." The following spot for Ricoh cameras demonstrates how effective one voice can be. It was written by Jackie Eng of Chiat/Day, New York, and produced by Pat Faw at Doppler Recording, Atlanta:

ANNCR: A couple of weeks ago I bought myself a Ricoh 35mm Auto-Focus camera.

And I take out the instruction folder, and it says, "It's the camera that thinks."

So I think about this, you know, and I realize it's true. When you're taking a picture with a Ricoh, it's thinking about the right exposure; it's thinking about the right focus, thinking about the film speed. It's thinking about all the things that give you a terrific picture. But let me ask you this . . .

What do you think a Ricoh camera thinks about when it isn't taking pictures? Does it wonder if you're gonna keep it for yourself or give it away for Christmas? Does it believe in

Santa Claus? Does it think you believe in Santa Claus? Do you? When it thinks, does it think in Japanese?

Does it dream? And, if so, does it dream in color or black and white? Or does that depend on the film you're using? Does it worry about being dropped? I would. Does it think you've got a screw loose thinking about all this? Think about it . . .

This spot is an example of one-voice exposition, in which the announcer speaks directly to the listener.

Another approach is one-voice internal dialog, which sounds like we're listening in on someone's private thoughts. Here's an example:

SFX:	SOUND OF WRITING
WOMAN:	Dear Tom. I completely understand why you stood me up last night. You're too good for me. How could I ever expect to hang on to a guy like you? After all, those hair transplants are really starting to take hold, and the dime size bulbs on your forehead are barely noticeable now. You're quite a catch. So what if you're 36 and still live with your mom. I was just lucky you asked me out in the first place. Well, I could write a lot more, but I'm running out of lipstick and there's no more room left on your windshield.
ANNCR:	If you ever need a squeegee, remember at Unocal 76 you can always find one waiting in clean, soapy water. 76. We get it.

Dialog

Two people talking. Sounds simple, doesn't it? But be careful. Some product categories don't lend themselves to a dialog format. When's the last time you chatted with someone about toilet paper or canned vegetables? It's likely that the dialog you create for such products will sound stilted and phony.

It's also easy to fall into the trap of having an expert talking to a naïf. The naïf says dumb things like "Why isn't my uniform as white as yours?" while the expert responds with something along these lines: "Brand X detergent has a water-soluble bleaching agent that seeps through dirt to render fabrics brighter than ever!" The commercial closes with the naïf asking, "Gee, where can I buy Brand X detergent?"

How do you make the dialog sound real while still getting across a selling message? Use the dialog to set the stage and let the announcer do the selling. Try this one from TBWA, New York, written for Carlsberg beer by Jeff Epstein and produced by Ed Pollack at 12 East Recording, New York:

SHE:	Honey?
HE:	Yes, Precious.

SHE:	I have a confession, Dearest.
HE:	What, Buttercup?
SHE:	You know the clock in the hall?
HE:	The 17th-century fruitwood grandfather clock?
SHE:	I knocked it over.
HE:	Not to worry, Lambykins.
SHE:	Oh, Pork chop, you're so understanding.
HE:	It's only money.
SHE:	Sweet Pea?
HE:	Yes.
SHE:	You know the rug in the den?
HE:	The leopard skin throw in my study?
SHE:	Well, when I shampooed it, the spots came out.
HE:	Don't worry your pretty little head.
SHE:	I'm so relieved.
HE:	What's mine is yours.
SHE:	Cream Puff?
HE:	Yes, Marshmallow?
SHE:	You know those cigars in the fridge?
HE:	The hand-rolled Hondurans?
SHE:	They got wet.
HE:	Pray tell how, Carrot Stick?
SHE:	Well, when I moved the Carlsberg beer in the . . .
HE:	(interrupting): I told you not to touch my Carlsberg.
SHE:	Cucumber.
HE:	Just have your lawyer call my lawyer in the morning . . . Sugar . . . Plum.
ANNCR:	Carlsberg beer. The imported taste that can't be touched. Carlsberg Breweries, Copenhagen, Denmark.

Multivoice

A number of voices speak, not to one another but to the listener. A commercial for AIDS awareness used a variety of voices to make young people aware of the number of misconceptions about the disease and its victims. For this spot, college students were asked to speak candidly about their chances of getting AIDS. The producers edited small sound bites from each of the participants:

VOICE 1:	It can't happen to me . . .
VOICE 2:	There's no way he's got it.
VOICE 3:	You can't get it from a girl . . .
VOICE 4:	Isn't there already a cure?
VOICE 5:	I know she doesn't have it . . .
VOICE 6:	I just want to have fun.
VOICE 7:	But I'm not gay.
VOICE 8:	I hope it doesn't happen to me.

A message about AIDS was read by an announcer and appeared within the commercial.

Dramatization

A dramatization uses the structure of a play, with a beginning, a conflict, and a resolution. You can use sound effects and several voices to act out the story, or you can use a narrator to tell the entire story.

Sound Device

With this approach, a sound or sounds are used repeatedly or intermittently to make the main point. For example, in one ad you can hear someone trying to start a car. The engine goes, "EEEERRRRR . . . EEEERRRRR . . . EEEERRRRR." As the person continues to try to start the car, it sounds weaker and weaker. "Eeeerrrrr . . . eeeerrrrr . . . eeeerrrrr." The sound of military taps fades in as the sound of the engine fades out. The battery finally dies. A voice-over announces that Sears is having a sale on DieHard batteries.

Sometimes music is used as the big idea for a commercial. For example, one spot opens to the sound of a man singing in the shower. His voice is dreadful—but he keeps on singing, and singing. You can't imagine what's going on until an announcer interrupts and asks, "Think this has gone on long enough? So do we. Take shorter showers and save water."

Vignette

A vignette is a series of short situations linked by a repeated device (for example: announcer line, musical bridge, or sound effect). After the first vignette makes the point, the ensuing situations need not be as long. An announcer usually wraps up the spot near the end, followed by a quick closing vignette. To illustrate, here's a portion of the commercial for George Schlatter's Comedy Club:

ANNCR:	Number 17. The chuckle.
SFX:	MAN CHUCKLING.
ANNCR:	Number 22. The giggle.
SFX:	WOMAN GIGGLING.
ANNCR:	Number 56. The snort.
SFX:	WOMAN SNORTING WHILE LAUGHING.
ANNCR:	Number 61. The nasal burst.
SFX:	MAN LAUGHING THROUGH HIS NOSE.

Interviews

With this approach, someone is interviewing someone or groups of people, somewhere—on a busy street, at the North Pole, in outer space. In one spot, the interview takes place under a house where the interviewer talks to two termites as they casually chew up the wood subflooring.

Jingles

David Ogilvy said, "When you have nothing to say, sing it." Not everyone agrees with that, however. A catchy jingle can make a lasting impression in our minds. For example, there's a good chance you can sing the lyrics to "Oh, I wish I were an Oscar Mayer wiener . . ." and "Hot dogs, Armour hot dogs, what kind of kids eat Armour hot dogs?" Most copywriters are not lyricists or composers, so you'll probably want a professional songwriter to develop the jingle. But you'll need to supply the songwriter with your key selling point and the attitude you want to convey (upbeat, sexy, whimsical, and so on).

Live Versus Produced

Most national radio spots and a growing number of local spots are recorded in a digital format, ready to be aired. But some commercials are sent in script form and are either read live or recorded for airplay by a staff announcer. Other advertisers don't even furnish a script; instead, they send a fact sheet describing the major selling points and benefits of their product, service, or place of business. Which should you choose? Here's a general guide to what works and when:

1. *Use a fact sheet when the radio station has a popular on-air personality.* Number the facts in descending order of importance, and you may get more than your paid minute's worth if the personality is having fun chatting about your product or place. A donut shop did just that. The shop sent a dozen donuts each morning to a local announcer who was known to love his food. Each morning, the announcer would lovingly describe every bite and rhapsodize on the flavor, texture, and so on. The spots ran during morning drive time, when people are most likely to buy donuts. The campaign was a tremendous success.

2. *Use a script read live only if you're using straight copy with no sound effects, music, or multiple speaking parts.* A problem with this approach is that many radio personalities are flippant by nature and can have too much fun being cynical or sarcastic with live copy. Therefore, use this approach primarily when you must make last-minute changes to your advertising: a store announcing an extended sale or a promotion that changes daily.

3. *Use a live-recorded commercial when you want to be able to update copy on a regular basis.* The advertiser records a musical introduction. At some point, the music "fades under" or is reduced in volume so that a local announcer can read copy over the music. At the end, the music swells to its conclusion, usually with a recorded closing line. Because the

middle of the spot contains this "hole," this format is called a "live donut." While the music provides continuity for the entire campaign, the scripted inserts keep the ad up-to-date. Obviously, the inserts must be timed so that they fit the hole in the music.

4. *Use a produced commercial when your script calls for multiple speaking parts, sound effects, music, or any combination of these and when you want assurance that the quality of the spot will never waver.* You can imagine why many advertisers prefer this approach. Like a print ad that arrives ready to run, the produced radio commercial allows little room for human error once it leaves the advertiser. Some produced commercials allow a 5-second space at the end for the local announcer to voice a local tag (where to buy it, when it goes on sale).

Most local radio stations provide basic production for free, but you may prefer to use a production house that specializes in a particular style. During production, the writer should be present to review and approve script adjustments and to work with the production staff on ways to enhance the spot. Some of the best commercials result from last-minute ideas in the studio. That's fine, as long as the essential message and strategy remain unchanged. For example, the slogan for Motel 6 came about through a fortuitous accident. After Tom Bodett finished his folksy monolog, there was still a smidgen of time left on the tape, so he ad-libbed, "We'll leave the light on for you."

Radio Script Format

Like all copy, a radio script begins with a tag in the upper-left corner (see Figure 8-1). In this instance, you should indicate on the second line, after the timing, whether the spot is a fact sheet, live announcer copy, or to be produced. Because radio scripts typically go through many revisions before being produced, many writers also indicate the date the script was written or the script revision number to ensure that everyone is working with the same version.

All radio copy should be double-spaced to facilitate reading and should leave room for notes and alterations during production.

The designation for a sound effect is SFX. This is capitalized and underscored, along with the entire sound-effect direction, to alert the producer to the effect and its position within the script. For the same reason, all effects are entered on a separate line. If the effect should come in the middle of a line of dialog, use ellipses (. . .) to break from the first part of the line, drop to a new line for the SFX, and then continue the dialog on the following line with additional ellipses at the beginning to indicate resumption of the dialog.

Names of speakers should be typed in capital letters. Note the abbreviation for announcer is ANNCR. Directions to the speaker should be typed in upper- and lowercase and enclosed in parentheses after the speaker's name. Dialog should be typed in upper- and lowercase.

Figure 8-1

Here's what an actual radio script looks like. This one also provides a wonderful example of how sounds can be used to bring an idea to life. Notice how the sound effects are capitalized and underscored for quick identification. Also notice how the spot wraps with a restatement of the theme line.

RENT.NET "Vampires" :60 Radio	
SFX	COFFIN CREAKS OPEN. SPOOKY MUSIC BEGINS TO PLAY, THEN FADES UNDER.
VAMPIRE 1:	Hey! What are ya doing?! You know we can't go out in the daylight! Vampire Code 6!
VAMPIRE 2:	Relax! I'm just trying to find us a new apartment . . . Maybe a *nicer* one?!
SFX:	DRIPPING FAUCET
VAMPIRE 1:	I'm tellin' ya—this is the only place where the landlady would meet us *after dark!*
VAMPIRE 2	(sarcastically): Yeah! Crazy ol' bat!
VAMPIRE 1	(nervously): But anyway, you can't do this NOW! I mean, how you gonna get a newspaper out there in the sunlight! You can't go out there, man!
VAMPIRE 2:	Relax! I'm using rent.net!
SFX:	MODEM DIALING IN
VAMPIRE 1:	What?!
VAMPIRE 2	(exasperated): Have you been living in a cave? Rent.net! It's the most comprehensive rental guide on the net! We can search for an apartment right here online by city, number of bedrooms—we can even choose our price range and view photos and check out the apartment's amenities!
VAMPIRE 1:	Oh! Hey—do a search for a place that allows pets—you know those juicy little, uh, I mean cute little puppies!
VAMPIRE 2:	(typing): You're sick man, really sick . . .
VAMPIRE 1:	Hey a vampire's gotta eat!
ANNCR:	Rent.net—the easiest way to find a new apartment in any city. Find your new home without leaving the . . . (SFX: CREEPY APARTMENT NOISES) . . . *comfort* of yours.

Courtesy of Kathy Van Nostrand.

Music is simply another type of sound effect and should be treated as such. If a commercial is to begin with music, which is then to fade under the speakers (play softly in the background), a direction might read like this:

SFX:	HARP INSTRUMENTAL AND FADE UNDER.
TIM:	Sometimes late at night, when you wish you could talk to a special voice far away, it's nice to know long distance rates are lower after 11 p.m.

If the music is to disappear at some point, you should indicate this through another sound-effect cue:

SFX:	MUSIC OUT.
TIM:	Because when you can pick up the phone . . .
SFX:	CLICK OF RECEIVER.
TIM:	. . . and dial your favorite person thousands of miles away . . .

Often, especially if your commercial consists of a conversation between two or more people, you may want to wrap up the message by bringing in an authoritative announcer (ANNCR) at the very end. This is a good way to bring your audience back to earth (especially if you've been treating the subject with humor) and to reinforce what you want remembered about your message.

Checklist for Radio Copy

✓ Is there one major premise?

✓ Is the structure appropriate for the message?

✓ Are voices, music, and sounds described clearly?

✓ If you used copyrighted music, is it essential, affordable, and available?

✓ Do music or sound effects help support the selling message?

✓ Is there sufficient time for comfortable, believable delivery of the lines?

✓ Is there time for all sound effects and musical bridges?

✓ Does the commercial time correctly?

✓ Is brand recognition achieved through mention of the brand, music, or sounds that trigger awareness?

Radio is fun and challenging at the same time. As with all advertising copy, it isn't always easy to find the best solution. But when you hear your commercial in finished form, you'll know if it's right. A well-written, well-produced radio spot can have a tremendous impact on its target audience.

Suggested Activities

1. Using the campaign theme from your print ads, write a radio commercial for the same product or service. Write it as if it were to be produced. Note as you are doing this that merely paraphrasing the text from a print ad may not work because of the essential differences between the media. What sort of voices will work best for your message? What will be the appropriate tone? These are but a few of the new issues you need to consider.

2. Visit a local business and interview the person in charge. Devise a creative strategy for this business, indicating how radio might be used. Cover approaches, target audience, mood, and expected results. Then write two or three radio spots based on your strategy and tie them together using a specific theme or device.

3. Listen to a different radio station every day for the next week. Make mental notes of the types of commercials you hear on each station. What did you learn?

4. Practice your editing skills. Take a print ad from this book and use the information to create a 30-second radio commercial.

Search Online! Discovering More About Radio Commercials

Use InfoTrac College Edition to discover more about radio commercials. Try these phrases and others for Key Words and Subject Guide searches: *radio commercials, radio commercial format, radio audiences, radio + visuals, theater of the mind, sound effects, mood music, writing for the ear, humor + radio, vignette, classic radio commercials.*

For sample scripts and winning commercials, go to the Radio Advertising Bureau Web site (www.rab.com) and click on "Mercury Awards."

BRIEFCASE

Tom Bodett Sells Affordability and Comfort for Motel 6

Motel 6 helped define the budget motel sector when it opened its first property in Santa Barbara, California in 1962. Its "no-frills" concept offered a cheap alternative to the pricey full-service hotels that then dominated the market. However, in 1980 occupancy rates for Motel 6 began to decline at an average of nearly 2 percentage points per year. Finally, in 1986, with no end to the decline in sight, the company set out to overhaul its business and turned to The Richards Group for help to reverse the occupancy decline, boost revenue, and regain share.

The Richards Group nosed around the properties and talked to a few customers and found a partial reason for the decline—the product itself. It was woefully out of step with the modern traveler. There were no phones in the rooms. There were televisions, but you had to pay to watch. The Richards Group recommended putting advertising on hold (imagine an agency saying that!) and fixing these problems. Motel 6 agreed and it was done.

Meanwhile, The Richards Group continued their dialog with consumers, and a curious thing happened. In focus groups with people who had stayed at Motel 6, no one mentioned the brand when they were asked where they had stayed. Only after probing did someone finally step forward and admit having stayed at Motel 6; then everyone in the group acknowledged a stay. Why had they held back? Simply because they feared being perceived as cheap for selecting Motel 6. What they really felt was that they were frugal, even virtuous. And they were proud of it.

Pride in frugality. There it was. So simple, but so hidden from view. This insight became the foundation of The Richards Group Spherical brand-development process, where positioning, personality, and affiliation are written in stone. The positioning statement became: "To frugal people, Motel 6 is the comfortable place to stay that's always the lowest price of any national chain." The personality for the brand was defined as "Honest. Simple. Friendly and fun. Humble. Unpretentious. Good-humored and commonsensical." And affiliation was described as follows: "People who stay at Motel 6

Courtesy of Motel 6 and The Richards Group.

are solid citizens with enough common sense not to throw away their hard-earned money. Regardless of how much money they make, they take pride in finding ways to save a buck."

From that day forward, these brand strategies have driven much more than the communication of Motel 6; they have driven critical business strategies. Spherical Branding drives price. The lowest price is unassailable territory for Motel 6. Only one can be the lowest. Motel 6 adjusts its price market by market, but it is always the lowest price of any national chain. It also drives renovation strategy because of the promise of a clean, comfortable room. Motel 6 spent $600 million from 1993 to 1998 in renovations to make certain this promise is not an empty one.

Spherical Branding also drives the communication strategy. Tom Bodett, an obscure carpenter from Homer, Alaska, and occasional commentator on National Public Radio, became the poster boy for frugality. Bodett took the new Motel 6 to the airwaves in 1987, granting permission to stay at Motel 6 and even to brag about your "smart choice." One time when Bodett finished his folksy monolog, there was still a smidgen of time left on the tape, so he ad libbed, "We'll leave the light on for you." Since then, the line became the familiar ending to Motel 6 commercials.

Spherical Branding paid an enormous media dividend too. As one sage said, no one ever arrives at Motel 6 by air. They are in their car, which led the agency to radio. So while the competition went head-to-head in television, Motel 6 underspent and outflanked them.

Today, no matter where you run into Motel 6, from listening to their commercials to walking into the lobby, you get the same message, the same personality. Try it. Call Motel 6 and listen to the on-hold message. Check out their Click 6 Web bargains. Or better yet, stay there and enjoy a wake-up call.

The Richards Group has won numerous awards for their work. *Advertising Age* magazine picked the Motel 6 campaign as one of the 100 best of the 20th century. Perhaps the most meaningful award is the dramatic rise in Motel 6 revenues, which are now more than three times their 1986 level. Motel 6 is now, with 76,000 rooms, the largest owner-operated economy lodging chain in the United States.

Here is a small sample of how Bodett and The Richards group works their magic to create an honest, good-humored, and commonsensical personality for Motel 6:

MOTEL 6 "Pets" :60 radio

TOM: Hi, Tom Bodett here. I've always wondered what exactly dogs are dreaming about when they're moving their paws and grunting in their sleep. Some say that the dream state lets the soul slip free of its earthbound shell to resume a past life. That maybe Buster harbors the reincarnated spirit of Constantine the Eleventh, last of the Byzantine emperors, who each night gallops once again through the rubble, tears of rage falling from one eye, tears of sorrow from the other, as the ancient walls are breached. Personally, I'm betting dogs are just dreaming about table scraps or chasing the neighbor's cat. Something to contemplate as you watch your dog's paws twitch in your room at Motel 6, where they have the lowest price of any national chain, and where pets are always welcome. I'm Tom Bodett for Motel 6, and we'll leave the light on for you and your best friend Buster . . . the Eleventh.

ANNCR: Motel 6. An Accor Hotel.

MOTEL 6 "Business Talk" :60 radio

TOM: Hi, Tom Bodett for Motel 6, with a word for business travelers. Seems business has its own language these days, full of buzzwords. Like the word "buzzword" or "net-net." And after a day spent white-boarding a matrix of action items and deliverables, it's nice to know that you can always outsource your accommodation needs to the nearest Motel 6. You'll get a clean, comfortable room for the lowest price, net-net, of any national chain. Plus data-ports and free local calls in case you tabled your discussion and need to reconvene offline. So you can think of Motel 6 as your total business travel solution provider, vis-à-vis cost-effective lodging alternatives for Q-1 through Q-4. I think. Just call 1-800-4-MOTEL-6 or visit motel6 .com. I'm Tom Bodett for Motel 6, and we'll maintain the lighting device in its current state of illumination for you.

ANNCR: Motel 6. An Accor Hotel.

TELEVISION:
THE POWER OF SIGHT AND SOUND

In Alfred Hitchcock's classic 1959 thriller, *North by Northwest,* there's a 14-minute scene that's a self-contained movie-within-a-movie. Using the barest amount of dialog, the 14 minutes elapse with a story made unmistakably clear through the careful actions, sounds, camera angles, and editing of the legendary director. It goes something like this:

1. We open on an extreme long shot, aerial view, of the middle of nowhere: a dusty crossroads on the prairie. A bus rolls into the frame, stops, deposits a passenger, and drives off.

2. We cut to a medium shot of our hero, Thornhill, who has just left the bus. In the previous scene, we learned he was to travel to this spot alone and wait for a man named Kaplan. He looks around.

3. Through a succession of crosscuts between Thornhill and point-of-view shots showing what he's seeing, we realize his frustration that no one is in sight.

4. We cut back and forth as he watches; then we see what he's watching: cars whizzing by. No Kaplan.

5. Soon he looks toward the camera. We cut to what he sees: a long shot of a car just coming out of a dirt road onto the main highway across from where he's standing.

6. The car drops off a man and heads back where it came from.

7. Thornhill stares at the man.

8. The man halfheartedly stares at Thornhill.

9. Thornhill begins crossing the road toward the man as the camera dollies to parallel his movement.

10. We cut to what Thornhill sees as he crosses: The camera moves closer and closer to the stranger.

Once Thornhill discovers the man isn't Kaplan, he's left alone again as the man boards an arriving bus. The rest of the scene takes us through a harrowing episode in which a crop-dusting airplane begins firing shots and spraying insecticide at Thornhill. The scene culminates in a fiery crash when the out-of-control plane smashes into an oil truck.

What has all this to do with writing television commercials? Everything. Although the scene runs for about 14 minutes and your commercial will probably run no more than 30 seconds, one thing both have in common is the use of film "language" to tell a story. Rent the video *North by Northwest* and watch the scene (watch the whole film; it's terrific!) after reading the visual description at the beginning of this chapter. You'll begin to see why the director chose those shots and how they are connected to one another to heighten the impact of the story. In a commercial, you can do the same.

A Meaningful Message for Business Travelers[1]

In a United Airlines television commercial, a group of businesspeople are getting a pep talk from their supervisor about the way they've been doing business. "I got a phone call this morning from one of our oldest customers," says the supervisor. "Over 20 years. He fired us. Said he didn't know us any-more. We used to do business face-to-face. Now it's a phone call and a fax and get back to you later. Probably with another phone call or fax."

Then he reveals that he's sending the entire sales force out for face-to-face chats with every customer they have. "But that's over 200 cities," whines one man. Then comes the clincher. The supervisor hands out United Airlines tickets to all and tells his crew that he's going to personally call on the guy who fired them that morning. Although the spot clearly shows the United logo on the ticket envelopes, this is one airline commercial that shows no planes, inside or out.

Bud Watts adds:

The client said, "Demonstrate United's scope in a manner that will be meaningful to the business traveler." We said to ourselves, of course, fine. But just telling people United flies to a lot of places won't do the job. We need to cut through. Get people's attention. So, using modern-day busi-

---

[1] Thanks to Bud Watts, executive vice president, group creative director, Leo Burnett Company, Inc.

ness methods as the theme, an idea came: the growing popularity of doing business solely electronically and how that can fail you. There will never be a substitute for a face-to-face with a client or business associate. That's the idea. Face to face, that's real solid ground—and it worked. The story starts with a shocker, then empathetically drives home the idea and finishes with a real "Knute Rockne" tug.

The spot was a tremendous success for United. It demonstrated the airline's understanding of business fliers and the realities of business.

Getting Ready to Write Ads for TV

For the copywriter–art director team, it's especially important to remember this: Although the bag of computer-generated, interactive, digital tricks is growing almost daily, be careful. If it furthers the strategy, use it. If it doesn't, don't. When you have no more than 30 seconds to make an impression, strategy is where the television commercial begins.

Watching TV Commercials with a Critical Eye and Ear

If you think about it, you'll probably realize that the commercials you remember are few and far between. What makes you forget most commercials, and what makes you remember those rare gems? Sit down in front of the TV and start watching commercials. Watch at least ten. For each commercial, jot down answers to the following questions:

1. What was the single central message or idea?
2. What was the value of the opening shot with respect to that idea?
3. Did you get involved with the commercial? If so, at what point did it happen?
4. To what extent did the pictures, as opposed to the words, tell the story?
5. Were the words redundant, or did they add something? What did they add?
6. Were interesting, exciting, complicated, beautiful visuals on screen long enough for complete understanding or appreciation? Were dull, static visuals on too long? How would you make them better?
7. Was the story an irrelevant attention getter, or was the product an integral part of the story?
8. Did you enjoy the story? Did you believe it or find some other value in it? Or was it unrelated to the product story and just there to make you watch?
9. Afterward, could you say why you should care about the product or service in a sentence?

Questions to Ask Yourself Before You Write

Before you actually write a commercial, you need to answer these questions:

1. *What's the big idea you need to get across?* In 30 seconds, you'll barely have time to do much more than that. For Bell Helmets, everything in each commercial (soundless shots of bikers flipping and crashing as a lone whistler is heard on the soundtrack) suggests that when bikers' heads are protected they can be cool about riding.

2. *What's the benefit of that big idea, and whom does it benefit?* Now, in addition to thinking about what your target audience will want to hear, you need to think about what they'll be interested in seeing.

3. *How can you turn that benefit into a visual element that will stick in the viewer's mind?* The intrusive Bell Helmets signature at the end of each commercial merges movement, visuals, and sounds to deliver the main message. As a full-screen "Bell Helmets" tag line appears when the announcer voices the name, a huge helmet descends with a whoosh over a model of the human brain. The chin strap locks with a powerful click. The words "courage for your head" are voiced and seen at the same time. Prior footage includes pictures and full-screen titles that, in their whimsical way, take potentially disastrous situations, add self-deprecating humor, and make the whole thing work. You sweat, then you smile, and then you agree: With a Bell Helmet on your head, you can enjoy this sport to the fullest with fewer risks.

From Visual to Script

Now, taking that visual, how can you write a scenario that takes the story to its logical conclusion? Here are some tips:

1. *At this point, just use narrative to tell the story:* "We open with a guy flipping on his bike in grainy, slow motion. We follow with other shots of guys who look like they're hell-bent on a path of self-destruction. We intercut titles to let the viewer know there's something more here than meets the eye. Whatever we put on the titles tells a continuous story that leads to our tag, 'Bell Helmets. Courage for Your Head.'"

2. *Once you're happy with the scenario, put it in script form.* (See Figure 9-1 and the instructions later in this chapter.)

3. *Read the script out loud and listen carefully.* Check for timing, clarity, and continuity. (Do the words and pictures follow a logical sequence?) Check for product identity. (Is the product "buried" by needless over-production or story exposition?) Have you essentially confined your story to one major point? If not, try again.

Figure 9-1

Note that it's more what you see than what you hear in this script. And rightly so. This is television, where most good commercial ideas begin with the pictures, adding words and sounds to fortify the visual images. Each number on the left moves the visual story forward—title shots included. The audio on the right simply calls for a soft, easy whistling, which makes a surprising contrast to the mayhem on the screen. At the all-important close, the theme line literally wraps things up with a startling graphic along with sounds that bring the whole idea of "courage for your head" to a memorable finale.

Bell Helmets "Reason" :30 TV

1. (GRAINY FOOTAGE THROUGHOUT)   SFX: SOFT WHISTLING
   LS CAR CRASHING ON TRACK.   THROUGHOUT. NO OTHER NOISES.

2. LS GUY WEARING HELMET
   FLIPPING OFF BIKE.

3. TITLE (WHITE ON BLACK):
   "HUMANS ARE THE ONLY SPECIES"

4. LS GUY IN HELMET FLYING
   THROUGH THE AIR AS HE LEAVES BIKE.

5. TITLE (WHITE ON BLACK):
   "WITH THE ABILITY TO REASON"

6. LS SHOTS OF VARIOUS OTHER
   CRASH SITUATIONS.

7. TITLE (WHITE ON BLACK):
   "AND SOMETIMES"

8. GUY CRASHES BIKE FLIPPING OVER
   IN MIDAIR IN THE PROCESS.

9. TITLE (WHITE ON BLACK):
   "THEY EVEN USE IT."

10. CUT TO FULL SCREEN BELL   ANNCR (VO): Bell Helmets.
    HELMETS LOGO.

11. CUT TO REVOLVING "BRAIN."   SFX: WHOOSH OF HELMET
    HELMET WRAPS AROUND IT.   COVERING HEAD, CHIN
       STRAP LOCKING TIGHT

12. CUT TO TITLE: "COURAGE   ANNCR (VO): Courage for
    FOR YOUR HEAD."   your head.

Courtesy of Bell Sports, Inc.

---

4. *Revise. Revise. Revise.* Make sure it's not too long. Then ask yourself the following questions: How well does the opening shot command the attention of the viewer? How much does the opening relate to the main idea of the message? How well does the closing reinforce the main idea and drive home the point? How much time is spent on the product? How visual is the idea? Try telling the story in pictures only, leaving out the words, and see whether it still makes sense.

5. *Finalize.* Once you have a script, prepare your storyboard. (See Figure 9-2 and the accompanying instructions.)

Abalone Vintage Guitars
:30 TV
"Rock the Cradle"

VIDEO:
OPEN ON LS BABY'S NURSERY

SFX: SOFT, SOOTHING LULLABY MUSIC IN BACKGROUND

VIDEO:
CUT TO CU DOORKNOB. IT SLOWLY BEGINS TO TURN.

SFX: SOUND OF KNOB TURNING QUIETLY.

VIDEO:
SLOW ZOOM OUT TO MS AS DOOR GENTLY OPENS. ATTRACTIVE YOUNG MOTHER PEERS IN ADORINGLY.

AUDIO:
ANNCR (VO): Some things in life are just more precious than others.

VIDEO:
CUT TO LS WOMAN WALKING ACROSS ROOM TO CRIB. PAN L TO FOLLOW HER.

AUDIO:
ANNCR (VO): And those things are worth all of your attention, every single moment . . .

Courtesy Ray Tom.

Figure 9-2
Raymond Tom's storyboard for Abalone Guitars not only uses an unexpected analogy but also explains what he plans to shoot. Here the right column is used for video and audio, with space between so there's no confusion. As in all good commercials, it's best to stick to one big idea. Thirty seconds doesn't give you enough time to do much more.

Abalone Vintage Guitars
:30 TV
"Rock the Cradle"

VIDEO:
CUT TO LOW ANGLE CU WOMAN FROM POV INSIDE CRIB. SHE SMILES ADORINGLY.

AUDIO:
ANNCR (VO): . . . 'cause it's one of a kind, and there's not another one like it in the whole wide world.

VIDEO:
CUT TO CU ELECTRIC GUITAR RESTING INSIDE CRIB. STUFFED TOYS SURROUND IT.

AUDIO:
SFX: ELECTRIC GUITAR JOINS LULLABY MUSIC.

VIDEO:
DISS TO LS WOMAN SITTING IN ROCKING CHAIR, PLAYING GUITAR WITH WILD ABANDON.

AUDIO:
ANNCR (VO): We've always been there for top recording artists . . . and we'll always be there for you, too.

VIDEO:
SUPER TITLE: ABALONE VINTAGE GUITARS. THE GUITAR AUTHORITY (ADDRESS/PHONE)

AUDIO:
ANNCR (VO): Abalone Vintage Guitars. The Guitar Authority.

Figure 9-2 (continued)

Formats for Television Commercials

As with other types of advertising, the best way to begin thinking about a television commercial is to immerse yourself in facts and ideas about the product. Only then do you start writing. If nothing happens, these suggestions can get you jump-started:

Demonstration   Television can show what the product can do better than any other medium. Here are some examples:

- *Product in use:* A man swipes shoe polish on his handkerchief and cleans it by shaking it in a cocktail shaker filled with ice and a little bit of brand X laundry detergent.
- *Before and after:* A guy who looks to be about 100 years old shampoos some coloring into his hair. Presto! He's 35. (Okay, we admit we're exaggerating a bit, but you get the idea.)
- *Side by side:* Two identical battery-operated toys are entertaining the viewer. One of the toys dies, while the toy with brand X batteries keeps working.

Product as star   A bulldog sizes up a Mini automobile. After the stare down, the dog circles to the rear of the car and starts sniffing the tailpipe. Graphic: "Let's get acquainted." Tag line: "Mini. Let's motor."

Vignette   Several brief episodes are threaded together to drive home the same point over and over. Each episode usually involves different people at different places, but they all say something relevant to the product story. For example, a spot for ESPN shows people watching television and shouting instructions at their TV sets. "Get out of the crease!" a woman screams. "Basketball 101," says a man. "Tackle somebody!" yells another fan. Tag line: "Without sports, there'd be no one to coach."

Slice of life   The star of the commercial has a problem, and brand X is the solution. A Swedish commercial shows beautiful people at a wedding. The bride and groom walk up a staircase and wave goodbye to their wedding guests. The guests wave back, and some blow kisses. The groom lifts the bride to carry her over the threshold and . . . THUD! The bride's head hits the doorway as the groom tries to carry her through, and he drops her. The camera cuts to a close-up of two pills being plopped into water. The groom drinks the remedy, and a voice-over says, "Headaches can suddenly appear. Treo gives quick and effective relief."

Presenters   Someone looks into the camera and tells you why you should buy the product. It could be an expert, such as a nurse who recommends a certain brand of painkiller. Or a person associated with the company, such as a CEO. Or a celebrity who looks cool using your product (or any product, for that matter—see Chapter 1 for guidelines for using celebrities). Or an animated or animal character, such as the M&M characters or the Chick-fil-A cows (see Figure 9-3).

Figure 9-3
The Chick-fil-A cows convinced a lot of people to "eat mor chikin" by painting messages on billboards (see Chapter 4). Now they're creating their own television commercials!

CLIENT: CHICK-FIL-A
JOB: :30 TV
TITLE: "OVERHEAD"

Video		Audio
OPEN ON A SHOT OF A GIANT PAIR OF BOOTS. TYPE THAT SAYS "LEATHER BOOT-O-RAMA" SPINS ONTO SCREEN OVER IMAGE. CUT TO STATIC.		TWANGY MUSIC UNDER VO: The finest leather boots are at Big Bob's… SFX: (STATIC AND TV EMERGENCY SOUNDS INTERRUPT VO.)
CUT TO "COW TV" CARD. MORE STATIC.		SFX: (BARNYARD SOUNDS. COWS MOOING. CHICKENS SQUAWKING. COW HOOVES MOVING TRANSPARENCIES ON OVERHEAD PROJEC-TOR.)
CUT TO INTERIOR OF BARN. OVERHEAD PROJECTOR IS PROJECTING HEADLINE ON BARN WALL. IT SAYS "KNOW YER FOOD GROOPS."		
THAT CARD IS REMOVED AND REPLACED BY ANOTHER THAT READS, "FIG. 1 FOOD PYRUMID". UNDER THE HEADING IS A TRIANGLE THAT HAS A DRAWING OF A CHICKEN WITH THE WORD "CHIKIN" UNDER IT.		

Testimonials   "I use this product. So should you." Testimonials must be true and must be based on real experiences of real people. Professional golfer Nancy Lopez seems credible when she endorses Synvisc, a treatment for osteoarthritis (knee pain).

Stories   Think of them as 30-second television shows. For example, in one ad, a boy spots an attractive girl in class. He passes her a note that says "I love you. Do you love me?" There are two boxes ("Yes" and "No") for her to

Figure 9-3 (continued)

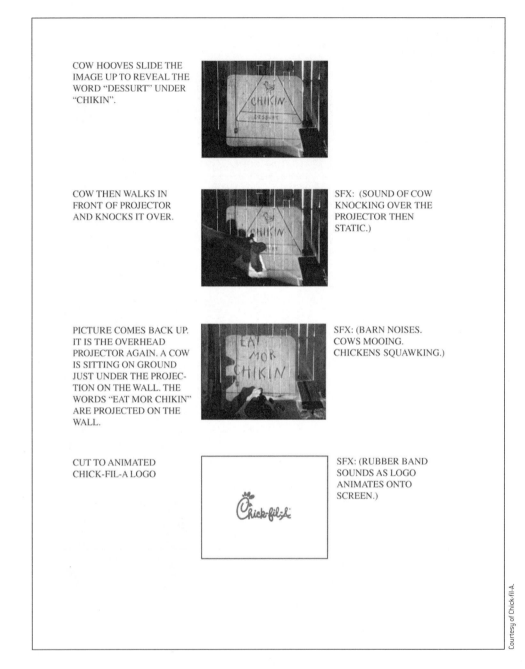

COW HOOVES SLIDE THE IMAGE UP TO REVEAL THE WORD "DESSURT" UNDER "CHIKIN".

COW THEN WALKS IN FRONT OF PROJECTOR AND KNOCKS IT OVER.

SFX: (SOUND OF COW KNOCKING OVER THE PROJECTOR THEN STATIC.)

PICTURE COMES BACK UP. IT IS THE OVERHEAD PROJECTOR AGAIN. A COW IS SITTING ON GROUND JUST UNDER THE PROJECTION ON THE WALL. THE WORDS "EAT MOR CHIKIN" ARE PROJECTED ON THE WALL.

SFX: (BARN NOISES. COWS MOOING. CHICKENS SQUAWKING.)

CUT TO ANIMATED CHICK-FIL-A LOGO

SFX: (RUBBER BAND SOUNDS AS LOGO ANIMATES ONTO SCREEN.)

Courtesy of Chick-fil-A.

check off her answer. The girl looks at him, scribbles her answer, and passes the note back. He opens it. The answer is no! He hangs his head. When he looks up, he spots another cute girl. He erases the no and passes her the note. The tag line appears on the screen: "You're never too young to start recycling. Weyerhaeuser."

Camera Shots, Camera Moves, and Transitions

Camera Shots

How many shots should you use in 30 seconds? It all depends on the story you want to tell and the best way to tell it. Each shot, however, should fulfill a specific need. Here are the basic shots to know.

Extreme close-up (ECU) In this shot, you get as close as you can and still show what needs showing: part of a face, a detail on a product. The ECU permits a bigger-than-life glimpse that can be used to dramatic advantage to further your story.

Close-up (CU) In this shot, a face fills the screen, or a product stands tall, commanding your attention. Early moviemakers such as D. W. Griffith invented this way of magnifying the emotional communication of the moving image, in part to compensate for the absence of sound. It's still a powerful way to provide visual emphasis. The CU contains no distractions; it shows only what you want the viewer to see. When we're this close, however, we rarely know where the action is taking place. So the choice of a CU or a wider shot depends on the purpose of the shot.

Medium shot (MS) A typical MS shows two people, from the waist up, engaged in dialog (also called a 2-shot, because it covers two people). In this shot, one can identify location to some degree, making it an ideal compromise in framing action. When a CU reveals too little and a long shot (LS) is too broad, the answer usually lies somewhere in-between.

Long shot (LS) Also known as an establishing shot, the LS broadly covers an area, revealing instantly where we are—flying in the clouds, working in the kitchen, exercising in the gym. Use an LS to open a commercial if your audience needs to know where it's taking place from the start. Or start with a CU to purposely hide the location until later. Again, it depends on the story you want to tell.

Camera Moves

Zoom in/out (dolly in/out) This involves a movement toward or away from the subject. In a zoom, the lens revolves to bring the image closer or to move it farther away. In a dolly, the camera actually moves forward or backward. A zoom is limited by the range of the lens, whereas a dolly is limited only by the imagination. Use either term in your script/storyboard and allow the director to make the final decision.

Pan R/L (truck R/L) This involves a movement to the right or left. In a pan, the camera turns to one side or the other or follows a moving object as it travels across the screen. In a trucking shot, the camera actually rolls sideways to follow or keep alongside the action—creating quite a different perspective than the pan.

Tilt U/D (boom or crane shot)   In a tilt, the camera "looks" up or down—like a vertical version of the pan. In a boom or crane shot, the entire camera and cinematographer are hydraulically raised or lowered while film or tape rolls. A famous boom shot is *Gone With the Wind*'s dramatic pullback as Scarlett O'Hara wanders aimlessly through rows of wounded soldiers at the Atlanta train depot. The camera finds her, swoops majestically upward to suggest her insignificance amid the thousands of casualties, and then comes to rest on a tattered Confederate flag. How many words do you think would be necessary to adequately relate what this single shot communicates?

Transitions

Like camera moves, transitions carry you from one point of action to another but usually in less time. When you have only 30 seconds, timing is critical.

Cut   The cut is the most basic transition, and one you should rely on. A cut is an instantaneous change from one shot to another—for example, from a CU to an MS. One second we're seeing a CU, and then suddenly we "cut" to an MS. It's essential that the two shots make visual sense when run together and that they carry the action forward with purpose.

Dissolve   The dissolve is a softer transition in which the first image gradually becomes more transparent as a second image, exactly behind the first, becomes more opaque. Stopping in mid-dissolve results in a shot where neither image is dominant. A dissolve can suggest the passage of time, freeing the writer to skip chunks of time in a sequence to focus on the most important elements. You don't want to watch someone washing her hair for 5 minutes (impossible in 30 seconds!), so you dissolve from her shampooing to her putting the final touches on her hairstyle. You can also use dissolves throughout a commercial to create a softer mood or to connect a series of shots unrelated in time and space, yet important in the telling of the story. (See the discussion of compilation cutting following.)

Fade   A fade is a dissolve that goes or comes from an image/title and black or white. This is the legendary "fade to black."

Editing for Continuity

Editing, which should begin with the writing of the commercial script, can accomplish a number of things. It can condense time, extend time, or jumble time. To condense time, you might show a man unable to sleep at night, dissolve to him sleeping soundly, and then dissolve to the reason his sleep habits are better—the product, of course. To extend time, you might show a speeding train approaching a car, cut to the driver's frenzied expression, cut back to the train, cut back to the driver attempting to get out of the way, back to the train, and so on. Trains move fast, and people in the path of trains don't linger, but extending the action makes the sequence more dramatic and involving to viewers. To jumble time, you might cut from present to past in a flashback or even "flash forward" to an imagined scene in the future.

Methods of Cutting

Compilation cutting   In this type of editing, the storytelling is dependent on the narration, usually voiced over the action, and each shot merely illustrates what is being said. The shots may be somewhat unrelated to each other, may occur in different places, or may consist of a series of different people or objects shot in similar fashion to one another.

Continuity cutting   Here the storytelling depends on matching consecutive scenes without a narrator to explain what is happening. Action flows from one shot to the next. Various angles and cutaways may not even be part of the previous shot. For example, a conversation between two people may consist of a 2-shot, several close-ups of each speaker, another 2-shot, and a cutaway to something happening elsewhere in the building that is related to the action within the room.

Crosscutting   Crosscutting combines two or more parallel actions in an alternating pattern. The actions may occur at the same time but in different places—as when we see a farmer driving a tractor, cut to his wife preparing dinner, cut back to the farmer, and cut again to the wife. The actions may also occur at different times in different places—as when scenes of a man enjoying a vigorous shower are intercut with shots of the same man at various times during the day to suggest that using the right soap helps him feel fresh for hours. (This was the idea behind a classic, long-running Dial Soap campaign.)

Crosscutting may also be used to suggest details of an action that occurs at one time in one place. For example, he runs toward her, she runs toward him, again he runs toward her, again she runs toward him, until—at last— we see both of them in one shot about to run into each other's arms. Their embrace is somehow more personal to us precisely because we've been watching their longing gazes for most of the commercial.

In one beer commercial, crosscutting makes us as thirsty as the man in the story. A bartender reaches for a frosty mug. A man leaves his office. The bartender begins to draw a draft. The man steps out of his building onto a busy street. The bartender has the mug almost topped off. The man walks down the street. The mug is filled. The man enters the bar. The bartender slides the draft down the polished bar top. The man reaches out and catches it just in time.

Point of View

Subjective versus objective   Although you won't always have to specify point of view, doing so often helps others understand your idea. Essentially, point of view is either objective or subjective. In the objective point of view (objective camera), the camera records the action from the viewpoint of an observer not involved in the action. Those on camera never look directly into the lens because this would destroy the objective relationship between them and the viewer.

In the subjective point of view (subjective camera), the camera involves the viewer in the action by representing the point of view of a person in the scene. An actor rages at the camera, but we know he's angry, not with us, but at the guy who just punched him out in the previous shot. The camera itself becomes the punch-happy guy. In an experiment in subjective camera, a late 1940s feature film used this point of view exclusively. The main character was rarely seen, unless he happened to walk by a mirror. Punches were thrown at the camera and were usually followed by a blackout. A hand would reach from the camera to grab someone. The film was probably too odd for most tastes, but it did show the power of subjective camera. Note Ray Tom's storyboard in Figure 9-2 to see how subjective camera is used briefly.

Camera angle   An eye-level camera angle presents a view as seen by most of us. A high-angle shot, looking down on the action, may be chosen because (1) it's the best way to say we're on, say, a football field, (2) it's a way to see something you couldn't see yourself, such as overhead shots of dance formations, or (3) it adds a psychological dimension to the story (looking down on something means we think little of it, whereas looking up means we are in awe of it). Low-angle shots can add importance to a product. High-angle shots can make competitors seem somehow diminished.

Music and Sound Effects

What would the movie *Jaws* be without the repetition of the two-note motif that gets faster and faster, letting the audience know danger is lurking, even though they're seeing a tranquil beach scene? What would *Psycho* be like without its sound track? Or *Star Wars?* Or any movie or television show, for that matter? The same is true for television commercials. Music and sound effects add meaning and texture to the story that's being told on the screen.

Music

A spot for Cheer laundry detergent opens on a couple talking to one another on the telephone. After the woman tells her boyfriend when her flight gets in, she asks, "Hey, do you ever wear that black sweater I gave you?" He gives the perfect response, "Like every time I miss you." She's delighted: "It must be gray by now." He answers, dutifully, "So gray." She has an idea: "Wear it tonight." He's dismayed. "Tonight?" As soon as he hangs up, he removes the sweater from the gift box and washes and rewashes it in an attempt to make it gray. As the action is taking place, we hear the lyrics, "Always thinking about you, 'cause a love like this won't fade away. . . ." Meantime, it turns out that the man is washing the sweater in Cheer, which "helps keep black from fading." The doorbell rings. As he heads to answer the door, the words "Dirt goes. Color stays. (Even black)" are superimposed on the screen.

People loved the music and began asking for copies of it. One woman even wanted to play it at her wedding. But there was a slight problem; there was no such song. The lyrics were originally a grand total of about 16 seconds and were written by a Leo Burnett copywriter just for the commercial. When Procter & Gamble (P&G), the parent company of Cheer, started getting emails and phone calls requesting the song, they asked the writer and production house to create a 4-minute version. With the full version of the song on hand, P&G produced an email message with an embedded MP3 file that consumers could download or burn into a CD. The commercial was supplemented with words superimposed on the screen directing them to the Cheer Web site to hear the full song. Before the song was added to the Web site, Cheer.com was getting from 500 to 1500 hits a day. With the addition of the song, hits increased to 2000 to 2500. Copies of the CD were also sent to radio stations, and within weeks there were 580 broadcasts on stations with an estimated reach of 4 million listeners.[2]

As the Cheer commercial illustrates, music can help put viewers in a right state of mind. It can make them feel romantic, relaxed, filled with fear. Sometimes playing music with opposite emotions can make your message even more effective. For example, a powerful commercial that addresses the problem of spousal abuse shows images of battered women while the song, "Stand by Your Man," plays in the background. The irony of the song helps illustrate the absurdity of staying with an abusive partner.

Music can also help narrate the story. JanSport introduced its Euphonic Pack, a backpack with built-in earphones and volume controls, with a tune from *The Sound of Music*. The 1959 Rodgers and Hammerstein Broadway musical may seem like an unlikely choice to reach the MTV crowd, but it worked. The version of "Do-Re-Mi" was updated and produced by Tomandandy Music to narrate a boy-meets-girl story. The commercial opens on a young man wearing a Euphonic Pack. He meets an attractive young woman who is wearing a T-shirt that has a cartoon of a doe. They part and, as he pursues her through city streets, he puts on the earphones. Each line from the song comes to life. For "Ray, a golden drop of sun," the sun shines. For "Me, a name I call myself," the boy catches a glimpse of himself in a window. "Far, a long, long way to run" plays as he pursues her. "Sew, a needle pulling thread" is heard as he passes a tailor shop. As he passes a coffee shop, a

---

[2] Adapted from Stuart Elliott, "Procter & Gamble's Hit Song," *New York Times,* 3 March 2003, NYTDirect@nytimes.com.

neon sign reading "Café Latte" blinks, and most of the letters burn out, leaving "La, a note to follow Sew." Next comes "Tea, a drink with jam and bread that will bring us back to doe," which it does. The couple reunites at a sidewalk café, drinking tea and eating jam and bread.

Sound Effects

Sound effects (SFX) can help reinforce your message and help paint the scenery. A Pepsi commercial opens with a mysterious mechanical sound. It turns out that a guy, desperate for a Pepsi, keeps trying to feed his dollar into a vending machine that keeps sucking in the money, then spitting it right back out. The guy keeps trying, from dawn until dusk, as Ricky Nelson's "Lonesome Town" plays, adding another layer of ambiance to the commercial.

Voice-over

A voice-over (VO), where someone speaks but isn't seen, can give the final sales pitch or help narrate the entire spot. A commercial for Dawn dish detergent shows an oil-covered duck getting washed at a wildlife-rescue center. VO: "If this bird could talk, she'd tell you how Dawn saved her life. If this bird could talk, she'd tell you how experts choose Dawn because it's so gentle. If this bird could talk, she'd tell you how happy she is to be alive today." Graphic: "Dawn. Saving wildlife for over 20 years."

A voice-over can emphasize the message that appears on the screen by reading it out loud, exactly as it appears on the screen. Note that words that are to be superimposed over the action on the screen are indicated by the word *SUPER*. Words that are to appear on the screen against a solid background are indicated by the word *TITLE*.

Getting It on Paper: The TV Script

Look at the script for the Bell Helmets commercial in Figure 9-1. The idea behind the whole campaign (see the BriefCase in Chapter 3), remember, was to show that a quality helmet like Bell gives you more courage to enjoy your sport. Here's how the TV script guides readers through the idea.

Everything on the left side is video, or what we will see. Everything on the right side is audio, or what we will hear. The audio and video are aligned so that we know how they relate to each other. Scenes are numbered down the left side of the page to guide us through the action. Scene 3 is a title, as are scenes 5, 7, 9, and 12. The words of the titles appear exactly as they will in the finished commercial.

As in radio, use SFX to denote music and other sounds. Underline all SFX directions for clarity. Because all we hear in this commercial is that cool whistling, the right side is blank till we get to scene 10. Then the announcer voices the words "Bell Helmets" over a full-screen logo. The sound of a whoosh (more like the squish of a brain about to be protected), followed by a locking sound as the chin strap snaps together, is simultaneous with the action in scene 11.

Finally, the announcer says "Courage for your head" as the exact same words appear in the title on the screen. Specify voice-over (VO) prior to dialog when the words are to be "voiced over" as opposed to spoken on camera. VO lines are usually recorded after footage is shot. They can also help others understand your concept in script/storyboard form.

Note that this commercial used words that are superimposed over the action on the screen, which also appear exactly as they will in the finished spot.

Making It Clear: The TV Storyboard

In Figure 9-2 notice how Ray Tom suggests that a certain guitar shop in town understands what your guitar means to you and how the frames help you understand more fully what the finished spot is meant to be. In storyboard format, the right-hand side contains both video and audio directions, with audio running beneath video. Leave space between the two to make things clear.

Tom opens with an LS to let us know we're in a nursery. He cuts to a CU of a doorknob turning. He's confident we'll know that it's in the same room (and that the baby isn't opening it!). He zooms in to an MS as a young mom peeks in adoringly. He cuts to an LS as she walks toward the crib, panning right to follow her. He cuts to a point-of-view (from baby's view) CU of the woman's face as she smiles with love and pride. Now comes the shock as we see what she's beaming at in a reverse point-of-view shot; it's not her baby, it's her guitar! A dissolve allows us to accept that she's been enjoying her performance for some time, while a supertitle reminds us where to go if we're hankering for a new guitar or a repair on our present one.

In sketching frames, indicate zooms, pans, and tilts, as well as the movement of things or people by using arrows (see Figure 9-4). To save frames, draw a smaller frame within the full frame to show zooms. Keep the number of frames conservative but don't leave out important actions, transitions, or other significant moments.

TV Production

Once the client approves a commercial for production, the agency normally seeks competitive bids from a number of sources. A copy of the storyboard is sent as the basis for the bid, along with production notes that cover all aspects of the commercial not specified in the storyboard. Production notes describe in detail casting preferences, wardrobe considerations, sets to be built, special effects needed, specific sizes and packages of the product to be photographed, and other aspects of production. It's also a good idea to

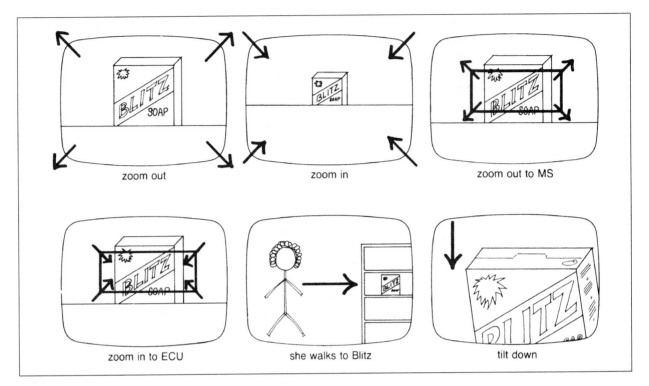

Figure 9-4
Using arrows will help others understand what is happening in your storyboard.

discuss the strategy of the campaign with the production house to further clarify the purpose of the commercial.

Once the agency accepts a bid, production begins. Most commercials take several working days to shoot. Prior to actual shooting, agency personnel, along with the commercial director, audition actors for parts, agree on locations, and work with crews to locate props, products, and other necessities. After the shoot comes the postproduction work of screening dailies or rushes (all the takes from production), choosing the best takes, and editing them down to the required time frame.

Checklist for Television

✓ Did you think pictures first and add the words later?

✓ Did you choose a format that best expresses what you want to say?

✓ Did you rely on the entertainment value of your commercial to sell the product?

✓ Did you ask if the opening shot will command attention?

✓ Did you check to see that the product is afforded enough visibility, in terms of time and closeness to the camera?

✓ Did you ask if you can get closer to the action to make the action more involving?

✓ Did you use supertitles to help viewers remember important points and, especially, the product name and the campaign theme?

✓ Did you choose words that add to the picture's meaning, not that mean the same thing as the picture?

✓ Did you make certain that important words are related to the pictures that they've been chosen to represent?

✓ Did you choose music or sound effects that enhance the message?

Suggested Activities

1. Watch at least five commercials on television this week and take notes on the following:

   a. Was the product shown prominently the first time it was mentioned?

   b. Was the product featured visually in or near the final shot?

   c. Did the first shot get your attention? How?

   d. Was the first shot related to the product story? How?

   e. Which shot was most memorable? Why?

   f. How did you feel about the product as a result of the commercial? Did it change your feelings at all? How and why?

2. Write a television commercial. Begin with a scenario, progress to a script, and present it to the class in storyboard form. Use your classmates' suggestions to make revisions.

Search Online!
Discovering More About Television Commercials

Use InfoTrac College Edition to discover more about television commercials. Try these phrases and others for Key Words and Subject Guide searches: *visual storytelling, writing with pictures, scenario writing, slice of life, testimonial + advertising, camera framing, camera moves, video editing, camera point of view, classic TV commercials.*

The following Web sites allow you to view new and classic television commercials:

www.adcritic.com (requires a paid subscription)

www.adforum.com

Pepsi Finds a New Way to Poke Fun at "the Other Cola"

Michael Patti, executive creative director, and Don Snyder, senior vice president and senior creative director, were the team at BBDO/NY, along with co-CEO and chief creative officer Ted Sann, who crafted the memorable "Security Camera" television commercial for client Pepsi Cola. Patti tells how they came up with the idea:

We have a history of doing competitive ads that poke fun at Coca-Cola, but it seems every year it gets harder and harder to do a great one. Don and I work together as a team, one-on-one in my office day in and day out on Pepsi. Ted comes in as often as he can and sits down with us to throw ideas around. It's an ongoing process. Ted can stick his head in for five minutes and say, "Jelly beans, I got an idea," and walk away. And Don and I will sit there and think about it.

One day he came in around lunchtime. He didn't have a lot of time. We were working on a bunch of other stuff, and he said, "Security camera. I don't know what it means, but security camera."

He had just installed a security system in his house or something, and that was the real germ of the idea. We told him, "Come on. That's boring. That's stupid." Then he walked away. Then he came back, and we sat down. We talked about the spot as being a single-take thing, something that happened with no cuts. And we thought that was interesting for Pepsi, because we never do anything that simple and that focused.

We thought it had competitive qualities. Don came up with the idea of putting the two coolers next to each other, and I think it took a day or two before we came up with maybe having the Coke guy going for a Pepsi. And we let it sit for a week.

Don drew a key frame of these two coolers with this Coke guy there. The thing we settled on would be that the Coke delivery guy would go for a Pepsi, and at that moment he would be caught in the act by a woman coming around the corner with a shopping cart. He would get embarrassed and leave the frame and you would stay and stay on that empty

Reprinted from *Agency* magazine, Spring 1996. Used with permission.

frame. Then all of a sudden, from underneath the security camera, he would sneak back in, grab a Pepsi, and run like hell.

The "Cheatin' Heart" music—I don't know who came up with it. We might have been talking about music and bounced a bunch of titles around. Once we played it, we knew that if we ever shot the spot, it would be perfect. It just felt good.

We thought the spot was okay, but it wasn't great. The CEO at Pepsi liked it a lot and said, "Gee I think it could be a little funnier." So we came up with an alternative ending. We said, "Well, maybe it would be funny if he pulled one can and maybe 20 cans fell on him and he had to pick them up and he got embarrassed."

As a result, we created the spot with more than 20 cans. Which was Joe Pytka, the director, saying, "Let's make it the mother of all spills! Let's keep it going until it's beyond belief."

Two takes was all we did. And we knew we had it in the can.

DIRECT MARKETING:
THE CONVENIENCE OF SHOPPING AT HOME

A Lands' End ad cuts to the chase: "Like, who has time to shop anymore? Maybe shopping at the mall was fun once. But not these days. You're too busy working, chauffeuring the kids around, doing a thousand other things. You simply can't afford the time to shop, can you?"

With the explosion of mass-media advertising and a continuing trend toward segmentation of target audiences, it's not difficult to understand why direct marketing is growing rapidly. Not only does direct marketing, of all advertising venues, inherently make it easiest to purchase products, but it also delivers its messages to a highly targeted and therefore user-friendly group of prospects. More brands are competing for the same customers, and the market continues to fragment. So, as marketers peg more and more subgroups of consumers by demographics, lifestyles, and purchasing habits, companies need to be ever more specific in their marketing campaigns. Information-driven marketing helps companies do this by targeting prospects with far greater accuracy than other mass-media efforts.

Direct Marketing: An Old Idea Improved Through Technology

Although the computer, the checkout scanner, the credit card, and the Internet have breathed new life into direct marketing, it has been a healthy and active industry for more than 150 years. Direct marketing got its start at about the same time that the U.S. Postal Service established coast-to-coast delivery in 1847. Early purveyors of direct-response advertising, called mail order in those days, were Sears, Roebuck & Company, founded in 1886, and the Montgomery Ward Company, established in 1872. Their early hand-illustrated, black-and-white catalogs brought the products of the industrialized world—in the form of appliances, farm tools, clothing, and even do-it-yourself home-building kits—to the most isolated farmhouses in America. And America never looked back. Direct marketing is one reason U.S. marketing techniques are eagerly emulated all over the world.

Early in the 20th century, pioneers in industrial sales, such as National Cash Register, used letters to attract sales prospects. But little of the present revolution in direct marketing would have been possible without the computer, the credit card, and the 800 number. Computers and checkout scanners capture and assimilate detailed information about businesses and individuals and then compile that information in narrowly targeted mailing lists. Names of individuals are now isolated not only by age, name, education, and other demographics but also by credit history, hobbies, and buying habits. Prospects are also targeted by size and type of business and exact job function.

How Direct Marketing Differs from Mass-Media Advertising

Whereas the goal of advertising is to build brand awareness or to create demand for a new product category, direct marketing is structured to sell now. Urgency is the key component. Also, the information flows two ways: from prospect to advertiser and back to the prospect. It's purposely interactive so that the lists that produce the greatest response can be identified early on. Once the list is analyzed by sociographic/demographic characteristics, marketers can obtain lists with the same characteristics but with new names. In a sense, direct response is a way to obtain marketing information through sales. Advertising sells products. Direct marketing sells offers, using deadlines to produce swift responses. Most important, subsequent efforts to sell to the same prospect work to strengthen the relationship between consumer and company. If, as we claimed in Chapter 1, all advertising works to build a relationship between the brand and the prospect, direct marketing works the hardest and is generally the most successful in building long-term brand loyalty.

Direct marketing is growing rapidly because it keeps bringing home the business. In a recent year, more than half of the U.S. adult population ordered merchandise or services by phone, mail, or the Internet. More women ordered than men, and the greatest growth by age group was in the 18- to 24-year-old category, followed by 45–54, and 55+. Buyers from all income classes participate, however, with annual growth skewing slightly toward incomes of $50,000 or more.

Even more interesting is what companies and marketers can find out about their customers:

- The dollar value of purchases
- The number of purchases annually
- The length of customer–company relationships
- Information on other purchase influencers at the same address
- Promotions aimed at customers
- Rentals of customers' names to other companies
- Nonresponders
- Sociographic/demographic information on customers

More than half the businesses that participate in direct-response mailings make their lists available for a price to other businesses, usually in the form of rentals or exchanges.

Advantages of Direct Marketing over Other Forms of Advertising

Direct marketing has several distinct advantages over other forms of advertising, including the following:

- *Pinpointing of prospects.* A well-targeted database enables marketers to pinpoint a select group of prospects by lifestyles, demographics, purchasing patterns, and so forth.
- *Personalized messages.* The design and tone of the message can be easily personalized.
- *Faster sales.* Sales can be made sooner than through traditional advertising media.
- *A wide variety of packaging options.* Except for minor regulations imposed by the U.S. Postal Service, the creative team can develop a range of exciting packages, from multifold self-mailers to odd-shaped boxes and from tear-open packs to actual product samples.
- *Less "competition" from other media content.* Unfettered by the editorial environment of print and broadcast media, the direct-marketing piece must compete only with other messages in the mail. If the design and copy are successful in getting recipients to look inside, the message has their attention as long as they find something interesting in it.

Computer Databases: The Key to Targeting the Best Prospects

Thanks to the computer, advertisers can accurately locate their best prospects. Once they "merge and purge" names from a number of databases—trades with other companies, motor vehicle records, warranty card data from their own files, birth announcements, lists of college students, subscribers to selected magazines, and on and on—they can compile an ever-growing list of ideal prospects for their goods and services. Buy fat-free salad dressing and yogurt at the checkout, and a scanner labels you as a prospect for exercise equipment or fitness magazines. Join an airline's frequent-flyer plan, and your gasoline credit card statement arrives with an offer for luggage. Buy a new car, and you hear periodically from the manufacturer asking you to complete a satisfaction questionnaire and reminding you it's time for servicing. Purchase a new home, and a lawn-care service mails you a "welcome to the neighborhood" offer for a trial weeding and feeding.

Companies use databases to expand sales into new market segments. As we noted in Chapter 2, research shows that gays and lesbians are a loyal audience. To win business from gay business owners, MCI chose direct marketing. Their direct-mail piece is delivered to a list obtained through the Gay & Lesbian Business Alliance. It rewards gay business owners who sign up by a certain date with free membership in the alliance, plus an offer for a new MCI calling card with the alliance logo, a 5-percent discount on volume calling, and one free month of MCI long-distance calling. The mailing includes both a letter from an openly gay MCI employee (who describes MCI as a workplace free of discrimination) and material describing various discounts and special offers for gay business owners.

Direct-mail campaigns can also be vehicles for market research. To get Singapore teens to divulge information about their pimple-control product usage—a sensitive issue in this age group—Ogilvy & Mather Direct created a questionnaire mailer that offered trendy prizes. Using point-of-sale leaflets, direct-response ads in teen magazines, and names of previous promotion respondents, the agency amassed over 10,000 names for its mailing. The control group (5000 names) then received a free gift (a small sample of the product), while the test group (the remaining 5000 names) received the gift and a "Skinformation Kit" with skin care advice and information on Oxy products. Adding the information in the test-group mailing upped the brand-purchase intention to three times that of the control group, while the overall result of the mailing was a 34-percent increase in correct usage of the product by teenagers.

In New Zealand, Ogilvy & Mather Direct used a mailing list of 350 current owners of BMW or rival luxury cars to introduce its new 7-series. This seven-part mailing was designed to "treat, spoil, and reward prospective buyers just as the new 7-series would." Seven months before actual introduction of the car, the first of the seven mailers was delivered. Each appealed to one of the senses, such as the chance to win an all-expense-paid trip to the Auckland Flower Show, an appeal to the sense of smell. The final mailing offered a test drive of the $150,000 car, an appeal to "pure driving pleasure."

Direct Marketing: A More Personalized Relationship

Jerry Pickholz, former chairman of Ogilvy & Mather Direct Worldwide and a leader in the field of direct marketing, says that consumers have rejected many aspects of the mass-marketing approach in favor of a more personalized and intimate one-on-one relationship, a relationship made possible by visionary concepts and modern information technology. Among currently hot trends, he cites the following:[1]

- *Using traditional media to generate new leads*—as the California division of the American Automobile Association did with a television commercial aimed at increasing AAA membership among female drivers.

- *Using compelling offers to upgrade customers*—as the American Association of Retired Persons did when it used its vast membership database to promote related products such as insurance and credit cards.

- *Using high-impact mail to build traffic at the place of business*—as Jaguar did when it offered an upscale writing pen to members of a highly affluent prospect list for visiting the Jaguar dealership. Simply offering a prestigious item of small value compared to the cost of the car brought this elite audience to dealers in droves.

- *Gathering a list while increasing usage*—as Miracle Whip did when it invited TV viewers to contribute recipes using Miracle Whip to a newsletter that featured a photo of the recipe's creator. By including coupons for Miracle Whip and related products in each issue, the marketer not only increased consumption but also was able to track future sales.

- *Building loyalty*—as Ikea furniture stores did by mailing an informative home-decorating newsletter to its "family" of customers. The newsletter included a questionnaire to track changes in the family unit and discount coupons to bring customers back.

- *Enhancing value*—as Microsoft did when it mailed a 30-minute videotape of its president, Bill Gates, talking "face to face" about the superiority of Microsoft programs, to convince "tekkies" who influence major software decisions for their companies. Because of specific targeting, Gates was able to use technical language that only this audience could appreciate.

For Emily Soell, former vice chairwoman and chief creative officer of Rapp Collins Worldwide, the winners in direct marketing today are those who recognize that consumers have turned the tables on marketers. Suspicious of claims that promised they could "have it all," Soell maintains, consumers now have less faith not only in advertisers but also in physicians, police officers, teachers, financial advisors, and even religious leaders.

Soell contends that a perceptive direct marketer knows how to change old rules to conform to new consumer values. Instead of showing the product, she says, "show the promise." A woman's magazine found that showing glamour alone is not as powerful as promising that the magazine will help subscribers contain the costs of face creams, haircuts, and other, often overpriced, accoutrements of glamour. Instead of bribing the prospect, Soell

---

[1] Courtesy of Jerome Pickholz.

adds, contemporary marketing endeavors to *involve* the prospect. To attract possible convention business, the city of Memphis sent a dog-eared package to a select list with a hand-scrawled address and the line "We found your wallet in Memphis" on the outside. Inside was a real wallet, stuffed with simulated "credit cards" that gave recipients numerous reasons to consider Tennessee's largest city as a convention site. While the claims were compelling, it was the magic of the highly involving package that made the difference.

Being personal is good but not enough. Soell stresses that marketers must also be relevant. Computer-generated statements that read "New York's best-dressed women: Ivana and (consumer's name here)" will draw only derision and contempt from today's consumers. A much more savvy way to personalize is Gillette's mailing to young men on their eighteenth birthday, which includes a Sensor razor and a can of Foamy shaving cream, plus a coupon offering a reduced price on the next purchase of Sensor blades.

Finally, Soell says that, while "making the sale" may be old-fashioned, "building the relationship" certainly is not. It is this relationship that holds the promise of making many more sales.[2]

The Three Musts for Successful Direct Marketing

The list   As the most important element of a direct campaign, the list should be narrowed to prime prospects for the product or service. The cost of outgoing and incoming messages and telephone calls constitutes the largest single expense of a direct-marketing campaign. There's no room for names that don't fit the target profile and won't offer the chance of a response.

The message   Copywriters estimate that they have only seconds to grab a consumer's attention with direct mail. As you will discover in Chapter 11, direct marketing on the Internet carries similar limitations. This is why great care should be devoted to the design of the envelope. Make it oversized. Print a message in boldface type on the front. Laser-print the recipient's name into the message on the envelope. Customize the shape of your mailer—make it in the shape of a hula doll, sports car, or hamburger.

Inside the envelope, a majority of offers contain a personalized letter, a brochure, and a response card. Stickers for yes or no responses may be used to involve the consumer further.

The letter carries the letterhead of the company and a salutation in keeping with the list: "Dear Music Lover," "Dear Traveler," or simply, "Dear Friend." To grab attention, the letter digresses from a personal letter by adding a message in large boldface type before the salutation, a message linking the lure on the envelope to the letter that follows. This headline also takes advantage of its prominence to sell the third essential, the offer.

---

[2] Courtesy of Emily Soell.

The offer   The mailing always asks for a response, often in the form of a limited-time offer. This may be as simple as coupons offering reduced prices if you buy before the expiration date, merchandise at a reduced price for a limited time, or a chance to participate in a contest should you buy something now. To raise the odds for a response, use a prepaid business-reply card or envelope or a toll-free number. The recipient must be told how to respond in the letter, in the brochure, and especially on the order blank or catalog page. Here, repetition makes sense because the average direct-mail reader just skims the mailing. A significant number of prospects will read only the response coupon, ignoring the letter and brochure, because they know they will find a short summary of the entire offer there. In addition to mentioning the offer in the letter's headline, you have other opportunities to urge the reader to respond as soon as possible. Look at the *Mother Jones* example in Figure 10-1 and note that the offer is mentioned practically throughout the message. The offer is made (1) in the letter's headline, (2) near the bottom of the first page (in the underlined subhead "*It's yours free*"), (3) near the end of the third page (beginning with "So—waste not a second" and even adding more incentive in the following paragraph), (4) toward the end of the letter on page 4, and (5, 6) twice in the P.S., or postscript, which is one of the most highly read portions of a direct-response letter. Six repetitions of the offer drive the point home even to skimmers.

Designing the Direct-Marketing Package

Want to try your hand at this? Perhaps the most common—and least expensive—design for direct marketing is the mailer designed on standard 8½- by 11-inch paper and folded into thirds. And this is where you begin. Fold a piece of paper this size and rough in the design for each panel. In preparing your rough, you may wish to use the front panel for a teaser headline, with or without a visual. Consider continuing the message on the right-hand panel— or "flap"—which is where the eye generally looks next. The left-hand panel will become part of the inside once the flap is lifted, so whatever you place there must work with the flap opened or closed. It's not always necessary to put something major on the back because this gets the lowest readership, but you should at least include a logo and perhaps an accompanying tag line.

Prepare your letter and envelope and—voilà—you have a direct mailer. Place the letter, brochure, and reply card inside the envelope and mount the back of the envelope, with the flap open, on black matte board for presentation.

Direct Marketing as Part of a Total Advertising Campaign

Research indicates that a direct-marketing ad campaign launched in conjunction with a mass-media blitz produces a higher response than an isolated direct campaign. Also, when the direct campaign includes three

Envelope

Brochure

Figure 10-1

Mother Jones, the liberal investigative magazine published in San Francisco, has won the hearts (and subscriptions) of its readers by admitting exactly what it is: a publication unafraid of big business or big government. Note the provocative envelope, the attention-getting headline in the brochure, and especially the "tell it like it is" letter that contradicts the "satanic image" of the envelope by chronicling the success of the magazine in exposing questionable practices and products. Note how consistent the voice (a flippant kind of intellectual) is in these various parts: (1) the headline at the start of the letter, (2) the opening paragraph, which sets the tone and delivers the message instantly, (3) the offer on pages 1, 3, and 4, (4) the "handwritten" signature, and (5) the repeated offer in the postscript.

MOTHERJONES

First they dismissed us as flaky and hysterical.
Then they branded us a threat to internal security.
Now they're calling us an instrument of satan.
Find out why. FREE

Dear Reader,

Ever get the queasy feeling you've just read the same six articles over and over again in a half-dozen different magazines?

Wackos in Waco. Yattering with Yeltsin. Soaping up with Schwarzkopf. Hobnobbing with Hillary. Disrobing (yawn) with Demi.

The same torpid insights from the same cast of "experts." The same shallow gossip. The same stale spin.

What's more, you have to wade through 40 glossy ad spreads for floral bed linen, designer perfume and Italian luggage... before you get to one slim nugget of real news.

When you're done, what more do you really know about the world? How will it help you put things in perspective?

No wonder things often look as bleak as a *thirty-something* rerun.

Now -- here's a prescription that will decidedly improve your outlook. Intrigue you. Enlighten you. Empower you. And give a lively new boost to your political IQ.

(In this dramatic year of Washington turnover, it might just make a difference.)

Just fire off the order card in this envelope, and I'll rush you, with my compliments, the latest issue of the all-new MOTHER JONES.

It's yours free. An uncompromising, uncensored, unapologetic journal teeming with the real people, politics and passions that have a daily impact on your world.

Plus some hardheaded tips on how you can make a daily impact for peace, social justice and a safer environment.

It's also a damn good read.

-2-

MOTHER JONES? Isn't she that feisty old gal who pulled the plug on the lethally defective Ford Pinto?...

Yanked the chain on the corporate criminals who were dumping hazardous junk in the Third World?...

Blew the whistle on federal bureaucrats who twiddled their thumbs while millions of Americans came down with AIDS?

Yep, yep and yep.

Like our namesake, orator and agitator Mary Harris "Mother" Jones, we have a bit of a history. (Including three National Magazine Awards in our first four years.)

Also like the original article, we get results. (In the case of Ford Pinto, a homicide indictment, $20 million in consumer lawsuits and the largest auto recall in history.)

How do we do it? By sponsoring the kind of gritty, time-consuming, often dangerous investigative journalism that the rest of the press just doesn't have the stomach for.

(Or doesn't respect your smarts enough to dig for.)

Result? In an era when corporate megamergers have gobbled up most news sources... tainting what you see, read and hear with fluff, euphemism or outright distortion...

MOTHER JONES remains the unchallenged leader in hard-hitting, between-the-lines, no-holds-barred, nose-to-the-street, no-nonsense news, analysis and consumer advocacy.

The kind you simply won't find in the New York Times, the Wall Street Journal, Esquire, Newsweek or Vanity Fair.

And today we're doing our job with more chutzpah, punch and audacity than ever before.

Just ask our quarter-million avid readers. Or the media pros polled by the American Journalism Review, who voted us the nation's "Best Magazine for Investigative Journalism."

What do they find in every issue of MOTHER JONES?

In-Depth Exposés. Like the ones that awakened America to the health-threatening Dalkon Shield. Toxic breast implants. The pesticide peril at your breakfast table. The electronics industry's calculated decision to shred the ozone layer.

-3-

██

Thoughtful Essays. Like our level-headed look at black urban poverty and America's growing trailer-home population. Gays in the military and the crisis in the Balkans. Women in the Men's Movement. Congressional reform.

Practical Advice. Like what to do when job options and principles collide. How to conduct an ecological audit of your home. Protect yourself from skin cancer. Seize back the airwaves. Act up against AIDS. Lead a shareholder revolt.

Also an unabashed point of view. A passion for uncovering government corruption and corporate shenanigans. An aversion to gridlock. A commitment to the little guy.

Needless to say, all this attitude and insight doesn't sit very well with some of the self-appointed legislators of political correctitude and public morality.

Demagogues on the right... who've branded us pro-terrorist, pro-feminist, pro-socialist, pro-hedonist, pro-humanist, pro-communist, pro-gay.

Ideologues on the left... who've squealed when we skewered a few of their sacred cows.

Or the fundamentalist kooks at the Coalition on Revival who denounced our coverage as "a powerful blow by Satan."

Are we going to let this gutter-baiting gall us?... Naaah. You see, the old lady's still got her teeth, and she knows how to bite back.

But she sure could use a few more independent thinkers like you along for the ride. After all, you're the reason we keep raking up the muck.

So -- waste not a second. All you need do is return the enclosed card. Your trial issue comes FREE.

If you like it, I'll round out your year with five more bimonthly issues of MOTHER JONES (6 total) for a full 33% off our regular subscription rate.

Send no payment now, if you like. We'll bill you later.

But --.if you do send payment with your order, I'll sweeten the deal. Extending your subscription by two more issues (that's 8 in all) for the same low price.

-4-

██

And if at any time you're not thoroughly enthused, engaged and galvanized, simply cancel your subscription. I'll send you a full refund on all unserved issues.

MOTHER JONES. We're not just a mirror of events, but a catalyst. A Molotov cocktail of ideas. A prairie fire of inspiration.

Are we also an instrument of Satan? Well, perhaps not. (The fellow on the envelope is actually a Chippewa spear-fisher named Tom Maulson, one of our 1991 grassroots activist award-winners.)

But we <u>can</u> assure you a devilish good time. While we make things mighty hot for the powers that be.

Can you afford <u>just 23¢ a week</u> to put yourself in the know, and keep America's best investigative machinery humming? ... That depends.

Are you the kind of person who's a little disgruntled with the status quo? Ready for a fresh outlook?

The kind who's willing to read between the lines? See the writing on the wall? Punch a hole in some platitudes?

Are you really? ... Then come on. Take a chance. Fill out the card. Cross the median. Welcome to the other side.

Cheers,

Jeffrey Klein
Editor

P. S. <u>Act now, risk nothing</u>. 33% off the regular subscription rate! And if you don't find MOTHER JONES completely indispensable, cancel at any time for a full refund on all unserved issues.

<u>Pay now, get more</u>. Two extra issues (that's 8 in all) for the same low price!

mailings, varying in terms of the copy but not the offer, that continue over the duration of the media schedule, the response will be at least double that of a campaign with only a single mailing.

Fund-raising Through Direct Marketing

Nonprofit organizations such as the March of Dimes and the American Lung Association use direct marketing as their major fund-raising tool. In recent years, using creative and aggressive direct-mail campaigns, more than $104 billion has been raised annually for such causes. As state and federal funds for nonprofit organizations dwindle, more and more charities and cultural groups are turning to direct marketing for support. Competition for consumer donations is fierce and will only become more so. Those organizations that cultivate current givers and prove that donations directly benefit their causes will be the winners.

Another factor in the surge in direct-marketing pleas for donations is the attempt by advocacy and social-change organizations to rid themselves of corporate support and large donors, turning instead to hundreds of thousands of dedicated small donors. Such organizations have discovered that, with 85 percent of their contributions coming from small donors, direct marketing is a democratic way to fund social change.

Sophisticated fund-raisers spend heavily to acquire donors. They know that, even if the initial donation fails to cover the marketing expense, people who donate that first time are highly likely to donate again. Accordingly, when a donor is first acquired, the contribution is swiftly and "personally" acknowledged to secure the donor's loyalty to the organization. Subsequently, the donor will be asked annually to renew the donation, even as the organization attempts to increase the amount of the donation each year.

Fund-raising solicitations pose peculiar problems. Remember that a fund-raiser asks for money without offering something in return (other than perhaps a tax deduction). Unless the case for support is made absolutely clear, the appeal may fall on deaf ears. Often, the benefit to the giver is a sense of helping the needy. In other cases, givers will respond to support a service, like public television, that they themselves enjoy.

Catalogs: Bringing the Retail Store into the Home and Office

Catalog advertising has come a long way since the early days of Sears, Roebuck. Some tightening is evident in sales, and a number of marginal catalogs have fallen by the wayside, yet catalog sales have emerged as a major contender in the battle for the retail dollar. Figure 10-2 shows how Lands' End, one of the leading catalog companies, connects with its customers.

Successful catalogs follow the trend of all successful direct advertising today: They target specific groups of buyers. So Americans' mailboxes are loaded with catalogs touting products to beautify their homes, control stress,

Figure 10-2
Selling through direct-response catalogs, Lands' End publicizes its goods through print ads such as this. Even the typeface used in the ads mirrors that used in the catalogs, but the similarities hardly end there. Consider the personal tone of the copy in this ad, as well as in the catalogs themselves, a style responsible in part for the overwhelming success of this company. The Lands' End charm is nowhere more self-disparaging than in this headline. Here, the writer compares the misplaced apostrophe in the company name ("a boo-boo from the early days") to the quality control that "was (obviously) a little skimpy" in the early days of the company but that resulted in the company's unconditional guarantee of quality.

To err is human.
To guarantee, divine.

That misplaced apostrophe in our name is a boo-boo from the early days, when our quality control was (obviously) a little skimpy.

Lots of people, especially English teachers, have taken us to task for it. It makes us cringe today. But in a funny way, that out-of-place apostrophe has served our customers very well.

You see, every time we think about it, it reminds us that we're only human. And that we can't ever be *too* careful about what we sell or how we deal with the good folks who favor us with their business.

Truth is, we depend on their trust. As direct merchants, we sell by catalog—classic clothing, soft luggage, home furnishings. Folks have to feel that anything they see in our catalog will deliver as promised.

Still, we know that occasionally we *will* goof. So, we add one more feature to our product line, the Lands' End guarantee:

We accept any return, for any reason, at any time. Without any conditions.

We want no mistakes about *that*.

Guaranteed. Period.® ©1993, Lands' End, Inc.

If you'd like a free catalog, call us any time, 24 hours a day, at **1-800-356-4444** Or mail this coupon to: 1 Lands' End Lane, Dept. JV, Dodgeville, WI 53595

Name _____

Address _____ Apt. _____

City _____ State _____ Zip _____

Phone (____) _____ Day/Night (*circle one*)

organize their lives, groom their pets, update their computers, and so on. Each has a particular audience in mind for the types of goods it offers. There are catalogs for movie lovers, music lovers, cat lovers, and dog lovers. Catalogs for new parents, for older travelers, for gift givers, and for designer collections. And the list goes on and on. In 2002 catalog sales totaled $126 billion, according to the Direct Marketing Association.[3]

One of the most spectacular catalogs is the Neiman Marcus Christmas catalog which contains everything money can buy. Gifts in the 2003 catalog included a pair of opera-singing, hip-hop dancing robots priced at $400,000; a $10,000 mermaid costume, complete with a lesson on how to swim in it; a 44.6-carat fancy yellow diamond ring for $800,000; a limited edition 2004 BMW 645Ci Coupe for $75,170; and a $12 million Learjet. Not on the Neiman Marcus mailing list? You can buy a copy of the catalog by calling or visiting the store.

To order merchandise from a catalog, you don't even have to fill out an order form. You simply dial a toll-free number, place your order, and charge it to a major credit card. Return policies are generally liberal, so you need not be concerned about buying sight unseen.

In addition to being persuasive and interesting, catalog copy must anticipate questions and provide all the answers. Prospects who can't examine a knit shirt in person must know it's 100-percent washable cotton and comes in sixteen colors and four sizes.

Personalizing the Direct-Marketing Message

Specialists in writing direct-marketing copy claim that the key to success is the element of one-to-one human contact. Emily Soell explains, "As direct marketers, we need to show we understand the prospect's problem and his/her dream. We must know the prospect's perceptions of the client company before we can address that prospect in a way that will be meaningful."[4]

Keeping the List of Lists shown in the box on page 231 in mind, collect several direct-mail packages from friends and family. Choose one to analyze, paying particular attention to the following questions:

1. How well does the message on the envelope motivate the targeted audience to open it and read farther? Inside the mailing, how strong is the relationship between the envelope message and the opening of the letter?

2. How is the letter put together? Specifically:

   a. If a headline begins the letter, does it succeed in getting the reader to read on?

   b. How does the salutation address the audience targeted?

   c. How are color, indented phrases or paragraphs, and subheadings used to break up the letter? What types of information are highlighted by such devices?

   d. What is the offer? How well does it relate to the product or service being offered? To the audience targeted?

   e. How much incentive is there to respond promptly?

---

[3] Keith Benman, "Catalog Sales Stack Up Well," nwitimes.com, 30 November 2003.
[4] Shira Linden, "Emily Soell Delights HVDMA with Wit and Wisdom," HVDMA.com, 5 November 2003.

3. What clues you into the sociographic/demographic characteristics of this mailing list? (Possibilities include age; gender; marital status; occupation; family income; level of education; own or rent home; special events such as just got married, had baby, bought home, remodeled home, moved, changed jobs, or retired; hobbies or special interests.)

4. Based on the List of Lists, what does the sender already know about the prospect? How does this knowledge strengthen the relationship value of the message?

Now select a product that lends itself to the sort of narrow targeting that direct marketing does so efficiently:

1. Who is your target? Can you narrow this description even further?

2. How can you narrow the field so as to mail to the prospects most likely to respond?

3. What incentive will you offer them so that they respond quickly?

4. Assuming you have a budget, what lists will you buy to find your best prospects?

5. What will your offer consist of? How will you connect it to the product, and what you already know about the prospect?

6. What will your package say/show to gain their attention and make them want to read on?

Ethical Aspects of Direct Marketing

Although direct marketing represents the ultimate way to establish a relationship with a prospect, its detractors claim that computer technology has caused an unprecedented invasion of privacy. Not only can marketers amass data on your age, name, and address, but they can also easily find out what your buying habits are and what your favorite charities are. Every time you pay with a credit card or check, every time you fill out the lifestyle section of a product warranty card or do any number of seemingly innocuous things, you are most likely contributing to a database. Your age, weight, and hair color come from driver's license records, your political leanings from your contributions, and the due date of your baby from the guest register at the maternity store where you shop. Marketers may know you have a weakness for Haagen-Dazs ice cream or prefer Naturalamb condoms, for every time you pay by check or credit card, the electronic scanner that totals your bill links each purchase to your name. Some fear that even your prescription drugs—birth control pills, tranquilizers, heart remedies—may be the next frontier for list harvesters. As you work on your direct-response package, keep such thoughts in mind.

LIST OF LISTS

To demonstrate the vast amount of data available from list sellers, here is a sample breakdown by lifestyles and demographic data available from a typical organization. Lists are not free. Generally, the more names on the list, the higher the cost. List buyers may request that lists be narrowed by merging demographic characteristics with lifestyle and geographic data in virtually any combination to help the advertiser pinpoint the best potential market for the mailing.

LIFESTYLES

Affluent/Good Life

Community activities	Stock/Bond
Charities/Volunteer	investments
activities	Travel for business
Cultural/Arts events	Travel for pleasure
Fine art/Antiques	Foreign travel
Gourmet cooking	Frequent flyers
Own vacation home	Wine purchases
Shop by catalog	

Community/Civic

Current affairs/	Donate to charita-
Politics	ble causes
Military veteran	Wildlife/Environ-
	mental issues

Domestic

Automotive work	Grandchildren
Bible reading	Home decorating
Book reading	Own cat/Own dog
Fashion clothing	Own microwave
by size	
Gourmet cooking	

Entertainment

Buy prerecorded	Own DVD
videos	Stereo/Tapes/CDs
Cable TV subscriber	Watch sports on TV
Casino gambling	Home video
Home video games	recording

High-Tech

Personal/Home computers
Use PC/Use Macintosh
New technology
Photography
Science fiction

Hobbies

Automotive work	Fishing
Camping and hiking	Gardening
Coin/Stamp collecting	Gourmet cooking
Crossword puzzles	Needlework
Do-it-yourself repairs	

Self-Improvement

Dieting/Weight control
Exercise: walking for health
Health/Natural foods
Health improvement

Sports

Bicycling	Hunting/Shooting
Boating/Sailing	Motorcycling
Fishing	Snow skiing
Golf	Tennis

DEMOGRAPHICS

Gender: Male/Female
(Mrs., Ms., or Miss)

Location: State, County, Zip Code

Age: 18–24, 25–34, 35–44, 45–54, 55–64, 65–74, 75+ (Year of birth available)

Home: Own or Rent

Marital Status: Married or Unmarried

Household Income: Increments from Under $15,000 to $100,000+

Occupation

Professional/Technical	Craftsman/
Upper management	Bluecollar
Middle management	Student
Sales and Marketing	Homemaker
Clerical	Retired
Working women	Self-employed
(Spouse's occupation	business
available)	

Credit Cards: Travel/Entertainment, Bank, Other

Children at Home: Exact ages of children from infant to 18 years by selection; gender also available

Religion/Ethnicity: Asian, Catholic, Hispanic, Jewish, Protestant

Education: Some high school, finished high school, technical school, some college, completed college, some graduate school, completed graduate school

Other Available Information

Motor vehicle registration
Census data
Your own company's consumer database
Competitive-purchase information (from other list sources)

Suggested Activities

1. To demonstrate how much you can learn from databases, assume that you are also the target consumer for your product and fill out the form in Figure 3-1. Then answer the following questions: For what products or services might this "person" be a good prospect? What clues, if any, suggest a basis for the relationship you might build with this person? What sort of offer/merchandise would appeal to this person? How would you work with this information to create an integrated marketing campaign?

2. Write a direct-response letter based on the List of Lists on page 231. Use all available tactics to get the prospect interested. And don't forget the offer—develop one that will make the prospect want to respond. Don't "give away the store," but suggest a premium, special price, limited deal, or other device that relates to your prospect and also to what your product represents to the prospect. Check how specifically you are targeting the direct-response package for your product. Remember, you can target much more narrowly using a good list than you can through typical mass media. That means you can restrict your appeal through direct response to the "ideal prospect." To narrow your search, assume that you can buy any type of list you might dream of. Beside each applicable entry, specify precisely what characteristics you are seeking in that particular category. Now summarize who is going to be on your list. How will this affect the nature and tone of your copy?

3. You have been hired to attract subscribers to a monthly newsletter, *Wine Lines*. The mission of *Wine Lines* is to provide an up-to-the-minute guide that helps subscribers become connoisseurs of fine wines. Subscribers will learn how to select, store, serve, and savor the finest vintages; they'll be able to enjoy the history of wine making; and they'll discover what to look for in texture, taste, body, and shelf life. Add other features that you think a wine newsletter should include. The price for twelve monthly issues is $12.99. The offer is three months free when the reader subscribes by a specified date (you choose). The offer also includes a premium: a wine bottle coaster that looks expensive (but is actually cheap when purchased in volume). You are targeting upscale men and women 35–50 years of age, urban and urbane. You have three testimonials (from Harrison Ford, Martha Stewart, and Julia Child)—use any or all of them. Design and produce (a) an envelope, (b) a letter, (c) a brochure, and (d) the response card.

4. Develop a direct-marketing piece for a nonprofit campus organization. Target your mailing to college students who are most likely to become members or supporters of the organization. Before you begin, interview the staff of the organization, asking what might compel other students to use the services of this organization, join the organization, or donate money to it.

Search Online! Discovering More About Direct Marketing

Use InfoTrac College Edition to discover more about direct marketing. Try these phrases and others for Key Words and Subject Guide searches: *catalog shopping, Internet shopping, online shopping, direct marketing, universal product code, checkout scanner, relationship marketing, consumer database, gathering consumer data, direct-marketing offer, direct-mail letter, direct-mail envelope, fundraising, list of lists, direct-marketing lists.*

To find out more about direct marketing, visit the Direct Marketing Association Web site:

www.the-dma.org

BRIEFCASE

Father Seeks Revenge After Daughter Loses Virginity (or Just Another Night at the Baltimore Opera)

You like this story line? Then you'll like *Rigoletto*. How about this story line: "Impotent blind man kills hundreds of pagans" (*Samson et Dalila*). Or "Young woman headed for convent gets steamy with two jealous lovers" (*Manon Lescaut*). Decadence? Immorality? Loose morals? Looks like Baltimore Opera's season is going to be fun. So you check the box alongside. Or you refuse (as if anyone could) by checking where it reads, "Call me a prude, but I'm not quite ready for your particular brand of entertainment."

What's going on here? Opera is boring stuff, isn't it? That's what a random phone survey by the Baltimore Opera of arts preferences and habits revealed. Subscriptions were down, single-ticket sales were down, and corresponding revenues were dropping dramatically. Furthermore, the subscriber base was stagnant, consisting mostly of long-time, aging devotees whose numbers were naturally decreasing.

To reverse this downward trend, the general director and the Board of Trustees took "dramatic" steps to rejuvenate the company by broadening the audience of both subscribers and single-ticket buyers. The opera company used a repositioning campaign that embraced research, public education, new media choices, and a tongue-in-cheek approach.

On the positive side, the phone survey had confirmed that patrons of the arts really do love opera music and that current subscribers were continuing to pledge their support. But outweighing these positives was a long list of negatives—reasons why many Baltimoreans couldn't imagine themselves enjoying opera: "foreign language," "hard to follow," "not for me," "boring," "not my kind of music." So instead of "preaching to the converted," the new campaign focused its energies on this uninitiated majority.

Using humor, showcasing the beautiful music, and communicating that English surtitles are displayed at every performance, the Baltimore Opera worked a miracle through direct-response, telemarketing, public service TV spots, and a radio campaign.

Used with special thanks to Deborah Goetz.

Celebrating our 45th year of seduction, intrigue, human sacrifice and revenge.

Women who *fake* it.

Next on

He loves her. She loves him not. She marries him. She cheats on him. He catches her. *La Gioconda* saves the day. October 1996. Featuring: Ghena Dimitrova, Nina Terentieva and Ermanno Mauro.

Is she a he or isn't she? Only *Fidelio* knows for sure. See what happens when a woman bends her gender to break her better half out of the big house. November 1996. Featuring: Frances Ginzer, Jan Grissom, Wolfgang Fassler and Gran Wilson.

She's not really his mom, she just plays it in *Il Trovatore*. Later, when junior gets reunited with his blood relatives, well let's just say things definitely get bloody. March 1997. Featuring: Chris Merritt, Stefka Evstatieva and Irina Mishura.

Everyone knows the story of *Roméo et Juliette*. Everyone except poor Roméo. When he realizes that his beloved Juliette is just pretending to be dead, it's too late. May 1997. Featuring: Leontina Vaduva and Fernando de la Mora.

1996-97 promises to be another exciting, dramatic and colorful season for The Baltimore Opera. So, in addition to a bit of feminine fakery, these four operas will share another common feature: fast selling tickets.

Don't you fool around. Become a season ticket holder. You'll save on the price of each opera, be guaranteed a better seat and have ticket exchange privileges. Just return the card below for complete season ticket information.

THE *Baltimore* Opera
Opera. It's better than you think. It has to be.

All performances at the Lyric Opera House, 140 West Mount Royal Avenue, Baltimore.

The results? Revenues are up, the subscriber base has grown 33 percent, subscriber retention is up by 10 percent to an all-time high of 80 percent, and single-ticket sales have risen 28 percent. Each year, the promotions become more irresistible. For a recent season, a square envelope teased the recipient with "Baltimore Opera on Disc." Inside, a paper disc with a rotating overlay allowed readers to review the four operas for the season in an interactive manner. (And without computers!) Turn the inner wheel to *La Traviata* and you read, "A handsome guy gets together with a beautiful girl who has a questionable past. But she has a good heart—it's just the rest of her that's not in such great shape. In all, a consuming tale."

Opera was always like this. It's just that most of us never knew it. Now all of Baltimore knows that grand opera and great entertainment can coexist in pure harmony.

THE INTERNET:
THE ULTIMATE DIRECT
By Jim Speelmon

In the beginning, the Internet gave people information, and a lot of it. Anyone who created a Web site knew that people would visit. Today, people are more sophisticated about their use of information, and companies are more sophisticated about providing it. Rather than using the Internet exclusively, those companies who are reaping the full benefits of this medium are integrating their advertising efforts across most or all media forms to create a more engaging relationship between their brands and their customers.

When Frito-Lay wanted to reach 12- to 20-year-olds, they partnered their Doritos brand with other teen-oriented brands including Microsoft XBox and MTV. Additionally, they sponsored co-promotions with movies like *Austin Powers: Goldmember* and bands like OutKast. By drawing their target to the Web through game pieces found in bags of Doritos, they built a large database. Approximately 350,000 teens opted to receive news on future products and promotions. Doritos commercials posted on the Web site were downloaded an average of 60,000 times each. And the ultimate proof that an interactive approach such as this really works? Frito-Lay saw a 5-percent increase in sales of Doritos while spending less on advertising in 2002.[1]

This chapter is designed to give you your first peek into the world of Internet advertising design and development. At the end, you may not be creating the ultimate online brand experience, but you should be better at it.

---

[1] "Frito-Lay Inc.: Using Interactive to Talk to Their Target," Interactive Advertising Bureau Web site, iab.net.

The Interactive Team

When you design ads for the Internet, your team is a bit larger than one for traditional advertising. You still need an art director and a copywriter, but you need a couple of other people as well. You'll need a programmer for technical expertise. You don't want the technology to overwhelm your creative thinking, but at some point you'll need to know whether your ideas are technically feasible. You'll also want to have a producer on hand. Internet sites and banner ads can be like jigsaw puzzles, and it's not unusual to have ten or fifteen people working on a project. The producer makes sure that everyone is on the same "page" and keeps track of the many details involved in completing the project.

Designing for the Internet: A Four-Stage Process

Whether it's a 100-page Internet site or an advertising banner, there is a method to the madness of Internet design. As you read this chapter, you'll notice that much of the Internet design process is similar to that for print and TV. The Internet is not as different as you might think.

Stage 1: Research and Planning

Anytime you see a great ad campaign, you'll find a great strategy behind it. Does this sound familiar? It should. In Chapter 4, you learned that good ads start with good strategies. Successful Internet sites and banner ads start the same way. Over the course of your career in advertising, you'll find that almost every project starts with research. After working on a couple of projects without a clear strategy, you will understand why it's so important.

Designing a Web Site: The Site Map

Suppose someone asked you to build a house. How would you start? Would you dash off to a building supply store for bricks, lumber, and plumbing supplies? Install the heating system and then build the walls? Shingle the roof before you poured the foundation? Probably not. You would likely start by asking some questions. How big will the house be? How many bedrooms will there be? Will the dining room be formal or just an extension of the kitchen? Will there be one bathroom or two? If you didn't ask questions, then you wouldn't know what to build or how to build it.

Designing for the Internet is a lot like building a house. One of the first things you need to do is get your idea down on paper. Look at the high-level site map shown in Figure 11-1. Just as a blueprint tells a construction manager how many rooms the house will have, where the doors and windows will go, and so on, the site map helps a creative team decide how many

Figure 11-1
This high-level site map provides an overview of the different sections planned for this Internet site. The universal navigation options identified at the top of the map would appear on every page. From the home page, major content sections are identified, giving the creative team a better understanding of the amount of information they have to work with.

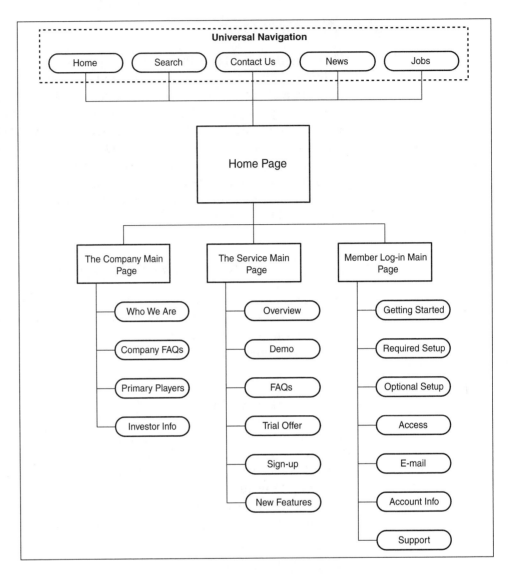

pages will be needed and how people will move through them. The map helps them make better decisions about how the site will look and work.

Understanding how people will move through a Web site is important. Your design approach will vary depending on how many options from which people have to select. Look at the detailed site map shown in Figure 11-2. This version outlines all the specific details for the "demo" section. Not only does the site map identify the different pieces of content, but it also makes recommendations for using technology. The Demo tab under The Service Main Page leads to an indicator for Flash. When developing concepts for this section, the creative team will know that they need to design a demo using Macromedia Flash. They also know that the content window will need to be

Figure 11-2
The detailed site map provides the specific details about how the pages will work. In this example, boxes with rounded corners identify primary navigation options, and the rectangular boxes identify specific pages.

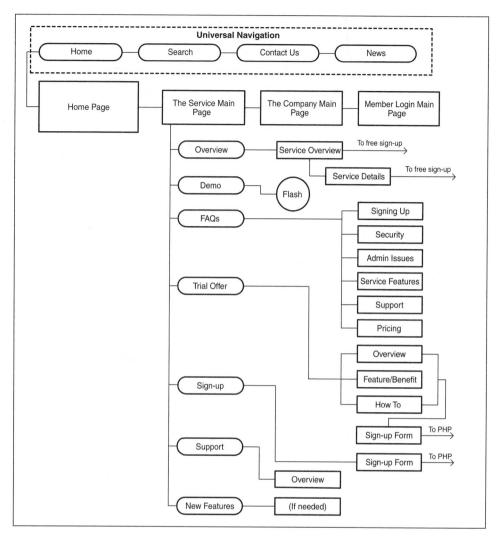

big enough to play the Flash movie. The demo will have a storyboard and script of its own.

Stage 2: Concepts

Once you have an approved site map, you're ready to start developing design concepts. Because of the way Internet sites are built, you actually have to develop concepts for both the content and the page template. Think of it as developing the "look and feel" (page template) of a magazine first and then coming up with this month's editorial material (content).

Some art directors prefer to create their concepts, or roughs, as a simple sketch. Others prefer using a computer with illustration or design software. Whatever your preference, the idea is the same: You start by putting together a rough version of your design. This is not the time to be precise.

It's more important to capture the basic concept than it is to come up with a completed design.

You might find it helpful to start with your page template, deciding where you want to place the constant elements like logos and navigation features. This helps you determine how much space you have for the actual content. Don't worry about whether your initial ideas are possible. At this stage, you want to give yourself plenty of options. Don't let the technology limit your thinking.

Remember that you're looking for interaction, not just a reaction. In traditional advertising, your ad is often considered successful if you stimulate a reaction in your audience. Janine Carlson, director of strategic marketing and principal at Icon Communications, points out the greater challenge facing online marketers: "You can't be satisfied with getting a reaction. You have to spark an interaction. One is simply a split-second exchange with your audience. The other opens the door for an ongoing relationship. And that should be the goal for anyone working in advertising or marketing."

Here are some guidelines to keep in mind as you start developing your rough concepts:

1. *Make sure your design works across a series of pages.* Internet sites almost always have more than one page, and not every page functions the same way. That means that your design for the page template has to be flexible. Some pages might have graphic headlines, text, and supporting images. Other pages might include a Flash movie, a submit form, or some other kind of Internet technology. Your template has to accommodate all these elements. It's usually easiest to start with your most complicated page. Figure 11-3 illustrates how a design works on both the home page and a secondary page.

2. *Keep some parts of the template constant.* When you design a page template, it's important to remember that some design elements won't change as you move from one page to the next. For example, you want to keep navigation elements in the same area on each page so people can find them. Logos are another design element that should stay in one place. Consistency makes your site easier to access and follow. Identifying the location of your constant elements first helps you determine how much space you have left over for everything else.

3. *Keep the most important elements in first view.* There really is no limit to how long an Internet page can be, but there is a limit to how much of the page a person will see at one time. A person's first view of an Internet page depends on the screen resolution, or size, of the Web site. Your template design should put the most important elements at the top so that they're easy for people to find.

4. *Pay attention to navigation.* Think of navigation as the highway system for your Web site, helping people to quickly get to the information they're looking for. Just like a real highway system, the navigational highway uses both primary and secondary systems. Primary navigation provides

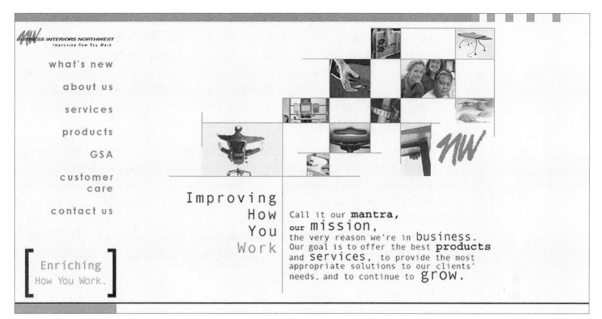

Home Page

Secondary Page

Figure 11-3
This home-page design uses a navigation-focused approach, providing visitors with an overview of the information that they can find on the site. The goal of this home page is to quickly move users to the page that best meets their needs. The secondary page provides more specific information about the company's services. Notice that there are not huge design differences between the home page and the secondary page. Although they are not exactly the same, the art director for this site continued the initial theme to the lower-level pages, keeping brand and navigation elements in the same location on each page. The result is a consistent and attractive page that is easy to navigate.

access to the major sections of content on a Web site. Secondary navigation helps users move around within a specific content section. Some sites also include universal navigation. These navigational options apply to all users on all pages. Examples of universal navigation include a Home option for returning to the home page, a Search option for accessing a site's search capability, and a Contact Us option for sending an email or finding a phone number or address.

A lot of options can sometimes create problems. Remember that technology will never be a good substitute for solid strategic planning. Just because you can make a logo spin doesn't mean that doing so is a good idea. Julie Johnson, executive producer for Web design firm Elusive Little Fish, advises creative teams to strive for elegant simplicity, noting that too often the message gets lost in the technology. Movement for the sake of movement doesn't do anything to make your message more memorable or effective. It can, however, be incredibly distracting.

Stage 3: Development

Refining the Design

Now it's time to start making decisions about your design and ironing out the details. An important part of development is comparing your concepts to the site map. You need to make sure that the final design works well on all pages in your site. Sometimes, you find the right design quickly. Other times, you don't and find yourself back at the drawing board looking for a better idea.

You'll likely revise your design more than once before you finalize it. The more complex your project, the more likely will be the need for revisions. When you're designing a complex Web site, it's a good idea to do a functional proof-of-concept before you get too far along in the project. You'll need your programmer for this. With your help, the programmer can mock up a section of the site and make sure that your design is technically feasible.

As you move through the development process and refine your design, you'll probably end up adding additional pages. Make sure that you consider the impact this will have on the rest of the site. A Web page is useful only if people can get to it, and introducing new pages at the end of the development phase can cause problems with the rest of the site.

Writing Copy for the Internet

The development phase is also the stage at which the copywriter really starts working. If you start writing too early in the process, you won't know how the pages work, and your copy won't make sense. By waiting until you're a little further along in the design process, you save yourself from having to do a lot of rewriting.

Writing copy for the Internet is very different from writing for print. Why? Because people don't read on the Internet. They scan. According to usability expert Jacob Nielsen, principal partner of the Nielsen Norman Group, people rarely read Web pages word for word. Instead, they scan the page, picking out individual words and sentences. This means that, when you write copy for the Internet, you need to adjust your style to match how people read online.

Although it's important to realize that writing for the Internet is different from conventional writing, it's equally important to note the similarities. Remember the guidelines for writing copy given in Chapter 6? They still apply. If you adhere to those guidelines and to the following guidelines for the Internet, your copy should be enjoyable and effective.

1. *Use highlighted keywords.* Adding visual emphasis to important words helps catch the scanning eye of the reader. Using boldface or italics is an effective way of highlighting keywords. If you have more detail related to a specific word, turning it into a hyperlink not only catches the reader's eye but also provides easy access to additional information on a subsequent page. However, use highlights sparingly. If every other word is a link or is boldfaced, the reader will ignore them and move on.

2. *Make sure your subheads are meaningful and not just clever.* Subheads are a lot like highway signs. Just as motorists use highway signs to find their way through an unfamiliar city, readers on the Internet use subheads to find their way through your site. If your subheads aren't instructive, people will abandon your site and go somewhere else.

3. *Aim for one idea per paragraph.* Having a single idea makes it easier to get your point across. Readers will skip over any additional ideas if they're not captivated by the first few words in the paragraph. In traditional advertising, you shouldn't try to say everything in one ad. On the Internet, you should avoid trying to say it all in one paragraph.

4. *Present complex ideas with bulleted lists.* Sometimes, a single idea will have multiple parts, making it difficult to get the main idea across quickly and easily. A bulleted list is a great way of organizing complex ideas and presenting the major points. Another benefit is that the specific bulleted items can be turned into hyperlinks so that additional details are just a mouse click away. Consider the "great deal" in this paragraph:

   The Acme Super Home Computer has everything you need. A 6-Gig hard drive, 64 MB of RAM, a 128 front-side bus, a DVD player, and tons of software. Only $1999 at Acme Super Computer City.

   Difficult to read, isn't it? Now see how a bulleted list makes this information much easier to read:

   - $1999 Acme Super Computer City Special
   - 6-Gig hard drive
   - 64 MB RAM

- 128 front-side bus
- DVD player
- Tons of software

5. *Write your copy using an inverted pyramid style.* Start with the conclusion and then add the details. If people have to read the entire paragraph to get to your main point, they won't. Putting the conclusion or benefit right up front makes it easy for your readers to determine whether they're interested in this information.

6. *Use half as many words (or less) as you would with conventional writing.* Reading on a computer screen is a different experience from reading on paper. Studies show that people read about 25-percent slower on a computer than they do when they read from paper. Cutting the length of your copy helps compensate for the slower reading time. Another problem is that reading from a computer screen is hard on the eyes. Think about the last time you spent a lot of time reading from your computer screen. It probably didn't take very long before your eyes felt dry and tired. By writing concise copy and tightly focusing your ideas, you can get your point across before your reader wears out.

Stage 4: Production

The final stage in designing an Internet site is putting together all the pieces. With the help of the producer and the programmer, you'll assemble the text, images, and various other parts of the site into the finished product. The programmer will address technological issues such as screen resolutions, operating systems, browsers, and plug-ins. After production is finished, the Web site is ready for the public. This last step doesn't require you to do anything except move the fully programmed Web site to the host server.

Banner Ads

Many people on the Internet consider banners annoying and go out of their way to ignore them. With the right approach, however, banners can be a very effective means of advertising. Consider the following story of a banner that doubled traffic to the destination Internet site:

You're browsing an online store looking for a Christmas gift for your best friend. You can't help but notice the banner at the top of the Web page: "Need CA$H for the holidays?" The banner animates to the second frame: "Sell last year's gifts." Finally comes the call to action: "Online auctions everyday." You click on the banner and go to an online auction, where you buy the perfect gift for your friend.

Why was this banner so effective? First, it asked a question. It's more difficult to ignore a question than a statement because even a stupid question makes you pause and think about it. In this case, the use of a question was even more effective because many readers identified with the subject. Who hasn't needed extra cash for the holidays?

Second, it used humor. You certainly don't expect the second frame of this banner. Most of us have probably wished we could sell last year's presents. We just wouldn't say that out loud.

Third, it took a different approach. This banner's objective was to funnel traffic to an online auction. Most banner ads about online auctions focus on the "buy." This banner focused on the "sell," setting this auction apart from the competition and creating an intriguing invitation for both buyers and sellers.

Guidelines for Creating Banner Ads

Sometimes the simplest ideas turn out to be the most effective. Here are some guidelines that will help make your banner ads more effective:

1. *Keep it short and simple.* People usually don't visit a Web site to see banner ads, and they probably won't take the time to notice a complex message. You have only a few seconds to catch people's attention before they move on to the next page and away from your banner. That's not much time to grab their attention. Short and simple messages have a stronger focus and are more likely to result in a click-through. As a general rule, each frame of a banner ad should have at most seven words.

2. *Animate three times and then stop.* If you've spent much time on the Internet, you've probably noticed that constantly animating banners are annoying. Even if the site doesn't have an animation limit, it's a good idea to use one. After all, you don't want people's reactions to your ad to be negative.

3. *End with the logo or the name.* If someone doesn't click on your banner, they might at least notice the name of your company. Although it's not the best response that you could hope for, it's better than nothing. Banner ads may not be the best tool for creating awareness about a brand, but every impression helps.

Suggested Activities

1. You've been hired by a new company that sells socks. Create a site map for your new client, outlining how the site would come together.

2. Visit at least five different Web sites and ask yourself the following questions:

   a. Was the navigation consistent from one page to the next, making it easy for you to move through the site?

   b. Was it easy to find what you were looking for? Why?

c. Which site did you think had the best design? Why?

d. If you could change anything about the sites, what would it be?

Search Online! Discovering More About Internet Advertising

Use InfoTrac College Edition to discover more about Internet advertising. Try these phrases and others for Key Words and Subject Guide searches: *Internet advertising, Internet banners, Internet marketing, Web programmer, Web sites + design, Macromedia Flash, Macromedia Shockwave, interactive advertising + Internet, Web site home page, Web site secondary page, HTML, writing for Internet, Internet links, Netscape Navigator, Microsoft Internet Explorer, Internet animation.*

Find out more about interactive advertising at:

Association for Interactive Marketing: www.imarketing.org

Best of the Web: http://botw.org

Interactive Advertising Bureau: www.iab.net

Spend Spring Break in Iceland

One of the packages Icelandair offers is a spring-break trip to Reykjavik, targeted at college students. In 2000, advanced bookings were much lower than anticipated. Competition from more traditional, warm-weather destinations, such as Jamaica, the Bahamas, and Cancun, was heating up, so Icelandair turned to Nasuti & Hinkle for a creative solution.

It was quite apparent that this was no ordinary assignment. It was important that both the medium and the message reflect how different it is to go to Iceland for spring break. After all, selling vacations in Iceland to people who've just come off a long winter is about as close as you can get to selling iceboxes to Eskimos.

Because of a limited budget, Nasuti & Hinkle decided on a one-week schedule in college newspapers and a two-week run of banners on www .studentadvantage.com and the Icelandair site.

Informal research conducted among college students about how they decide where to go for spring break yielded some surprising answers. Although Nasuti & Hinkle expected "Because I want to get a great tan" and "Because I heard they have a lot of great bars there," they also heard answers along the lines of "Well, my boyfriend/girlfriend is going to such-and-such place, so I want to go somewhere else." Nasuti & Hinkle decided to address those college students who wanted to go somewhere and do something different for spring break—different in particular from her or his boyfriend/girlfriend.

The creative consisted of banner ads and full-page ads in college student newspapers proclaiming this line of reasoning for going to Iceland for spring break: "Because your boyfriend is going to Jamaica," "Because your girlfriend is going to Cancun," "Because any fool can go to Florida," and "Because you never looked good with a tan anyway."

The results of the campaign were beyond anything the client had anticipated. Spring-break packages from Icelandair sold out—a 40-percent increase from the previous year—for a total budget outlay of $25,000.

With special thanks to Woody Hinkle of Nasuti & Hinkle.

To see how Nasuti & Hinkle solved another problem for Icelandair, read the BriefCase in Chapter 1.

Iceland for Spring Break.

Because you can actually afford it.

And any fool can go to Florida.

Discover our World   ICELANDAIR Holidays

Iceland for Spring Break.

Because you can actually afford it.

And you never looked good with a tan.

Discover our World   ICELANDAIR Holidays

INTEGRATED MARKETING COMMUNICATIONS:
BUILDING STRONG RELATIONSHIPS
BETWEEN THE BRAND AND THE CONSUMER

Grade school teachers recently taught their students to sing, "My bologna has a first name, It's O-S-C-A-R," and "Oh, I wish I were an Oscar Mayer wiener." To assist teachers, the National Association for Music Education (MENC) developed lesson plans using the Oscar Mayer jingles.

Why would teachers and MENC do something so commercial? Simple. It was for the money. Schools could win $25,000 and a visit by the famous Wienermobile by singing the popular jingles. As John J. Mahlmann, executive director of MENC, explained on the MENC Web site:

> *At a time when music programs are threatened and young students denied the opportunities of a complete education that includes music, it is encouraging to see a company like Oscar Mayer step forward in a generous way to make a significant difference. We applaud their efforts to help bring the benefits and joy of music making to students as a vital part of their education. These generous gifts will help the winning schools provide the resources necessary to retain and enhance the music program that will provide life long value to the schools fortunate enough to benefit from this present from Oscar Mayer.*[1]

---

[1] "Oscar Mayer Donates $25,000 to MENC's Fund for the Advancement of Music Education," www.menc.org, 4 June 2002.

A group of fourth graders from Little Rock, Arkansas hit the right chord with their rendition of the Oscar Mayer Bologna song in the 2003 Oscar Mayer Talent Search School House Jam™. Their winning entry earned them the grand prize of $25,000 for their school's music program plus a starring role in a print advertisement in *People* magazine. Schools from 49 other states were each awarded $10,000. Additionally, Oscar Mayer gave MENC a $25,000 donation for its Fund for the Advancement of Music Education.

The Oscar Mayer promotion is an example of how advertising, public relations, sales promotion, and cause-related marketing can work synergistically to reinforce a brand's image. Does it work? You bet. The Oscar Mayer brand is recognized by 97 percent of consumers.

Integrated Marketing Communications

Integrated Marketing Communications (IMC) is the coordination and integration of all marketing communications tools within a company into a seamless program that maximizes the impact on consumers and other end users at a minimal cost.[2] IMC includes direct marketing, Internet marketing, sales promotion, public relations, promotional products, sponsorships, cause-related marketing, guerilla marketing, and, of course, advertising.

Sales Promotion

A consumer may prefer brand X, yet buy brand Y or Z. One explanation for this seemingly odd behavior is sales promotion, the use of short-term incentives such as coupons, rebates, sampling, free offers, special packaging, and sweepstakes. Done right, sales promotion can inspire trial of your brand, reinvigorate the relationship between your brand and loyal customers, and help reinforce your advertising message.

Ivory Soap's famous slogan, "99 44/100% Pure . . . It Floats," inspired a promotion celebrating the brand's 120th anniversary. Customers were asked to find the sinking bar of Ivory Soap to win a grand prize of $100,000. To commemorate this important anniversary, individual bars of Ivory Soap were wrapped in limited edition wrappers that looked like the original package (Figure 12-1). Multiple bars of soap were packaged together with outer wrapping that gave a little tweak to the brand's slogan: "Ivory Soap: 120 Years and Still Floating."

Kraft Foods offered pizza lovers an opportunity to win a "job" as the DiGiorno Delivery Guy. The grand prizewinner got a $100,000 "salary," a Chrysler PT Cruiser, a customized DiGiorno Delivery Guy uniform, and all the

---

[2] Kenneth E. Clow and Donald Baack, *Integrated Advertising, Promotion, and Marketing Communications* (Upper Saddle River, NJ: Pearson Prentice Hall, 2004), p. 322.

Figure 12-1
Ivory Soap brought back an original package design for a limited time. This old design helped break through the clutter on the store shelves and helped reinforce the brand's image of purity.

Photo by Debbie Garris.

pizza one could possibly eat for an entire year. And, because "It's not delivery. It's DiGiorno," the winner never had to deliver a single pizza. Not bad work, if you can get it.

Contests, Sweepstakes, and Games

Contests require skill, ability, or some other attribute. For example, Oscar Mayer sponsors contests among its local sales mangers to see who can generate the most publicity when the Wienermobile visits their areas. The results of this type of contest are fairly easy to tally through press clippings and tapes of local news shows. Also, the relatively small number of sales managers involved makes the contest manageable.

However, just imagine how difficult it would be to judge the thousands of entries sent by grade schools across the nation, each vying for $25,000 and the chance for the Wienermobile™ to roll onto their school grounds. The sheer volume of interest in this competition made it infeasible for Oscar Mayer to judge each entry. To get around this obstacle, Oscar Mayer hired an external firm to judge the competition. Additionally, the jingle promotion also involved a random drawing where the names of 50 schools were selected to win a visit from the Wienermobile.

The random drawing in the Oscar Mayer jingle promotion is an example of a sweepstakes, which is based on luck, not skill. Likewise, the Ivory Soap

"Find the Sinking Bar" and DiGiorno Delivery Guy promotions are also examples of sweepstakes because everyone has an equal chance of winning. Unlike a contest, you don't need to have anyone judge the merits of a sweepstakes entry, other than to ensure that the entry form is filled out properly.

Games are also based on luck but reward repeat visits. McDonald's Monopoly game requires customers to collect letters and spell out a word to win a prize.

Law requires that people can enter a sweepstakes, game, or contest without buying anything. The rules will tell consumers how to get a free entry piece, which often requires sending a self-addressed envelope. If a customer must pay to enter, then that's a lottery, which is illegal (unless it's a state lottery).

Premiums

A premium is an item given free, or greatly discounted, to entice you to purchase a brand. If you've ever ordered a Happy Meal at McDonald's for the toy, dug through a box of Cracker Jack's for the prize, or collected proofs of purchase for a gift, you know what a premium is.

A self-liquidating premium offers consumers something at a reduced price when they buy the primary brand. During the Christmas holiday season, many retailers offer stuffed toys at a nominal charge when customers spend a certain amount in the store. The stuffed toys Macy's offers as a premium during the holiday season are inspired by the balloons from the store's annual Thanksgiving Day Parade.

Sometimes the packaging itself can be a premium. Keebler packages their cookies in a container that looks like one of their elves. Planters Peanuts put their nuts in a glass jar that resembles Mr. Peanut. Tootsie Rolls come in a bank that looks like a giant Tootsie Roll. Popular advertising icons can make great premiums, too.

Coupons

Approximately 78 percent of all U.S. households use coupons, and 64 percent are willing to switch brands with coupons.[3] An advertisement for the Gynecological Cancer Foundation uses the power of a coupon to attract the attention of its target audience (see Figure 12-2).

However, coupons are not foolproof. Brand-loyal users may be the ones redeeming the coupon, not new users. Also, if you run coupons too often, you may "train" customers not to buy your brand when it's full price. Additional problems include counterfeiting, improper redemptions, and, last but not least, reduced revenues.

[3] Clow and Baack, *Integrated Advertising,* p. 322.

Figure 12-2
Before this pro bono (for the public good) ad for the Gynecological Cancer Foundation ran in space donated by *People Weekly,* the foundation was receiving an average of 500 calls monthly to its 800 number. The month the ad ran, 1278 women called for information, and an additional 425 responded by mail. Even two months later, the number of calls (974) was still well above the monthly average prior to the ad. Despite budget restraints on production and the absence of visuals, the ad worked. What made so many women respond to this ad?

Courtesy Gynecological Cancer Foundation. Pro bono work donated by Susan Fowler Credle (copy) and Steve Rutter (art direction).

Odds are a woman is more likely

to cut out a coupon to save 25 cents

than one to save her life.

Of course, we've never chosen to do what we do

based on odds. After all, 20 years ago,

the chances were a woman diagnosed with cancer

would die.

That didn't stop doctors from trying.

And the result has been that the statistics

have changed dramatically.

Cancer is no longer a death sentence. Today, women

can continue to increase the odds of beating cancer,

simply by taking the time

to find out

how to get

the best care.

For a free brochure on gynecologic cancers and a directory of specialists, call 1-800-444-4441, or write: Gynecological Cancer Foundation, 401 N. Michigan Avenue, Chicago, IL 60611-4267

Name_____

Address_____

City_____ State _____ Zip _____

Sampling

As the saying goes, "Try it. You'll like it." Sampling can be distributed at special events, given in-store, inserted on or in packages of related products, mailed, or delivered directly to the consumer's home.

Ferrero U.S.A. developed an innovative approach to get college students to sample Nutella, a chocolate hazelnut spread that's very popular in Europe but less known in the United States. Working with the Public Relations Society of America, they developed a case study and invited public relations students to develop and implement a plan for their Nutella brand. Schools that formed teams of four or five students were sent samples to distribute at their campus events. Students summarized their results in plan books, and the top three teams presented their plans in person to Ferrero executives. The students gained great experience (some may have gained a pound or two in the process as well). Public relations programs got an interesting case study to use as a teaching tool and the opportunity to gain recognition for their school. In return, Ferrero got college students to sample their brand. As a bonus, they got some great ideas for future events.

To get people to sample their products, Procter & Gamble (P&G) created Potty Palooza, portable restrooms that are driven to outdoor festivals. Unlike the typical portable potty, P&G's versions are immaculate and come equipped with running water, wallpaper, hardwood floors, and, of course, Charmin Ultra toilet paper, Safeguard hand soap, and Bounty paper towels. P&G estimates that Potty Palooza reached 30 million people in 2002. More important, Charmin sales increased by 14 percent among those consumers who used the facilities.[4]

Continuity Programs

These promotions instill repeat purchases and help brand loyalty. Rent twelve movies and your thirteenth rental is free. Buy $25 worth of groceries each week for four weeks and get a turkey at Thanksgiving. Use a certain charge card and accumulate air miles on your favorite airline.

Kirshenbaum Bond & Partners uncovered an interesting insight about members of frequent miles programs. Some people love the thrill of racking up the miles, even if they never use them.[5] This insight led to an ad for the Citibank American Aadvantage card that showed a bouquet of roses with the headline, "Was he sorry? Or was it the miles?"

Rebates

Send in required proofs of purchase, and you'll get a rebate check in the mail. It sounds simple enough. However, many people fail to redeem the

---

[4] Jack Neff, "P&G Brings Potty to Parties," *Advertising Age,* 17 February 2003, p. 22.
[5] Jonathan Bond and Richard Kirshenbaum, *Under the Radar: Talking to Today's Cynical Consumer* (New York: Wiley, 1998), p. 34.

offer, so they end up paying more than they originally planned. Others take the time to cut out bar codes, photocopy sales receipts, fill out forms, and mail it in, only to wait months for the rebate check. Sometimes it never comes. The rebate application may be rejected if there is missing information or if the consumer has failed to comply with an offer's conditions. According to Peter Kastner, an analyst with the Aberdeen Group in Boston, approximately 60 percent of purchasers never get a rebate because they don't send it in or don't supply the necessary information.[6]

Many consumer advocates have ethical concerns about rebates. Manufacturers that take too long to send out rebate checks sometimes attract the attention of the Federal Trade Commission, who may charge offenders with unfair and deceptive practices. Some companies have abandoned rebate offers altogether to avoid tampering with customer goodwill.

Point-of-Purchase (POP) Advertising

Advertising at the point of sale—in the store where the buyer is about to choose between one brand and another—represents the last chance the advertiser has to affect the purchasing decision. Common forms of POP advertising include window posters, permanent signs inside and outside the store, special display racks and cases, wall posters and "shelf talkers" (those ubiquitous reminders popping from the place where the product is shelved), coupon dispensers at the point of sale and checkout, shopping cart signs, and even signs on aisle floors.

POP displays can be very effective because many purchasing decisions are made at the store. In fact, 50 percent of the money spent at supermarkets and mass merchandisers is unplanned.[7] The right display can motivate consumers to make an impulse purchase or choose one brand over another. To be effective, the display needs to be attention grabbing and have a clear selling message that ties into other advertising and promotional messages. But even the most creative display won't work if the retailer won't put it in the store. Your display should be easy to assemble, easy to stock, and versatile so that retailers can adapt it to their individual needs.

Push/Pull Strategies

A push strategy encourages retailers and other intermediaries to promote, or push, the product to consumers. A pull strategy puts its emphasis on the consumer, who is expected to demand that the retailer offer the promoted product. Many successful plans combine these two approaches. For example, on days when the giant Wienermobile is parked outside a supermarket, Oscar

---

[6] Howard Millman, "Customers Tire of Excuses for Rebates That Never Arrive," *New York Times,* 17 April 2003, nytimes.com.

[7] Clow and Baack, *Integrated Advertising,* p. 322.

Mayer products fly off the shelves. In one promotion, customers got a free Oscar the Bean Bag toy by presenting the Wienermobile staff with a receipt for the purchase of three Oscar Mayer products. To drive excitement inside the stores, Wienermobile pedal cars were made available to retailers who agreed to erect 150-case displays. Plush toys were given to those who bought a minimum of 75-case displays.[8]

As the previous examples illustrate, sales promotion tactics can help an organization get immediate, measurable results. They can instill goodwill among consumers and intermediaries. And unlike traditional advertising, sales promotion tactics give consumers an incentive to buy now. But there are dangers with sales promotion. Luke Sullivan, chief creative director at WestWayne, likens the dependency on promotions to drug addiction:

> *Similarity No. 1: Both give short bursts of euphoria and a sense of popularity. Similarity No. 2: A promotion will likely get you through the night with lots of jovial activity, but when morning comes and money is needed for food and rent (or brand awareness), the coffers are empty. Similarity No. 3: After the stimuli are removed, depression ensues, and there is an overpowering need for another jolt of short-term spending.*[9]

Public Relations

Public relations practitioners manage the communication between an organization and its publics. For Oscar Mayer, publics include grocery store managers, restaurant owners, parents, children, food columnists, employees, unions, stockholders, financial analysts, and, as the previous example illustrates, music teachers.

News Releases

One of the most common ways of delivering an organization's message is through stories that run in the media. Before the Oscar Mayer Wienermobile rolls into any community, the public relations department sends news releases to the local media to help ensure that their story will run. The media seem happy to cover the giant hot dog because it's a fun human-interest story. Stories about the Wienermobile have appeared in the *Wall Street Journal, USA Today,* the *Los Angeles Times,* the *Chicago Tribune,* and in local papers from coast to coast. And when it comes to television coverage, Hotdoggers, the folks who drive the giant wiener, have appeared on *The Tonight Show with Jay Leno, MTV, Oprah,* and NBC's *Today Show.*

---

[8] Sonia Reyes, "Hotdoggin' Cross-Country," *Brandweek,* 3 April 2000, p. R16.
[9] Luke Sullivan, "Natural High: Getting Off Those Addictive Promotional Drugs," *Adweek,* 9 September 2002, p. 10.

Unfortunately, most releases aren't greeted with the same enthusiasm as are ones about the Wienermobile coming to town. In fact, 90 percent of releases are tossed away by editors and producers because they're too promotional or aren't relevant to the medium's audience.[10]

Like a news story, a release should have the tone of an impartial reporter and include the basics of who, what, when, where, and why. It should be written in an inverted pyramid, where the most important points come first and the least important facts last, to allow the editor to cut from the bottom without hurting the message. Follow the format shown in Figure 12-3 when writing your release.

Ann Wylie offers these additional suggestions[11] as a way to get your release published:

- Grab attention in the headline. Telegraph a single newsworthy story in eight words in less, so editors and reporters can understand your point at a glance.

- Sell the reporter on the story in the subhead or summary by offering a secondary news angle or reader benefit.

- Answer "What happened?" and "Why should the reader care?" in your first paragraph.

- Keep your release to 500 words or less.

In addition to a release you may also wish to send a media kit containing a fact sheet, backgrounder, brochure, photos, product samples, or any other item that will help the journalists make an informed decision about the newsworthiness of your story. A fact sheet is a who-what-when-where-why-how breakdown of the news release. Some journalists prefer a fact sheet to a release because they want to write the story themselves, without any bias. A backgrounder may contain information on the history of your organization, biographies of key people in your organization, and testimonials from satisfied customers. Photos can increase the chances of your story running and should have captions attached to them. You may also want to include a photo opportunity sheet, which lets the media's photographers know where and when they should be to capture a photo of a breaking story.

Video news releases, commonly known as VNRs, are distributed to television stations and are designed to look like television news stories, ready to air. Most VNRs include a section called b-roll, which contains unedited video footage of the story, thus allowing the station to create their own version. Actualities are sound bites for radio stations and are often accompanied by news releases.

Sometimes the story will be released in stages to pique the interest of the media and their audience. For instance, Jack Horner Communications Inc.

---

[10] David W. Guth and Charles Marsh, *Public Relations: A Values-Driven Approach* (Boston: Allyn and Bacon, 2003), p. 274.
[11] Ann Wylie, "Anatomy of a Press Release," *Public Relations Tactics,* September 2003, p. 16.

Figure 12-3
Follow this format when writing a release.

Format for News Releases

- *Use one side of the paper and double-space the copy.* Keep the release short, preferably one page. If the release continues onto a second page, write "more" at the bottom of the first page.
- *Identify your organization,* with your company name or logo at the top.
- *Identify when the story should be released.* Most stories are "for immediate release," but there are times when you want to specify an exact time and date. For example, a company may want to announce a new product to the public on a certain date but will want to prepare the media ahead of time. This information is usually set in capital letters and boldfaced type.
- *Date of release.* This is usually placed under the previous date.
- *Contact information.* Write "CONTACT:" followed by the name, title, phone number, and email address of the person to contact for additional information. This information may be single-spaced.
- *Headline.* Skip two lines after your contact information and give a summary of what your story is about. Boldfaced type is optional but suggested.
- *Dateline.* This is the city of origin for your press release, followed by the state abbreviation if it is not a major city or if it could be confused with another city by the same name. The dateline is written in capital letters plus a dash, followed by the first line of the lead.
- *Lead.* This is the opening line of your story and usually includes who, what, when, and where.
- *Body.* This is the rest of the story and may include quotes from a company official. In the last paragraph, you may include a Web site or other relevant source for information.
- *Ending.* Skip a line after the last sentence and type a symbol for the ending: "# # #" or "-30-" to indicate the conclusion.
- *Photos.* Attach a caption for each photo to the bottom border. The back of the photo should give the name, address, and phone number of the contact person. Scans of photos may be sent on disk or email in TIFF or JPEG format.

created buzz about Heinz's new purple ketchup in different stages. The first release featured the headline, "Grab your Buns and Brace Yourselves" and included a mystery photo, teasing a new but still unannounced ketchup color. The next phase of the campaign was a press kit that came in a box that was covered with different colored question marks to stir rumors about what the new color would be. Inside the box were bottles of Funky Purple ketchup, as well as regular red ketchup, dip cups, and bags of chips that reporters could use to conduct blind taste tests. Finally, a press release announcing Funky Purple as the new EZ Squirt color was distributed with two photos. In addition, b-roll was sent via national satellite. The campaign was a success, with nearly 2000 stories, including more than 1000 TV stories.[12]

Procter & Gamble hired Manning, Selvage & Lee (MS&L) to get media coverage for Potty Palooza. Concert-style T-shirts with the message "Potty Palooza 2002 . . . It's Loo-La-La" were sent to local media in advance of each appearance. The shirts were compressed and shrink-wrapped into the shape of an 18-wheel trailer, making them even more intriguing to reporters who, prior to Potty Palooza, may never have considered toilet paper and portable restrooms to be newsworthy. Additionally, MS&L sent press releases to local media two days before each festival or fair's opening day. A media alert inviting press to visit Potty Palooza was blast-faxed to the media the day before each event. The potty hoopla worked. Stories ran in TV and print in all local market stops. Additionally, three national news stories covered the "event." P&G and MS&L won a 2003 Bronze Anvil award from the Public Relations Society of America for this creative approach to media relations.[13]

Special Events

Whether it's a major event such as the Macy's Thanksgiving Day Parade or a community cookout to raise money for volunteer firefighters, you need to answer the following questions:

- How will the event benefit your organization? Will it get you more customers? Build goodwill in the community? Give you a venue for product sampling?

- How will you measure the success of the event? Will it be through formal research methods, such as surveys or focus groups? An increase in sales? Or the amount of media coverage you get?

- What is the best venue? For instance, Oscar Mayer brings its Wienermobile to state fairs, parades, and grocery store parking lots because that's where its publics eat and buy hot dogs. Macy's prefers to invite its

---

[12] "Bronze Anvil 2003 Winners," *Public Relations Tactics,* September 2003, p. 16.
[13] "Honoring the Best in PR Tactics," *Public Relations Tactics,* September 2003, p. 16.

valued customers to their store for private events to get them in a shopping mood. Syracuse University holds numerous receptions in Manhattan because that's home to many of their students and alumni.

- Who should be reached? You need to define your target audience, just as you would in an advertising campaign. Are you thanking loyal customers? Going after new customers? Trying to reach gatekeepers such as teachers and politicians?

- How many should be reached? Bigger is not always better. An exclusive retailer like Neiman-Marcus won't want a massive crowd traipsing through their store to see a fashion show because Neiman-Marcus isn't about serving the masses. Additionally, a large crowd could damage merchandise and raise security concerns.

- What can go wrong? You name it, bad things can happen even when you have the best of intentions. Speakers and celebrities can cancel on you. Guests can get food poisoning from your hors d'oeuvres. And Mother Nature can wreck your outdoor plans. By anticipating potential problems, you can take action to avoid them or know how to respond if they occur.

Crisis Management

One of the most important functions of public relations is that of crisis management. You hope that you'll never need it, but you should have a crisis-management plan prepared so that your organization will know how to respond to emergencies, which experts need to be consulted, and who should be in contact with the media and the various publics involved.

A crisis plan starts with a risk assessment. Food manufacturers need to know how to respond to food contamination, airlines need to know how to respond to plane crashes, and all companies need to know how to respond to financial difficulties, on-the-job accidents, fires, and natural disasters. Your plan should designate a media spokesperson and identify other experts you may need to call upon for counsel, including lawyers, technical experts, and financial advisers.

Once the crisis occurs, you need to tell the truth, tell it completely, and tell it promptly. Any delays or half-truths will only make the crisis worse. You should also identify ways to make the situation better, whether it's support for grieving family members, a product recall, or another appropriate action.

One of the best examples of crisis management is what Johnson & Johnson did after someone laced Tylenol capsules with cyanide, killing seven people. Johnson & Johnson's CEO responded immediately, admitted the problem, launched a nationwide recall, and presented the company's plan for dealing with the crisis: triple-sealed packaging and tamperproof caplets. The Tylenol brand could have gone into extinction if the crisis was handled differently. Today, Tylenol is back on top.

Promotional Products

Go to a job fair, outdoor concert, or any major event, and you're bound to get a load of free stuff with companies' logos plastered all over it. When you get home you may realize you've collected pens, pencils, coffee mugs, T-shirts, and coolers from companies you don't even know. Obviously, this isn't a very effective use of a promotional budget.

However, promotional products can help further your brand's image if they're used strategically. A newspaper that guarantees delivery by 6 a.m. may want to give subscribers an alarm clock with its delivery promise printed on it. A grocery store that promises great savings may want to give calculators to customers when they sign up for the store's savings card. A car dealer in the South may want to give automobile sun protectors, whereas northern dealers may want to give ice scrapers. The key is relevancy and consistency with the brand message.

Often, promotional products will be a part of a public relations effort. For example, Union Pacific Railroad wanted to bolster safety awareness among its 6200 employees, so it sent a direct mail piece to each employee's home. The mailer featured a photo frame magnet with a postcard and the message, "Be Safe. It's right for you and me." At work, the message was reinforced on posters, floor decals, and banners. Managers also presented scratch-off game cards to employees exhibiting safe workplace behavior. Prizes included Swiss Army knives, insulated coolers, thermoses, binoculars, and customized Fossil watches with the "Be Safe" logo. The campaign generated a 30-percent reduction of on-the-job injuries.[14]

Special Packaging

How do you make a brand that's been around since 1869 seem cool? That's the challenge Leo Burnett faced with Heinz ketchup, a brand that was losing market share. Research showed consumers knew and liked the brand but just weren't buying it as much as they once did. To add further insult, the ketchup category had dropped from the number one condiment to number two, with salsa leading the way. Something had to be done.

Heinz didn't want to lower the price or offer price incentives that might cheapen the image of the brand, nor did they want to allocate a huge advertising budget. The first thing Leo Burnett did was identify the target audience. Mothers were the buyers, but teenagers were the heavy users. Burnett needed to find a way to project the individualism teens covet by giving the brand a unique, quirky, self-confident voice. They needed to give the brand

[14] "Walk Like a Winner," *PROMO,* 1 April 2003, p. 16.

"attitude." Wisecracking labels did the trick. Funny lines appeared on the bottle labels, including:

Instructions: Put on food

Taller than mayonnaise

Will work with mustard if it has to

Desperately seeking Tater Tots

On a first name basis with onion rings

14 billion French fries can't be wrong

The Heinz campaign, which also included TV, print, and book covers, was a huge hit. Market share rose 15 percent, and the bottles are so popular people buy them on eBay (see Figure 12-4). The campaign won a 2002 gold Effie, an award presented annually by the New York American Marketing Association in recognition of the year's most effective advertising campaigns.[15]

Leo Burnett won another 2002 gold Effie for the heart-shaped tin it created for Altoids. The "love" tin was offered during Valentine's Day and played on the notion that Altoids mints can help spice up your love life. In 2003 Altoids packaged their mints in collectible tins with designs from popular ads (see Figure 12-5).

Innovative packaging is becoming increasingly important as a result of media fragmentation and the proliferation of new products on store shelves. Chris Maher, managing partner at Convergence Marketing, calls innovative new packaging the crucial "tiebreaker" in product categories where war is waged on the shelf instead of through price and advertising.[16]

Sponsorships

Corporations spent $25 billion in 2001 for the rights to put their names on everything from local AIDS walks to sports stadiums, and that's just for naming rights. Sergio Zyman reports that companies typically spend three times more than that to create, advertise, promote, and implement their sponsorship programs.[17] In his book *The End of Advertising as We Know It,* Zyman lists a series of questions companies need to answer before signing a sponsorship agreement:[18]

- Is the sponsorship relevant and persuasive to your consumers?
- What specific business results are you trying to achieve?

[15] Adapted from a lecture by Edward Russell at Syracuse University on 17 March 2003 and leoburnett.com.
[16] Kate Fitzgerald, "Packaging Is the Capper," *Advertising Age,* 5 May 2003, p. 22.
[17] Sergio Zyman, *The End of Advertising as We Know It* (Hoboken, NJ: Wiley, 2002), p. 145.
[18] Ibid., pp. 151–154.

Figure 12-4
How do you get people talking about a 100-year-old brand? By having the brand do the talking. Heinz first introduced "talking labels" on the world's best-selling ketchup in 1999. These 2003 versions feature winning statements from the "Say Something Ketchuppy" contest. The name of the person who came up with the expression appears under each quote.

Photo by Debbie Garris.

Figure 12-5
The idea for Altoids' famous ad slogan and positioning line, "The Curiously Strong Mints," came from a line on the package. In a twist, limited edition tins feature some of the most popular ads.

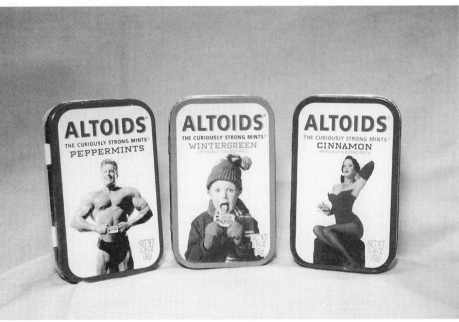

Photo by Debbie Garris.

- Does the sponsorship possess the associate equity you need to meet your objectives?
- What will the sponsorship cost, and how much business will it need to generate in order to achieve your objectives?
- What are the opportunity costs (how else could you be spending the money)?

The right sponsorship can expose your brand to your target audience, give you a venue for product sampling, and generate positive publicity. But sponsorships can get confusing to the average consumer. For example, do you know what beer company owns the sponsorship to the Super Bowl? Did you think it was Anheuser-Busch? If you did, there's a reason. Anheuser-Busch has been the exclusive Super Bowl beer advertiser for years. In 2003 alone, the company ran eleven commercials for Budweiser, Bud Light, and Michelob. But does that make them the sponsor? Not necessarily. Coors has a five-year agreement that makes them the "official beer sponsor of the NFL." Meanwhile, Miller has acquired the rights to associate its name with 20 individual teams, including the Buccaneers. To make things more confusing, Miller shares the rights to the Buccaneers' logo with Anheuser-Busch, which in turn, shares the rights to the Raiders' logo with Coors.[19] Confused? You're not alone.

Cause-Related Marketing

Cause-related marketing associates a company or brand with a social cause in an attempt to build customer goodwill. A Cone/Roper study found that consumers consider a company or brand's price, quality, and social involvement as major criteria in their decision of which brands to use.[20] A Roper Starch study confirmed this, with 92 percent of respondents agreeing it's important for marketers to seek out ways to become good corporate citizens.[21] A good example of cause-related marketing is Chiquita's commitment to the rain forest. *Audubon* magazine reported:

> *Her hat was adorned with a Carmen Miranda-esque assortment of fruit; her lipstick, fire-engine red. The real-life Miss Chiquita recently appeared at the Copacabana, New York City's tropical watering hole, to celebrate a milestone: The Rainforest Alliance has certified 100 percent of Chiquita's farms in Latin America as environmentally and socially responsible. Under the alliance's Better Banana Project, farmers follow strict guidelines to conserve soil and water and minimize the use of pesticides and other agrochemicals.*

Do you think Audubon Society members care about these issues? You bet they do. So do many average consumers. But do you think the average person even knows what an agrochemical is? Probably not. That's why Chiquita uses a different tactic when communicating their respect for the environment to moms and children. A Chiquita banana display in grocery stores

[19] Christopher Lawton, "This Super Bowl, It's All About the Beer," *The Post-Standard,* 26 January 2003, pp. E1, E8.
[20] Reyes, "Hotdoggin' Cross-Country," p. R16.
[21] Carol Krol, "Consumers Note Marketers' Good Causes: Roper," *Advertising Age,* 11 November 1996, p. 51.

Figure 12-6
AFLAC sells a stuffed toy duck on its Web site. Profits from the sales of the merchandise support the AFLAC Cancer and Blood Disorder Center at the Children's Heathcare of Atlanta hospital.

Photo by Debbie Garris.

promoted an opportunity to win a family vacation for four to a rain forest in Costa Rica. To enter, children under 12 years old were asked to color a rain-forest drawing that had images of tropical plants, birds, animals, and, of course, Miss Chiquita. Interesting facts about rain forests and Chiquita's good deeds appeared throughout the drawing.

AFLAC is another company that understands the importance of giving back. Consumers can buy a toy duck that quacks "Af-laccck!" by visiting the company's Web site. Proceeds support the AFLAC Cancer and Blood Disorder Center at the Children's Heathcare of Atlanta hospital (see Figure 12-6).

Unfortunately, there are bad examples of cause-related marketing. Some companies jump on the "cause du jour" and fail to make a relevant connection between the brand and the cause. These transparent efforts usually produce equally transparent results. Sometimes they can even backfire as a major retailer learned when it asked customers to bring in used jeans, and in return, the store would give them a discount on a new pair and then donate the old jeans to a charity. The concept sounds like a good idea. However, the store ran the ad before asking the charity. As it turned out, the charity had no way to distribute used clothing and sued the retailer for wrongfully using its name.

Before developing a cause-related program, answer the following questions:

- How does the cause relate to the brand? Is there a natural tie-in?
- How do consumers feel about the cause? Do you need to educate them about the importance of the issue?

- What are the expectations of the charitable organization?
- How may you promote your involvement with the cause?

Guerilla Marketing

Coined by Jay Conrad Levinson, guerilla marketing is the use of unconventional marketing intended to get maximum results from minimal resources. This approach is important not only for a new brand with a limited marketing communications budget but also can be an important branding tool for well-established companies. For instance, Marshall Field's sends Jingle Elves onto the streets of Chicago to perform random acts of kindness during the holiday season (Figure 12-7). These ambassadors of goodwill offer hot chocolate along Michigan Avenue, pay bus and subway fares for commuters, give lip balm and hand lotion to pedestrians, and read stories at local libraries. These kind gestures are far more persuasive than institutional ads that state "We care about our customers." As the adage goes, actions speak louder than words.

Sometimes the guerilla-marketing techniques will involve unconventional media. Kirshenbaum & Bond got people's attention by painting sidewalks with the message "From here it looks like you could use new underwear." Other agencies soon followed suit, plastering messages on sidewalks, subway entrances, and construction sites. But before you start covering your community, check the local ordinances. Nike learned its street decals violated a New York City code that states it is "unlawful to deface any street by painting, printing, or writing thereon, or attaching thereto, in any manner, any advertisement or other printed matter."[22] Right after the Nike faux pas, Microsoft plastered adhesive butterflies on subway entrances, telephone booths, and newspaper-vending machines throughout Manhattan. The transportation department ordered the butterfly decals to go into hibernation.[23]

Product Placement and Branded Content

Watch the James Bond movie *Die Another Day,* and you'll see at least 20 product pitches. Ford is reported to have paid $35 million to have Pierce Brosnan, who plays Bond, behind the wheel of its $228,000 Aston Martin Vanquish, and to have Halle Berry, who plays the Jinx, drive a Thunderbird whose coral color matches her bathing suit.[24] In the movie, Bond wears an

---

[22] "Keep the Sidewalks Ad-Free," *New York Times,* 23 October 2002, nytimes.com/opinion.
[23] David W. Dunlap, "New York Tells Microsoft to Get Its Butterfly Decals Out of Town," *New York Times,* 25 October 2002, nytimes.com/nyregion.
[24] Guy Trebay, "Make It a Finlandia and 7Up, Shaken, Not Stirred," *New York Times,* 27 October 2002, nytimes.com/weekinreview.

Figure 12-7
Marshall Field's gives back to the Chicago community in many ways. During the holidays, they send Jingle Elves into the streets of Chicago to perform random acts of kindness.

Omega wristwatch, drinks Finlandia martinis, flies first-class on British Airways, and wears Ballantyne turtleneck sweaters and suits from Brioni Roman Style.

Product placement can range from a background shot to a product-centered episode, such as when *Seinfeld* devoted an entire episode to Junior Mints. Some companies even produce their own movies, television shows, and video games. For example, BMW found a way to connect with their upscale target audience by creating mini movies for its Web site. The movies use famous actors and edgy directors to give BMW enthusiasts a thrilling ride. One, starring James Brown, goes along these lines: A boy sells his soul to the devil for fame and fortune. Years later he wants to renegotiate because he failed to address the aging process. He agrees to a drag race with the devil. If he wins, he gets another 50 years.

Branded content can be extremely expensive and is far from foolproof. Ford and its agency, J. Walter Thompson, created an outdoor-adventure TV series for the WB network. The show's title, *No Boundaries,* was the same as Ford's SUV ad slogan. The show bombed and was quickly yanked off the air. Product placement also has its share of risks, from being so subtle that most people don't even pick up on it, to being so blatant that it can turn off viewers and devalue the brand. The trick is to make the brand seem natural to the characters and plot of the story.

Suggested Activities

1. Develop an idea for a special event for a company you admire. Include details of the event, such as who will be reached, where the event will be held, how it will be promoted, and how much it will cost. Also, indicate how you will evaluate the success of the event.

2. Write a news release for the special event you described in Activity 1.

3. Develop a sales promotion idea for your favorite soft drink or snack food.

4. Go to a movie or watch 2 hours of prime-time television. Take note of how many brands were recognizable within the program and how they were incorporated into the storyline.

Search Online! Discovering More About Integrated Marketing

Use InfoTrac College Edition to discover more about integrated marketing communications. Try these phrases and others for Key Words and Subject Guide searches: *integrated marketing communications, sales promotion, public relations, guerilla marketing, product placement, events marketing, green marketing, cause related marketing.*

For more information on integrated marketing communications, visit the following Web sites:

Effie Awards: www.effie.org

Entertainment Resources and Marketing Association (product placement): www.erma.org

Guerilla Marketing: www.gmarketing.com

Point of Purchase Advertising Institute: www.popai.org

Council of Public Relations Firms: www.prfirms.org

Public Relations Society of America: www.prsa.org

PR Week magazine: www.prweek.net

Promotion Marketing Association: www.pmalink.com

How to Get New Yorkers Talking

New Yorkers are a tough audience because they're inundated with media messages every day. Whether it's the bright lights of Times Square, the colorful street vendors hawking designer knock-offs, or the mesmerizing store windows along Fifth Avenue, everywhere you look, someone's trying to grab your attention and sell you something. So what can a company do to get the attention of New Yorkers and get them talking? That's the challenge Cingular Wireless gave to agencies BBDO and Ketchum as it was about to introduce its brand in New York in the summer of 2002.

With 7.8 million cell phone users, the Big Apple is the country's largest wireless market. Already home to Cingular's national competitors including Verizon, AT&T Wireless, Sprint PCS, and T-Mobile, New York's saturation rate was at 50 percent, higher than any other city in the country.

Research showed that 40 percent (or 3.1 million users) had six months or less left on their current contracts with other wireless carriers. Furthermore, competitive assessment research revealed that customer-satisfaction scores among all carriers were very close, ranging from 7.3 (Verizon) to 7.6 (T-Mobile, Nextel) on a 10-point scale. This research demonstrated that there was not one carrier with strong overall customer satisfaction, indicating that consumers would be willing to switch carriers if Cingular were able to differentiate itself from the competition. Focus groups indicated New Yorkers would be more receptive to marketing messages that took an insider New York–centric perspective.

With the research in hand, Cingular and its agencies set the following objectives: (1) Generate 70,000 net activations from July 11 to December 31, 2002, (2) create and sustain 60-percent brand awareness via marketing activity during launch, and (3) generate buzz among NYC key influencers. To accomplish these objectives, BBDO and Ketchum created an integrated communications campaign that included advertising, public relations, special events, cause-related marketing, celebrity appearances, and guerilla-marketing tactics.

As part of the entry to NYC, Cingular wanted to show its support for the community by pairing with a charity that was New York–centric as well as in line with the self-expression brand platform. After considering several

Courtesy Cingular™ Wireless.

options, Cingular chose Art Start, an organization that provides an outlet for underserved children and teenagers to express themselves through arts and music. Cingular held a New York launch press conference at the Cingular Fifth Avenue retail store on July 11, 2002, and presented a $500,000 donation to help begin a project to develop a 24-hour safe haven, the Art Start Center, in Lower Manhattan. High profile community leaders, including former Mayor Giuliani and members of Mayor Bloomberg's staff, attended the event.

During the rest of the summer, New Yorkers could hardly walk a block without seeing signs of Cingular's arrival. New York was introduced to Cingular's "Jack" icon by the placement of 20- by 20-foot sculptures at locations around the city, including Grand Central Station and South Street Seaport.

Cingular-branded Gray Line buses were spotted all over town. Cingular hired a number of celebrities, including Spike Lee, Darrell Hammond, and Joan Rivers, to surprise tourists by jumping aboard buses at the Cingular Flagship Store on Fifth Avenue and cohosting the tours, sharing their personal New York experiences and stories with passengers.

Orange, the signature color of Cingular, became a branding device. Containers of orange juice carrying the Cingular logo and the message "Hey, who you calling half-pint?" were given away on street corners. Orange umbrellas adorned with the Cingular logo were handed out on rainy days. And orange M&Ms gave weary pedestrians a sweet pick-me-up.

Cingular sponsored the Central Park SummerStage, a free concert series that featured a diverse group of artists. The sponsorship leveraged the self-expression platform with "Express Yourself" stations at the concerts, where concertgoers could speak into a video camera and give their view about New York. Clips were posted at ny.cingular.com, a Web site developed by BBDOAtmosphere for the launch.

Cingular launched a humorous, highly creative New York–oriented advertising campaign, proclaiming the message "The company that champions self-expression nationwide is now in the most expressive city on Earth." Messages such as "We would have been here earlier, but we got stuck in traffic" and "If you can make it here, you can make it anywhere. A phone call, that is" were plastered across newspapers and television screens as well as out-of-home advertising outlets such as subways, taxicabs, bus stops, and the middle of Times Square.

The Cingular logo became the payoff in several ads. In a print ad, empty space on the New York Stock Exchange trading floor forms the jack figure. The ad's headline reads "When nearly half of the Fortune 1000 count on you, a pattern starts to emerge." A television commercial featured Yellow Taxis doing a synchronized "dance," similar to what you'd see at a Broadway musical. After the cabs zip around each other, they eventually form the Cingular logo.

The campaign generated a lot of buzz. Media coverage garnered a total 18,662,180 impressions, including placements with financial outlets such as *CNBC* and *Bloomberg* and other national outlets such as the *New York Times*, Reuters, Dow Jones, *BrandWeek, Ad Week, RCR Wireless News,* and *Wireless Week*. Brand-awareness levels in the New York metro area are up to 66

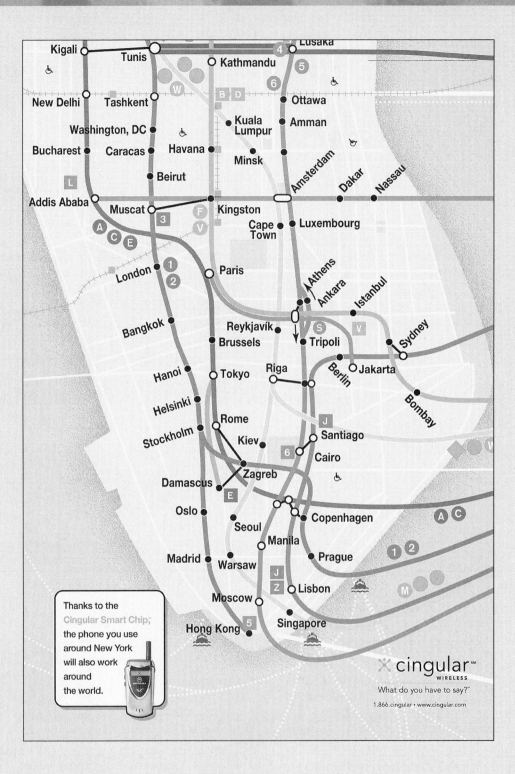

percent, growing 43 percent from the launch on July 11. And the ultimate payoff? Cingular generated 79,000 activations from July 11 to December 31, 2002. Now that's something worth talking about!

CLIENT PITCHES:
HOW TO SELL YOUR IDEAS

There's a wonderful scene in the British film *Honest, Decent, and True*—a send-up of advertising—in which the copywriter and art director do their best to convince the client that their TV commercial for his new brand of lager is just what the brand needs to become a success. If the scene didn't strike so close to home, we could enjoy the laughs less guiltily. But as in all good satire, this scene has been played, with variations, in nearly every advertising agency or client conference room. It goes something like this:

The writer ardently presents a TV storyboard, which is handsomely mounted and standing on an easel in full view of those present. These include, in addition to the client, members of the agency (the account executive, the planner or head of research, the media analyst, and, of course, the copywriter and art director, who have slaved feverishly for weeks to come up with this concept).

The commercial is a bit risky, however. It tells the story of a group of happy voyagers at the bar of a grand cruise ship. Some order embarrassingly toney drinks, while a few are "brave enough" to order what they really want—the client's new lager. Suddenly, there's a loud crash, and the ship begins to sink. In the final shot, we see survivors in a lifeboat, and they're all drinking the client's lager. Only then do we learn the name of the ship—it is the *Titanic*.

The client listens in silence and says nothing, even after the presentation is finished. The tense silence is at last broken by the researcher, who explains that this is a spoof, a big joke. The client answers, "Yes, I suppose some people would find this funny . . . Yes. Well it's just fine. Just fine." There is an audible sigh of relief. Then the client continues: "There are just a few very small things I'm having problems with. Nothing major, mind you. I wonder about the time frame here. After all, this is a contemporary product, and is it appropriate to do it in a period setting? Then there's the question of whether humor is appropriate to the selling of a lager. I also have a bit of a problem with the use of such a historic disaster to advertise our product. But nothing major." Silence again. A few clearings of throats. Then the various agency members attempt to brush these "small" problems aside, telling their conservative client that the young singles who are the market for this product don't care about the *Titanic,* that they will merely laugh at the disaster and get the message. But it's no use. He just isn't buying.

The Presentation Is Half of the Battle

Coming up with great ideas is a monumental task, but convincing your coworkers and your client to "buy" your ideas is no small task either. When you see great advertising, you can be fairly certain that those ideas saw the light of day because the client was willing to take a risk.

Regardless of your client's proclivity for taking risks, you must be prepared to sell the advertising just as thoroughly as you believe the advertising sells the goods. Generally, the presentation of the creative portion of an ad campaign should come after all other aspects of the campaign have been discussed. These other elements may include a summary of the marketing background for the product or service, a discussion of the research the agency has undertaken to conceive the strategy, and a proposed media plan that justifies the selection of certain media vehicles and the rejection of others.

Because your marketing summary will have touched on target markets and broad marketing goals, your presentation of the ad should be restricted to the communications aspects of your campaign. But where do you begin? Actually, you began weeks or months ago by establishing a comfortable, two-way relationship with your client. Clients don't like surprises. Nothing turns them off faster than walking into a presentation without the slightest inkling of what lies ahead. By staying in touch with your clients and making them feel that they are valued members of your team, you will put them in a more receptive frame of mind. This doesn't mean that you have to reveal your big ideas early, but you should certainly agree on the basic direction of the campaign before the actual presentation. Good clients are risk takers who try not to throw barriers in the way of sound, creative judgment. Part of your job is to nurture this attitude well before the day of the presentation. When that day arrives, here's what should happen:

1. *Begin with a brief recap of the assignment.* You were asked to solve a certain problem. Remind your client of the problem and share your creative exploration of it. You might even share ideas that you rejected; this can indicate that you are concerned about the success of the campaign and not merely about selling your ideas.

2. *Discuss your creative strategy thoroughly.* You're not talking to the consumer, who doesn't need to understand the strategy to like the ads. You're talking to the people who are going to be paying you handsomely for your efforts. Therefore, you must convince them in a highly logical manner that the ideas you are about to present—which may appear to be highly illogical—are the result of sound, perceptive thinking. So talk about what's going on in the minds of members of the target audience. Tell what they're saying now. Tell what you would like them to be saying. Tell why your campaign will stand out from the competition; you might even want to show competing ads to demonstrate how your campaign breaks through the clutter. Above all, when you get to your strategy, link it very clearly to the original goals of the project. Does it answer the problem? Exactly how does it do this?

3. *Make a big deal about the campaign's theme.* You may be so familiar with the theme by now that you forget that your client may never have seen or heard it before. Introduce the theme importantly by displaying it on a board or flashing it on a screen. If animation or music or sound is involved, use them as part of the presentation.

4. *Show how the big idea is expressed.* This involves the various advertisements and commercials, the sales promotion and collateral pieces, and everything else that is part of your campaign. For television and radio, try to have something as finished as possible (a demo CD for radio, a rough video or a set of computer-generated stills with an audio track for TV). With regard to the body copy in print ads, most seasoned presenters agree that it's best not to read it to your client. Instead, simply communicate what it expresses and invite their review at a later time. What you're striving to communicate, obviously, is that the big idea—the central theme—runs through all of these ads and that this theme is a result of a well-devised strategy that delivers the intended message perfectly.

5. *Close with a summary statement and ask for the order.* Remind the client how effective this campaign will be, how thoroughly it satisfies marketing and communications goals, and why it is the best choice for the problem at hand.

6. *Answer questions honestly.* If you don't know, say you don't know and promise to find out. Avoid direct confrontations, but don't come off as a "yes-man" or "yes-woman" to your client. Clients don't want that. If you disagree with your client's suggestions, explain why logically and politely. Compromise on minor issues and speak with conviction about those issues that you feel are essential to the spirit and intent of your work. If there is no agreement, your only choice may be to thank the client and go on to another job. Few good agencies will compromise their creative standards to produce what they feel is inferior work. It's a delicate situation. Knowing how to handle a client who disagrees demands a thorough understanding not only of that client's company culture but also of the personalities of the decision makers.

Pitching with Pizzazz

Advertising is a creative business, so don't try to bore a client into buying your big idea. Have fun with your presentation but make sure it's relevant. Consider this pitch from Merkley Newman Harty to members of the National Thoroughbred Racing Association. The Harty team started their presentation with a video that showed close-ups of a typical horse race—pounding hoofs, whips to the hindquarters, flaring nostrils, and a photo finish. Then came the line "The function of insanity is doing the same thing over and over again and expecting different results." This helped the agency make the point that the hackneyed approach that racetracks had used for years wasn't working. Racetracks needed a fresh, new approach. They needed Merkley Newman Harty. Members of the National Thoroughbred Racing Association agreed.

When Kevin Fisher presented his idea for a new ad campaign for the Riverbanks Zoo, he blared the song "Wild Thing" from a boom box and started dancing to the beat of the music. Mary Leverette, the zoo's marketing director, recalls her reaction: "When he was jumping around with the music just blasting, Satch (the director of the zoo) and I just cut our eyes at each other. It was a big departure from the sedate nature of the ads we had had in the past. But we loved it. We just loved it." Fisher's performance sold the zoo directors on the idea of running commercials that featured animals keeping time to rock music while humans cut loose at the zoo.[1]

Leo Burnett won the Heinz ketchup account by showing ads that made Heinz seem cool and teen-friendly. On the morning of the final pitch, the agency's team set up a hot dog stand in the lobby and lined the escalator walls with ketchup labels with catchy slogans. The conference room was turned into a diner with bar stools, a counter, and a short-order cook.

The Martin Agency's pitch for the advertising account of *Men's Health* magazine began even before the actual presentation. The magazine's representative encountered about 20 Martin Agency employees reading *Men's Health* on the sidewalk and throughout the agency's headquarters. When she got on the elevator, she found a framed sign that read, "If *Men's Health* was our client, your ad pages would go up faster than this elevator." The Martin Agency won the account.

Why do some agencies go to such elaborate lengths to win accounts? Consider this: According to the American Association of Advertising Agencies, the average account stays with an agency for 7.2 years. Harry Jacobs, the chairman emeritus of the Martin Agency, told the *Richmond Times-Dispatch,* "New business is the lifeblood of the advertising agency. Without perfecting it and being proficient at it, the agency is not going to grow."[2]

---

[1] Anna Velasco, "Swimming with the Big Fish: Fisher Communications Makes It Big, but Stays Small," *The State,* 29 August 1999, p. G1.

[2] Otesa Middleton, "Here's the Pitch: Ad Agencies Reveal Their Strategies for Getting Accounts," *Richmond Times-Dispatch,* 2 September 1996, p. D16.

A great way for prospective clients (and employees) to get a first impression of an agency is to visit its Web site, which will state the agency's business philosophy, list current clients, profile key personnel, and show examples of creative work (see Figure 13-1). However, even the best Web site can't compare to the impact of a face-to-face presentation.

Guidelines for Making Presentations

In whatever area of advertising you eventually choose, you're always going to have to present something to somebody. The more experience you have in presenting, the better you will become. A great place to start presenting is in your classes. The following tips will help you discover how to do so comfortably, enthusiastically, and convincingly:

1. *Get the attention of your audience right away.* Open your talk with something that not only gains the attention of your audience but also causes them to respect you as an authority and starts them thinking about your topic. Never apologize for yourself as an introduction—that only undermines your credibility.

2. *Remember how it feels to be a listener.* You have plenty of practice being a student. What do your most interesting professors do to keep your attention? Use them as role models.

3. *Be prepared for questions.* Don't let them throw you. No one is out to do that. If you don't know the answer, simply say you don't. Ask for others to answer.

4. *Rehearse out loud.* Practice before a mirror, unless that's uncomfortable. If it is, rehearse before a room and pretend the room is filled. Or rehearse by asking one or more friends to listen and give you comments.

5. *Listen to your words and inflections.* If they sound wrong to you, they probably are. Underscore words you want to stress. Indicate pauses for a breath if that will help your pacing.

6. *Stand tall.* Your arms should be comfortably at your sides. Avoid sweeping gestures. Don't fiddle with rubber bands, paper clips, or pen caps. It will be difficult at first, but you can learn to do it.

7. *Make eye contact.* If your audience is large, shift your focus now and then to a different person or a different side of the room. Include everyone. If one person is more important than the rest, spend a good deal of time making contact with him or her.

8. *Speak from your diaphragm.* Use one of the lower ranges of your voice. It will carry better and sound more authoritative.

9. *Use inflection for effect.* Avoid monotones. Emphasize important words as underscored in your notes. Pause for dramatic effect. A pause that seems eternal to you is probably short to your listeners.

Figure 13-1
Nasuti & Hinkle's Web site explains the agency's philosophy and shows examples of their creative work. Also notice the terrific sales results of the ads.

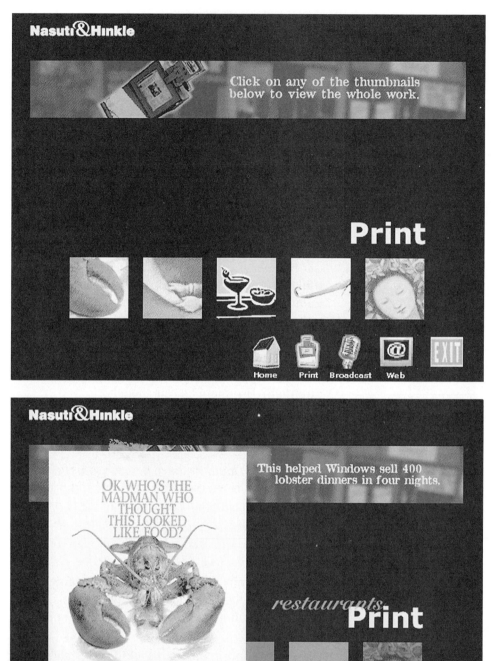

10. *Use appropriate facial expressions and gestures.* These should be congruent with your spoken words. If something is funny, smile.

11. *Check out the room before you speak.* There's nothing more disconcerting than discovering when you're in the midst of your presentation that you can't use your visual aids. Before you speak, make sure all the audio/visual equipment you'll need is in the room and in working order. Are the seats arranged the way you want them? Is there a podium or table for your notes? If you plan on writing key points throughout your presentation, is there an easel with a pad, a chalkboard, or overhead projector? Are there appropriate pens or chalk?

Perils and Pitfalls of Presenting

Ron Hoff, who in his long and distinguished career has been associated with Ogilvy & Mather and Foote Cone & Belding, has a lot of experience with the perils and pitfalls of presenting.[3] Here is what he says:

- The biggest problem we face is boring our audience. Sometimes, we even bore ourselves. Seldom do our true identities emerge in our professional selves. Perhaps this is why we're so boring when we make presentations.

- Visuals, when added to words, will more than double recall of your message. When you get the audience to participate in your presentation, recall will zoom to around 90 percent among the people who have actually taken part.

- The moment of judgment in presentations occurs within the first 90 seconds. That's when audiences decide to tune in or check out. If the presenter talks entirely about himself or herself, the audience disconnects or daydreams. Audiences are sitting there asking themselves, "When is that presenter going to start talking about me?"

Hoff identifies the following key strategies for effective presentations:

1. *Know the people in the opposition and know who is your best supporter.* Address your first words to the opponent. Then move to someone you know is favorable. You should feel refueled and reinforced at this point, so you can move on to the others. When you reach a seemingly negative person, go back to a friend. Keep warming up the group until it seems safe to invade the "enemy territory."

2. *Start with something you feel comfortable with.* It can be fun, but it must be relevant. Dr. Stephen Zipperblatt of the Pritikin Longevity Center in San Diego opens his workshop with these words: "Man doesn't die . . . he kills himself." He then goes on to tell participants how to live healthier lives. He's off and rolling.

---

[3] The authors thank Ron Hoff for granting them permission to use these ideas.

3. *Appoint a DSW—a director of "So what?"* This person represents the grubby, selfish interests of the audience. Whenever you say something irrelevant, he or she says, "So what?" and you know you're off course.

4. *Start your agency presentations about halfway through.* Halfway through is where most of us stop talking about ourselves and start talking about our clients. Start with the audience's issue of primary concern instead of your issue of concern (get the business). Ask yourself, "How can we help the poor devils?"

Hoff also identifies "what bugs people about presentations," explaining that these come from people in the business who've suffered through numerous presentations that flopped:

- "You know so much more about this than I do." (The client wants someone who knows more than he or she does.)

- "I'm so nervous. I hope you can't see how much my knees are shaking." (A true confidence builder.)

- "I've got my notes so screwed up, I don't know what I'm going to do." (The client thinks, "What am I doing here?")

- "We know you're waiting for the creative, so I'll try to fly through the media plan." (And therefore miss lots of opportunities to sell the package or set the stage for the big idea.)

Hoff also feels that every presentation should have a burning issue. Too often, we fall far short of this. We sputter. He adds that too many presenters act as if they don't know what slide is coming up next and that just as many don't know the first thing about eye contact. What is so interesting about that distant star they're looking at? Is it any wonder there's no connecting going on there?

How to Correct the Problems

Eye contact and connecting are extremely important. So keep the lights up and get near members of the audience. Reduce the distance between you and them, both geographically and ideologically. People are nervous at the start of a presentation, when the distance is the greatest.

Don't be upset by interruptions. Answer but never attack. Be professional. If there are rude people in the audience, continue to be polite. The group will take care of their own. Above all, never lose your temper; this is tantamount to losing the business.

How do you overcome nervousness? Tell yourself that you're the best—and believe it. Relax. Present to yourself in the mirror and watch and listen to yourself. Even better, videotape yourself presenting. Watch it once, a second time with the sound off, and a third time with sound only. Do you like your nonverbals? If not, take steps to improve them. Do you like your voice? What, if anything, could make you sound more convincing? Exercise your jaw just before presenting. Take several slow, deep breaths.

It all comes out in your voice—your joy, your nervousness, your anticipation, and your boredom. Your voice gives your audience its first real clue about you, yet we often neglect our voices. Deep voices communicate authority. Anyone can, with practice, present in a voice deeper than their normal speaking voice. Spend a day working on your voice by narrating your day into a cassette recorder: "It's 9 a.m. and I'm waiting for the bus. I see it coming now. A few people are here, but it's not a busy day. . . ." Then listen to it. Then do it again and listen again.

Most important of all, says Hoff, is to remember that the client may not always be right, but the client is always the client.

Using PowerPoint Effectively

Picture this: You're sitting in a darkened room. Slide after slide is swirling past you. The presenter is droning on in a monotonous voice, reading everything that appears on the screen. He tells you that he'll give you a handout of the PowerPoint presentation, so you don't have to take notes (or, as you realize, pay attention to what he's saying). Occasionally, a cute graphic or cartoon appears on the screen. You chuckle, even if you don't see the relevance. Finally, the presentation's over and the lights come up. As your eyes try to adjust to the light, the presenter asks, "Any questions?" You're too numb to respond.

Just as in the above example, the wrong visuals can sabotage a presentation. So what should you do?

1. *Remember you, not the screen, should be the focal point.* There's a reason you were invited to present in person. Otherwise, you would have been asked to email your presentation as an attachment. Use the screen to supplement what you're saying, not say it for you.

2. *Keep the bells and whistles to a minimum.* PowerPoint allows you to add all sorts of funky sounds and movements. Sometimes these gimmicks help you make a point, but all too often they're the sign of an inexperienced presenter.

3. *Remember the basics of good design.* Readability is key. Have one concept per slide and no more than eight lines per slide. Text should be set in 24-point or larger type and in upper- and lowercase letters to make it easier to read.

4. *Create a look for your presentation.* Select a typeface and color combination that is easy on the eyes. Sans serif typefaces work best because of their simplicity. Yellow, orange, and red are good for text and graphs; blue, green, and purple work best for the background.[4] Also, consider putting your logo in the corner of your slides.

---

[4] Morag Preston, "Slide Rules" *Kinkos Impress,* 2001, p. 48.

5. *Use numbers, bullets, and lists.* These devices help organize your material and make it easier for your audience to follow. But don't overwhelm your audience with a slide that has every point listed. Start by showing one point at first, then building until you've listed all the points.

6. *Keep the visual on screen in sync with what you're saying.* There's nothing more distracting than hearing someone describe the big idea and seeing a media flowchart, or some other unrelated message, on the screen. Even smaller inconsistencies can be irksome, such as hearing someone say, "Save 50 percent" when the screen says "half off."

7. *Remember, a slick PowerPoint presentation won't make up for a weak idea.* All the latest bells and whistles won't make up for a presentation that's not smart.

Suggested Activities

1. Contact an account executive or creative director in an advertising agency, or the advertising manager of a company, and ask that individual to explain how a particular creative strategy was devised. Make a presentation to your class on your findings.

2. Choose one of the case studies in this book and imagine that you've been chosen to sell the client on the idea. Make a presentation to the class as if you were selling the campaign to the client.

3. Read a book on salesmanship or interview a speech professor at your school and prepare a report that identifies the key elements in making a sale. How can you apply these principles to the selling of an idea?

Search Online! Discovering More About Convincing the Client

Use InfoTrac College Edition to discover more about convincing the client. Try these phrases and others for Key Words and Subject Guide searches: *advertising agency + client, presentation style, advertising campaign, unusual advertising presentations, presentation techniques, speaking tips, eye contact + presentation, posture + presentation, overcoming nervousness, rehearsing presentation.*

For more information on making presentations to clients, go to:

www.effectivemeetings.com

Reading This Will Make You Irrational

Here's part of a pitch from Henderson Advertising, the first agency outside of New York or Chicago to be named "Agency of the Year" by *Advertising Age:*

We awaken every morning to a choice of over 100 breakfast cereals.

We enter the bathroom, having chosen from an array of aloe vera–infused, anti-bacterial, deodorant soaps containing not one but two kinds of moisturizers, not to mention the lanolin-treated toilet paper that contains no dye but feels soft as a cirrus cloud.

We down a sports beverage that offers flavors ranging from Ice-Blue to Mountain Frost, even though no one can come up with the adjectives that best describe the extraordinary refreshment one encounters from gulping the taste of blue.

We pay huge sums of money to be like Mike, to have lips like Cindy, and to have a laptop in a color called grape.

It's kind of nuts.

And it's kind of beautiful.

Competition spurs choice, innovation, experimentation, and enormous opportunity.

It can cause consumers to dance from one competitor to the next.

Or, when marketed properly, can encourage an extraordinary, even irrational attachment^{SM} to one brand.

That's what we do.

We create that irrational attachment.

We marry consumers to your product or service. And we do it in a way that severely diminishes the possibility of divorce, that withstands pricing battles, competitors' promotions, and anything else an under-branded competitor might throw at you.

Courtesy of Henderson Advertising.

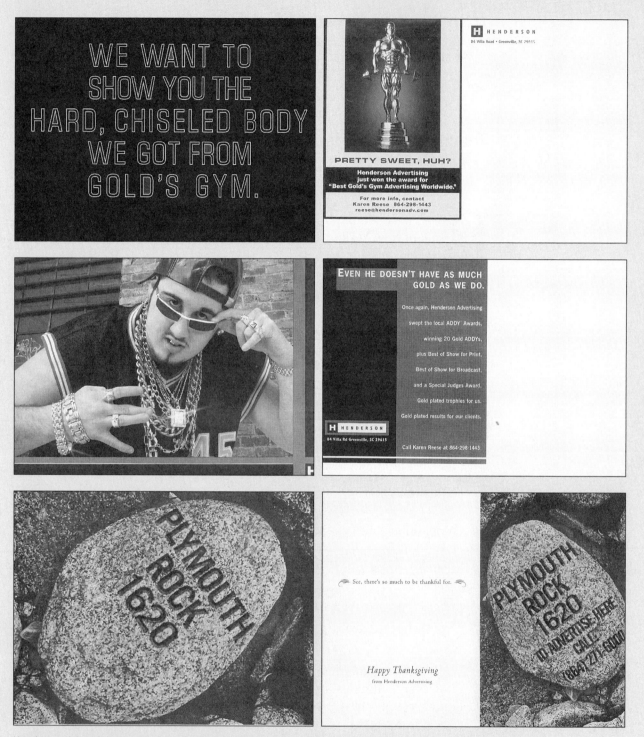

Henderson Advertising keeps their clients and vendors informed of their success stories through postcards such as these. Holidays, such as Thanksgiving, give the agency another reason to stay in touch.

We believe a brilliant strategy executed with style, insight, humanity, and consistency can draw a consumer to your product like metal to a magnet.

We also believe the opposite is true. A dull, vanilla, hand-me-the-remote execution might garner some immediate results, but holds no lasting sway over your customer. You've given them a reason to think about you today. And a reason to forget about you tomorrow.

Brilliant advertising, brilliant branding, can keep them coming. Those consumers are yours . . . unless you blow it.

After all, there is no rational reason why someone should pay $150 for sneakers that do no more than the $60 pair. But it happens. No reason why a little German car in the shape of a pimple should enjoy such loyal, cult status. But it does. No reason a beer company's product is considered the crème de la crème in this country, but a workingman's beer in Europe. But that's the case. Those companies have built brands using advertising as an atomic bomb against their competitors.

Never be bland. Never be who you aren't. Never assume a potential customer makes his or her decision for strictly rational reasons.

Rational reasons get you on the shelf. It's the price of entry. Irrational reasons are the tie-breaker.

Make them think.

Make them feel.

And you'll make them yours.

Henderson's ability to uncover consumer and brand insights and then act on them has made their clients' businesses flourish. Colonial Supplemental Insurance has enjoyed a 40-percent increase in sales in advertised markets. Costa Del Mar sunglasses has seen their sales increase by 23 percent, and FlexCheck has experienced a phenomenal 69-percent return on advertising investments.

In the process of making their clients' businesses grow, Henderson has grown, too. Billings have increased from $58 million in 2000 to $70 million in 2002. Henderson's success seems perfectly rational to us even if they do use some seemingly irrational methods to get there.

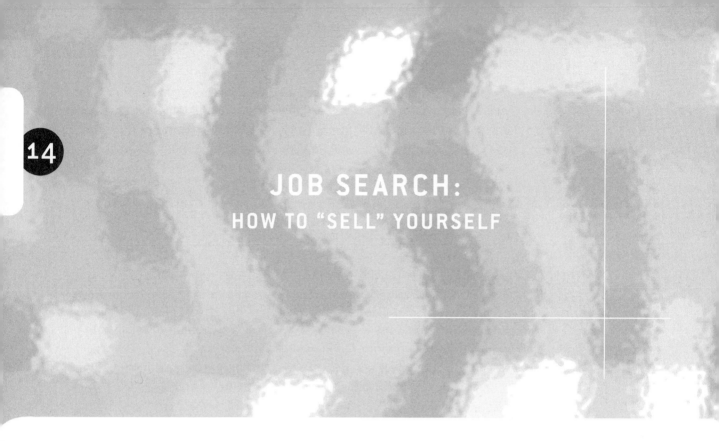

JOB SEARCH:
HOW TO "SELL" YOURSELF

If you know how to market products and services, you know how to market yourself. The principles you've learned in this book that help you sell frozen peas and laundry detergent also work when you're selling yourself. What do you do? The same thing, only now you are the product. So you develop objectives, pinpoint your strongest selling points, assess the competition, and research your target audience. Only then do you go about creating the message that will land you a job.

Step 1: State Your Objectives

Your career objectives should be as specific as possible. Do you want to work at a creative hot shop in Minneapolis? At a major agency in New York? For a small firm in your hometown? What about a Chicago agency that specializes in package-goods accounts? A direct-marketing company? The advertising department of a national retailer?

If you tell yourself that you'll settle for any job, that's just what you'll do. Settle. Why not go after the job you really want? After all, you can always regroup if your first choice doesn't work out, and you will have learned a lot in the process.

When Ed Chambliss graduated, he wanted to move to Atlanta and work for a major agency. After studying the *Red Book,* talking with professors, and reading the trade journals, Ed knew he wanted to work for BBDO in Atlanta. Rather than send a mass mailing of his résumé to every agency in Atlanta,

Ed targeted BBDO with a self-promotion piece, EDWEEK, a parody of the advertising trade publication, *Adweek,* where every article was about Ed and his accomplishments. The lead story was headlined "BBDO Hires Chambliss" and had made-up quotes from BBDO's executive creative director. Ed got the job and never had to fall back on his second or third choice. Ed believes his self-promotion piece worked for three reasons. First, everyone in advertising reads *Adweek,* so the creative directors understood the parody. Second, everyone loves to see his or her name in print. Third, it reinforces Ed's name and makes him stand out from the other job applicants.

Step 2: Pinpoint Your Strongest Selling Points

This is not the time to be modest. Jot down every compliment you've ever gotten from professors, employers, and peers. Jog your memory for ways that you've demonstrated creativity, leadership, and entrepreneurship. What's your greatest accomplishment? Your proudest moment? The biggest hurdle you've overcome? What would your best friend say about you? Your favorite professor? Your current employer or internship supervisor?

Jot down reasons why your educational or work background is superior. For example, if you've completed a journalism program that's accredited by the Accrediting Council on Education in Journalism and Mass Communications, you should have a well-rounded liberal arts education. This will be viewed as a plus by most employers, who want copywriters well versed in literature, history, the arts, and social sciences.

Step 3: Assess the Competition

Start by looking around your classes. How does your work compare? Do you consistently earn praise from your professors and peers? Does your work get displayed as an example of excellence?

Check out the competition outside your school. Many advertising programs display the work of their best students in their catalogs and Web sites. How does your work compare to the work done by advertising students at the Portfolio Center or the Creative Circus in Atlanta? The AdCenter at Virginia Commonwealth University? The Miami Ad School? Parsons School of Design or the School of Visual Arts in New York? The Art Center in Pasadena, California? Be forewarned. Many agency recruiters are sold on the polished portfolios of students from trade schools such as these. Examples of student work from the Creative Circus are found in Figures 5-1, 7-1, 14-1, and 14-2.

Study how your ads and designs compare to the work published in *CMYK,* a magazine devoted to student work. Also, compare your work to the industry's standard of excellence. Study the award books and publications devoted to creativity. *Communication Arts, Print, HOW, Advertising Age's Creativity,* and *Archive* are filled with creative work from the professionals. Pay attention to the agencies that are doing great work and see if your style and theirs are a good match.

Figure 14-1
Copy reads: No backseat. No backseat driver. The bigger the backseat, the more trouble there is. The Audi TT eliminates all 'You're going too fast' and 'Watch out for the biker' chatter. Comfort is good but minivan comfort isn't. The TT has forty cubic feet of room and a large trunk. You'll forget you don't have a backseat. Small enough to get you through your daily grind, but big enough for that weekend getaway to the beach. Hey, smaller is better.

Copy reads: Lots of elbow room if you hang one out the window. Just enough. No more. We at Audi purposely spent more time on the TT's design than contemplating how many bags of groceries you're hauling. Shouldn't luxurious, yet sporty cars be small? How else could a TT weave in and out of traffic while others sit in their SUV's and stare?

Courtesy of The Creative Circus. Cecily Herbst, student art director, and Dana Johns, student copywriter.

Step 4: Research Your Target Audience

Major agencies receive thousands of job inquiries every year. How do you set yourself apart from the hordes? By knowing your target audience. If you send a form letter, you're bound to receive a form rejection letter—or no response at all. However, if you demonstrate that you really want to work at a specific agency, you're more likely to capture its interest. Write to specific

Figure 14-2
This work from students at The Creative Circus is smart and unexpected. No wonder why so many agencies rave about the books that come out of this portfolio school in Atlanta.

individuals. In your letters, say something about them. Mention an account they just landed. Compliment them on an award they just won. Refer to a write-up about them you read in *Advertising Age* or *Adweek*. And if you learned about the opening through a personal contact, be sure to mention that right up front. A letter that starts outs "So-and-so suggested that I write to you" is bound to be noticed.

Also be sure that you're the right match for the company that you're targeting. If your creative style is outrageous and a bit irreverent, don't bother with an agency that is known for its conservative advertising. If you hope to land a job at a creative hot shop, make sure everything you show pushes the boundaries. If you want to work in New York, develop strong package-goods and print campaigns. Smaller markets want to see spots for things like hospitals and banks, plus some strong radio and newspaper ads. Direct marketers want to see copy that intrigues while containing a lot of detail. Retailers want to see a range of things, from high fashion to high tech.

How will you learn about the agency or company that you're targeting? The same way you learn about a product. Through research.

Secondary Research

As with any research project, you should start out by reviewing the information that already exists. There are excellent reference guides that will point your job search in the right direction, including the following:

- *The Red Book* has more than 8000 agency profiles and includes the names of key personnel.
- *The Adweek Directory* lists more than 6000 advertising agencies, public relations firms, and media-buying services.
- *Advertising Age* publishes special editions that are useful in a job search. Leading National Advertisers profiles the 100 top U.S. marketers by media spending and includes the names of their advertising agency and the names of key advertising and corporate personnel. The Agency Report lists gross income, volume, number of employees, and offices of the 25 largest global advertising organizations.

Annual publications are a great starting point, but they can't reflect all the changes that are constantly taking place. After all, agencies are winning and losing clients all the time. People are being promoted, retiring, and changing jobs. Therefore, you should set aside some time each week to peruse *Advertising Age, Adweek,* the marketing section of the *Wall Street Journal,* and the advertising column in the *New York Times.* These publications will keep you apprised of client moves, changes in agency personnel, and job openings. By being current, you'll show your passion for the business. You'll also save yourself the embarrassment of sending a letter to a person who no longer works at the agency or of complimenting the agency on work it did for a client it just lost.

Be sure to check out the agency's home page on the Web. Call the public relations department and ask for an annual report or clippings they have on file. Ask your professors and professional contacts what they know about the agency.

Primary Research

Now that you have a good foundation, it's time to customize your search. It's time to find out if you'll fit in with a particular agency or company. So where do you start?

1. *Go for an informational interview.* You may hear, "We don't have any positions open, but I'd be happy to talk to you." Do it. The feedback you receive on your portfolio will be worth it. Always end by asking for other names. Advertising is a small business; a name can get you over a variety of moats and walls, not to mention past the receptionist. And when you get home, be sure to write them a thank-you note.

2. *Network.* Networking is a key component of your job search. At first, some people are uncomfortable doing this because they think they'll be perceived as being pushy or obnoxious. Don't feel this way. Politely ask your professors, internship supervisors, parents' friends, and neighbors if they have contacts or know of any openings, and you may be pleasantly surprised. Also be sure to take advantage of every networking opportunity offered while you're in school. Join the student chapter of the American Advertising Federation, the American Marketing Association, the

Public Relations Student Society of America, or all three. If your school doesn't have one of these chapters, consider starting one—it'll be a great way to demonstrate your leadership abilities to prospective employers.

3. *Attend professional meetings.* Local advertising clubs will often invite students to attend their meetings for free or at a reduced rate. When you go to these meetings, don't stand in the corner. Mingle. Make contacts. Get business cards. You'll be surprised at how receptive most people will be. Even if you're not job hunting locally, there's a good chance you'll bump into someone who knows someone in the town that you want to move to. And contacts can open doors.

4. *Search online.* There are a variety of Web sites for jobs in advertising. Here are a few:

   - *Career Builder.* Career Builder has a vast job-search engine, but the jobs aren't necessarily aimed at recent college graduates. The site includes a résumé-posting service and a somewhat helpful college connection section. Go to www.careerbuilder.com.

   - *Monster.* The mother of all job-search sites lists job openings by location, category, and keyword. It also allows you to post your résumé and offers career advice. Go to www.monster.com.

   - *NationJob.* NationJob lists hundreds of jobs, ranging from entry-level to senior positions. For advertising and media jobs, go to www.nationjob.com/media. For marketing and sales jobs, go to www.nationjob.com/marketing.

   - *Talentzoo.* Talentzoo is devoted to advertising jobs. In addition to listing jobs, it offers important information on résumé writing and employment trends. Go to www.talentzoo.com.

Step 5: Develop a Creative Communication Message

You've got a clearly defined objective. You understand your target audience and the competition. You know your key selling points. Now it's time to launch your campaign. You will need a cover letter, a résumé, and a portfolio. You may also want to create a self-promotion piece. And you'll certainly want to develop your interviewing skills.

Your Cover Letter

Your letter must not merely say, "Here's my résumé, and do you have a job?" It must demonstrate how well you write, how passionate you are about advertising, and how much potential you have.

Thousands of applicants never make it to the interview because their letters are poor. So how do you enhance your chances for an interview? Start by addressing your letter to an actual person. Do not use "To whom it may concern." Find out the name of the creative director by looking up the

Figure 14-3

Here's what not to do: Don't send a letter to the personnel department—send it to the creative director. Don't send it to "sir or madam"—send it to a specific person. Don't bore this person with details about your past—intrigue him or her by showing how your past fits into the agency's future. Don't mention negative publicity about the agency. And don't expect this person to call you.

Personnel Department
McCann-Erickson Worldwide
485 Madison Avenue
New York, NY 10098

Dear Sir or Madam:

This spring I will earn my B.A. in Journalism from the University of South Carolina with a major in advertising and public relations and a cognate in marketing.

I will be seeking a position with an advertising agency in the New York area, preferably as a copywriter, and would like to talk with you about the possibility of employment with McCann-Erickson.

I really enjoy writing copy and have taken two courses in creative strategy with Professor A. Jerome Jewler at Carolina. I have also completed courses in media, campaigns, ad research, ad management, and graphic production. I believe I have much to offer your agency and could make important contributions with my unique ideas and marketing expertise.

By the way, I note in the trade press that you are in trouble with the Nescafe campaign. I have been working up some roughs for Nescafe and would be happy to share them with you, if you're interested.

I look forward to hearing from you.

Sincerely,

Victoria Smith

Victoria Smith

---

agency in the *Red Book* or by calling the agency. Be sure to get the spelling and the gender correct. Robin can be a man or woman. So can Leslie, Pat, Lee, Kim, Beverly, and many others. When in doubt, call the receptionist and ask.

Now you've got your salutation. Start your letter by telling why you are writing. Then mention something nice, but not phony, about the company you're writing to or simply plunge into your sales pitch. The main body of the letter should tell this person why you should get the job. Be sincere and forthright. Use plain English and avoid jargon. Personalize your letter by mentioning something about your background or personality that gives some insight into you, but don't be too flip or casual. In closing, state that you will provide additional information if required. Don't ask the recipient to call you. Tell the recipient you'll be calling him or her. And be sure to follow through. Look at the two letters shown in Figures 14-3 and 14-4. Which one do you think is more persuasive and why?

Figure 14-4
This letter's got it right. It's written to the creative director, demonstrates a passion for advertising, offers examples of creativity, and shows initiative.

Roger C. Franklin
Executive Creative Director
McCann-Erickson Worldwide
485 Madison Avenue
New York, NY 10098

Dear Mr. Franklin:

I am writing at the suggestion of Brad Cummings, who is a longtime friend and mentor, and who knows of my desire to enter the world of advertising.

To be perfectly honest, I want to be a copywriter, and I've prepared myself for this difficult task from the time I was about thirteen--devouring advertising on radio, TV, in magazines and newspapers every chance I could get. The walls of my bedroom were literally plastered with my favorite ads. It didn't make Mom happy, but I couldn't resist clipping 'em and hanging 'em.

It's no wonder I pursued a degree in advertising at the University of South Carolina. And while my peers were earning C's and B's, I was getting A's in creative strategy, graphic design, campaigns, and marketing. My professors told me I was one of the best students they had seen in years. I began to believe it.

Now I want you to judge me. I have a portfolio of what I consider to be my best work, and I would be honored if you would grant me a few brief moments to share this with you.

I'm planning to be in New York the week of April 27, and will call you that Monday to see if you can see me sometime during that week.

In the meantime, I'm enclosing my résumé and a few samples. Once again, thanks for hearing me out. I'm excited about the prospect of meeting you and having you critique my work.

Cordially,

Victoria Smith

Your Résumé

Employers want to know what you did, where, and for how long. Be thorough but don't overembellish. One page should be enough to convince an employer to invite you for an interview. More than two pages will indicate that you don't know how to be concise.

Writing your résumé   Your résumé should be attractive, with no misspellings or errors in either punctuation or grammar. Organize it with titles and block sections. At the top of your résumé, put your name, address, phone number, and email address. Should you include your career goals? Some say absolutely; others say never. If you can work your goals into your cover letter, you won't have to include them here. It's a good idea to list the position you are seeking, such as "copywriter." Most businesses will want to know at least that much. It confuses companies when you say that you'll take any kind of job with them.

Avoid "I" and "me" sentences. Start with such phrases as "improved the service procedures," "supervised ten people," "managed three departments," "created . . . ," "designed . . . ," "introduced . . . ," and so on. Emphasize your accomplishments, not your duties. Emphasize assets, not liabilities. Omit anything unfavorable, but always tell the truth. You will most likely be checked.

In terms of personal information, include only what is relevant. Do not include a photo or such things as number of children in your family or health. You may wish to include memberships in associations, travel, language fluency, and computer skills if they are relevant to the job that you seek. If you're applying for a job as an account executive, it's not relevant that you know how to design ads in Quark. References may or may not be included. If your references are prominent people and you have their permission, definitely include them. But avoid the generic line "references available upon request" because it says nothing.

Brad Karsh, President of Job Bound and former vice president/recruiting director at Leo Burnett, offers these important suggestions:[1]

- Write your résumé so that the most important information is read first—not only top to bottom, but also from left to right. If you waited tables at the Olive Garden last summer but interned in the marketing department at Procter & Gamble the summer before, put the P&G information first. Also, keep the same discipline in mind when listing experiences. Don't say, "Fall 2004–Summer 2005, Sigma Alpha Beta Fraternity, President." Instead, say, "President, Sigma Alpha Beta Fraternity, Fall 2004–Summer 2005."

- Keep in mind that résumés are not data dumps of everything you did in your life. You need to focus. Just as a good ad doesn't tell you every single thing about a product, the same holds true for a résumé.

- Craft a résumé that's full of accomplishments as opposed to job descriptions. Karsh says this is where virtually all résumés fall short. Your objective is to record your accomplishments. What did you do that was different? What results did you generate? What skills did you demonstrate or acquire? How were you selected? Whenever possible, use facts and figures to back up what you claim.

Almost any intern can claim something along the following lines:

Leo Burnett, USA, Intern, McDonald's, Summer 2004

- Assisted account executive on new product launch
- Prepared competitive analysis
- Attended brainstorming meetings and agency seminars

---

[1] Brad Karsh, "How to Write an Amazing Résumé," *AAF Communicator,* Spring 2003, pp. 2–4. Used by permission.

But few interns can say the following:

Leo Burnett, USA, Intern, McDonald's, Summer 2004

- Assisted account executive on most-successful burger launch in region's history
- Prepared 12-agency competitive analysis presented to client's upper management
- Selected as one of two interns from more than 150 applicants

The second version is much stronger. Karsh suggests that you talk to a friend, family member, college advisor, or industry professional and discuss in excruciating detail all of your experiences. Chances are that you'll find the good stuff. Karsh's rule is . . . if the person who did the job or held a position with you, after you, or before you can put the same thing down on a résumé, you haven't done yourself justice.

Posting your résumé online   A variety of sites allow you to post your résumé online. For example, Monster Board offers résumé posting and a personal job-search agent that allows you to specify the types of jobs in which you're interested and then sends you information about matching job openings.

Before you post your résumé online, be aware of the pitfalls. There are horror stories of employees being caught by their bosses who have access to online résumés. In some cases, it's a perfectly innocent mistake, such as when a résumé is posted before the person found the current job. In other cases, it can be the work of an unscrupulous headhunter who has duplicated and reposted the person's résumé.

To protect yourself, *Fortune* magazine[2] suggests doing the following:

1. Date your résumé.
2. Include a legend that forbids unauthorized transmission by headhunters.
3. Ask the job site's administrator if résumés are ever traded.
4. Keep your résumé off Usenet news groups.
5. Cloak your résumé by not including your name or employer.

Self-Promotion Ads

The same rules that apply for great advertising work for self-promotion pieces. Combine an unexpected headline and visual to make a relevant selling point. One such ad featured the headline "President Seeks Entry-Level Job." Your attention is captured right away, and you want to read further. In the body copy, you learn that the person was president of his fraternity and that this helped him learn how to motivate people. That's relevant and unexpected.

[2] Jerry Useem, "Read This Before You Put a Résumé Online," *Fortune,* 24 May 1999, p. 290.

Another ad had a Florida lottery ticket attached to it with the headline "Call Me on Monday to See If You Won." The ticket was for a multimillion-dollar lottery and was sent to a Dallas agency by a student from Florida who wanted to relocate. A mere investment of $1 got the student something money can't buy—a phone call from the creative director.

Toby Jenkins landed a summer internship driving the Oscar Mayer Wienermobile by writing new lyrics to the famous jingle "Oh I wish I were an Oscar Mayer Wiener." Her lyrics demonstrated that she had the kind of spunk that's needed to travel around the country in a 4-ton orange hot dog.

Some people try to stand out by doing something outrageous. One student sent a roll of toilet tissue with the message "They said advertising is full of shit. But I don't mind starting at the bottom." This concept won an award in *How* magazine's self-promotion contest. But be forewarned before you consider something over the top like this—not everyone will agree with this type of humor, and many will find it offensive.

Some people play on their own names to make an impression. Jennie Moore landed a job at Ogilvy & Mather with a brochure that showed she was "Moore intelligent. Moore passionate. Moore involved. And Moore dedicated." Each page elaborated on these qualities and showed why Jennie was perfect for a job in account management. If you use this approach, be certain your name makes a relevant connection to why you're perfect for the job. Musician Jim Brickman once sent bricks to production houses to get his name noticed. He laughs about it in hindsight. For starters, the bricks were costly to ship. Many arrived broken. And most recipients didn't have a clue what to do with their brick other than to toss it in the trash. But more important, the bricks failed to communicate why he would make a great jingle writer.

How should you go about creating an ad for yourself? Start by jotting down such attributes as these:

- Something unusual, unique, or interesting about yourself from any period in your life
- Your interests, hobbies, collections, and spare-time activities
- A compliment paid you by a friend, family member, professor, advisor, or employer
- Your passion for advertising
- Details about the agency or company you want to be hired by and how you will fit in

Your Portfolio, or "Book"

Students need more than "good" books—they need great books to even be considered by a major agency, according to top creative directors who spoke to a group of advertising educators in a weekend creative symposium. Agencies admire books that break rules instead of complying with them—books that stand apart in smart ways, just as great advertisements stand apart.

The person behind the portfolio   What are agencies looking for in beginning writers and art directors? Here are some key qualities:

- *Originality in thinking.* Granted, that's highly subjective, but you don't even get an interview unless your work is special. Furthermore, the work and the person being interviewed have to connect in the mind of the interviewer.

- *Passion for the work.* This involves the ability to enthuse about how you came up with the ideas and bounce back from mistakes.

- *Enthusiasm for the world.* More than a fleeting knowledge of music, film, theater, art, and current trends in humor is highly regarded. So is travel, especially to places that are off the beaten track. Such is the stuff that good ideas come from.

- *A love affair with words and design.* This affair should be ongoing and all consuming.

- *Raw imagination.* For the book, the ideas don't have to be feasible. The agency can pull you back. It's much harder to push you further.

- *Knowledge of research and marketing.* This means you can converse intelligently about those subjects, but not to the extent that it restrains your creative product.

- *The guts to try the dumbest ideas.* Strike the emotions. Touch people. But don't do too much of a good thing. Too many puns can hurt you. Bad puns can hurt you. Then again, it's subjective.

The look of your portfolio   What type of portfolio should you use? A spiral book with acetate pages is a popular choice because it allows you to arrange and rearrange your work until everything has the best flow. You may wish to place your mounted works in a compact portfolio or briefcase, arranging them in a way that shows off each piece to its best advantage. However, this approach can get cumbersome. Some students spend extra money to laminate their work so that it has a professional look. Some show off their design skills by creating a special package to hold samples of their work (see Figure 14-5). Others display their techno-savvy by putting their work on disk or CD-ROM.

Keep in mind that the quality of your work will be what lands you the job, not how much money you spend. A typo will hurt your chances whether the piece is laminated, on disk, or photocopied. However, given a choice between two would-be creatives who both have great books, the individual who puts in the extra effort will probably rate higher.

Also keep in mind that you will often be asked to leave your book for later review. Therefore, you may need to develop several books or create a small "leave-behind" piece consisting of photocopies of your work.

John Sweeney offers this advice about what to include in your book:[3]

---

[3] John Sweeney, "Step Up Persistence to Get in Agency Door," *Advertising Age,* 2 May 1985. Used by permission.

Figure 14-5
Kristin Gissendanner further demonstrated her creativity by wrapping her portfolio in gift paper and tying it with a ribbon. Inside were samples of her work and her résumé.

Courtesy of Kristin Gissendanner.

1. *Demonstrate the campaign concept.* Make sure your first campaign is absolutely your best, and close with a flourish. First and last impressions carry weight.

2. *Adjust your portfolio to meet the needs of the interview.* If you want a simple formula, try this: one package-goods campaign (toothpaste, deodorant, trash bags, and so on), one hard-goods campaign (stereos, cameras, computers, refrigerators, and so on), one food or fashion campaign, one public service or tourism campaign, and one new product idea and an introductory campaign for it. At least one campaign should include TV, print, radio, and outdoor—a complete demonstration of the campaign concept. Use music once, demonstration once, and testimonials once. Give a range of solutions to a range of products.

3. *Choose products you like when possible.* Be forewarned, however. It's easy to write for products you like. You won't always have such freedom in the business. Also, if you try to beat American Express, Coke, and Macintosh, you will probably fail. Choose products that are not currently celebrated for their creative work. Also, don't do work on one of the agency's accounts. You may choose a strategy that was rejected by research.

Figure 14-5 (continued)

4. *Include at least two long-copy campaigns.* Many creative directors are suspicious of beginners. They are leery of smooth-talking, glitzy TV types who have no fundamental writing skills. Demonstrate your ability to write body copy conclusively by including at least two long-copy print ads that are substantially different in content. Show your ability to handle at least 300 words per ad.

5. *Make sure your scripts time properly.* The first sign of an amateur is a 30-second commercial that runs 58 seconds. Learn the proper scripting format. It's an easy way to look professional.

6. *Keep audience and strategy statements brief.* Agencies are looking for original thinking and strong writing skills, not marketing or research potential.

7. *Monitor your feedback.* If you get the same comment in many interviews, listen to it. If you get a range of responses to the same ad, welcome to the business.

Mistakes to avoid   Based on a survey of top U.S. creative directors, Alice Kendrick and her colleagues report that the biggest mistakes students make in their portfolios include the following:[4]

- Creating fancy storyboards that couldn't be produced for under $500,000 (some even questioned the appropriateness of TV storyboards in portfolios)
- Offering weak ideas or clever pieces that don't demonstrate what advertising can do
- Failing to develop campaigns
- Doing what has already been done instead of taking risks with new ideas
- Doing ads for products that already have great campaigns
- Revealing a noticeable lack of writing, thinking, and conceptual skills
- Showing too much work—and having too much finished work
- Overemphasizing execution and underemphasizing content
- Overusing puns
- Forgetting that the real challenge of advertising often involves making small differences important to consumers
- Putting more weight on polished work than on creative work
- Showing work that does not apply to advertising

---

[4] Alice Kendrick, David Slayden, and Sheri Broyles, "Real Worlds and Ivory Towers: A Survey of Top U.S. Agency Creative Directors," *Journalism and Mass Communication Educator,* Summer 1996, pp. 63–74. Used by permission.

The Interview

Relax! You shouldn't be nervous in an interview. The reason you've been invited for an interview is because they're interested in you. Feel confident but don't be so relaxed that you look as if you don't care. You need to show professionalism through appropriate attire, proper attitude, and preparation for the interview. Recruiters from J. Walter Thompson recall an unfortunate occasion when a candidate started the interview by opening a can of soda and then consumed it during the interview. Don't be mannequin-stiff, but don't put your feet up on the desk and gulp down a soft drink either.

Many interviewers state you shouldn't rehearse answers to questions because they will sound rehearsed. Instead, they recommend that you carefully consider your answer at the time the question is asked. However, many employment consultants say the opposite and insist that you must prepare yourself for an interview by anticipating the questions. So what's the answer? It's probably somewhere in-between. Prepare for the interview, but don't memorize your answers.

Although no two interviewers are alike, here are some typical questions:

1. *"Why do you want to work here?"* In other words, what do you know about the company? Do you really want to work there, or will you jump at any job offer?

2. *"Tell me about yourself."* It's a simple request, but if you're not prepared you will probably either ramble on or shrug your shoulders and say something dumb like "Shucks! There's not much to tell" or "Gee, I don't know where to start."

3. *"What are your strong points?"* Talk about things such as your ability to work on a team, your willingness to work long hours on creative projects, and your inquisitive nature—whatever you feel are qualities that will help you succeed in the job. But be honest.

4. *"What are your weak points?"* Try to come up with a weak point that will somehow show off a strong point. For example, you may have little patience with incompetent people, or you may be terrible in math. Although this may hurt your chances of getting a job in the media or research department, most creative people aren't expected to have this talent.

5. *"What ad campaign do you love the most?"* You could choose one of the agency's campaigns, but don't do this unless you really think it's good. The next logical question is "Why?"

6. *"What's the last book you read?"* They're not looking for the title of a textbook; they want to get a sense of who you are. Other similar questions include, "What's your favorite movie? Your favorite artist?"

7. *"Why did you leave your last job?"* Never say anything negative about your former employers. Instead, say something about how you're looking for new opportunities. How you want to move to a larger/smaller city. Or

how you were caught in corporate downsizing, which happens to the best of people.

8. *"What questions do you have?"* This is usually the last question, and in your quest to end the interview, you may be tempted to say you don't have any questions. Don't do this. By asking no questions, it will seem as if you're not that interested in the job or that you're not inquisitive, a definite no-no in this business. Remember, this is the last impression in the interview, your last chance to shine. When in doubt, ask the interviewer about his or her career at the agency. Ask about future growth opportunities. Ask when the hiring decision will be made. Don't be shy here—show you want the job!

After the Interview

Send a follow-up letter within two days of the interview. Reaffirm your interest in the position. Highlight one or two interesting points from the interview. Call about a week later and ask about the status of the opening.

What do you do if you feel the job interview didn't go well? Is it possible to get a second chance? Yes. Consider what happened to Stacey Staaterman who interviewed for a position with *Sports Illustrated for Kids.* Stacey was working for another magazine within the same company, so the job seemed a sure thing—until the interview. Stacey could tell the person who interviewed her just wasn't interested. After some investigating, Stacey learned the interviewer already had someone else in mind. How could she convince him she was the best person? Why not pitch him like a client? Inspired by the trading cards that are found in *Sports Illustrated for Kids,* Stacey created an ad with the headline "Let's trade." The ad had a removable baseball card with—you guessed it—Stacey's picture. The back of the card featured her career highlights and positions played. After she won the job, Stacey informed her professional contacts through a self-promotion piece. This time, she was able to say, "I got traded" (see Figure 14-6).

Other Job-Hunting Suggestions

Enter the Award Shows

What's the first thing you see in the lobby and offices of just about every agency? Awards, awards, and more awards. According to an American Advertising Federation/*Advertising Age* poll, 60 percent of client/advertiser respondents felt that their ability to attract business was influenced by the awards they had won.[5] You don't need to have published work to win an

---

[5] "Awards Bring Laurels but No Guarantees," *Advertising Age,* 17 April 1995, p. 14.

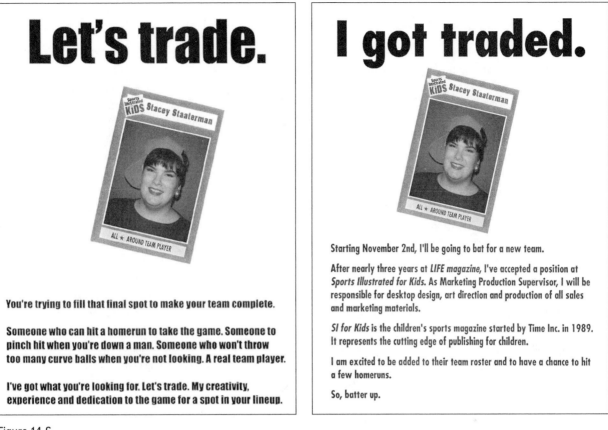

Figure 14-6
Stacey Staaterman used a feature found in *Sports Illustrated for Kids* to win a position with the magazine's promotions department. After she won the job, she let her professional contacts know she had been traded.

award. There are a number of competitions that allow speculative work. Some of the student competition sponsors include the American Advertising Federation, the Clios, the Direct Marketing Association, the Promotional Products Association, and *CMYK* magazine. Some competition sponsors reward the winners with cash prizes, trips, and internships. All of them give the winners an accomplishment to highlight on résumés. See the box on the next page for a listing of student competitions.

Practice Persistence

One creative director told all applicants that no jobs were available and then interviewed only those who called back despite the lack of jobs. Agencies can be closed to job applicants for months and suddenly be in desperate need of people. You have to get used to it.

CREATIVE COMPETITIONS

Does your work make the cut? There's one way to find out. Have professionals judge it against the best work of other students. The top creative directors judge the following competitions. Also, check with your professors and your local advertising club for other possible opportunities.

Andy Student Awards. Sponsored by the Advertising Club of New York, any student in an accredited institution of higher learning may enter and compete for a $5000 scholarship and an invitation to the Andy Awards show. For more information, go to www.andyawards.com.

Art Directors Club of New York Student Awards. Students enrolled in undergraduate or graduate programs in advertising, graphic design, photography, illustration, and new media may submit published or unpublished work. Winning work becomes a part of a traveling exhibition. For more information, go to www.adglobal.org.

Athena Student Awards. Sponsored by the Newspaper Association of America, students submit single ads and campaigns created for newspapers and compete for the grand prize of $5000. For more information, go to www.naa.org.

Clio Student Awards. Students enrolled in an accredited advertising, film, or design program compete for the opportunity to pick up a coveted Clio statue at the awards show. For more information, go to www.clioawards.com.

One Show. Undergraduate and graduate advertising majors create an ad from a brief supplied by the One Club. Winners get a One Show pencil, cash prizes, and publication in the One Show annual. For more information, go to www.oneclub.com.

Radio-Mercury Awards. Rewards excellence in college-produced radio commercials with a $2500 cash award. For more information, go to www.radiomercuryawards.com.

TEAM COMPETITIONS

The following competitions use a case study approach and require student teams to conduct research, make media recommendations, and of course develop outstanding creative work.

AAF National Student Advertising Competition. Student teams develop an integrated marketing communications campaign for a national client. To enter, students must be members of their college's chapter of the American Advertising Federation. Winning schools receive cash prizes, and students get tremendous networking opportunities. For more information, go to www.aaf.org/college.

Bateman Competition. Teams of four or five students develop a public relations campaign for a sponsoring client. Winning schools get cash prizes, and students get great experience and networking opportunities. Students must be members of their college's chapter of the Public Relations Student Society of America. For more information, go to www.prsa.org.

DMEF Collegiate Echo Competition. Teams of up to four students develop a direct marketing plan to solve the challenge presented by a national client. Winning teams go to a major industry conference and get promotional gifts. For more information, go to www.the-dma.org/dmef.

PUBLICATIONS

See your work in print. Better yet, have top creative directors see your work in print.

CMYK. A magazine devoted to student work and judged by professionals invites students to submit advertising, design, photography, and illustrations. For more information, go to www.cmykmag.com.

Communication Arts. The illustration and photography competitions accept unpublished work. The advertising and design competitions accept only published work seen by a substantial audience. For more information, go to www.commarts.com/CA/.

How. Annuals feature-winning work from the Interactive Design Competition, the International Design Competition, and the Self-Promotion Competition. For more information, go to www.howdesign.com.

I.D. The October issue publishes the best student work and is sent to leading design firms, along with a letter introducing the competition winners. The Best of Show winner receives $1000. For more information, go to www.idonline.com/sdr.

Explore All Options

The advertising agency is by no means the only place for a rewarding career in copy or design. Many manufacturing and service companies maintain in-house advertising departments. Likewise, many retailers have sizable advertising departments that offer impressive growth opportunities. Also, check the printing firms, which might need creative assistance for some of their clients. See what creative positions exist within the media—at newspapers and magazines, radio and TV stations, and cable TV companies. Consider the burgeoning fields of direct marketing and business-to-business advertising. Don't forget graphic design studios and production houses, which may need writers and art directors. Above all, be patient and persistent. If you know that you are talented, the right job will come along. Best of luck!

Suggested Activities

1. Write a résumé for a job in advertising. Now compare it to the résumé of a friend who is in your same class. Are your résumés interchangeable, or have you each highlighted your unique strengths and accomplishments?

2. Write a cover letter to accompany your résumé. In preparation, jot down anything unusual about yourself that might be of interest and carefully evaluate what you've written before you decide what to include. Remember that your cover letter should communicate something about the kind of person you are, as well as express your interest in and enthusiasm and qualifications for the position.

3. Create a self-promotion piece using the guidelines in Activity 2.

4. Interview a local advertising professional about the proper way to apply for a job. Assuming that you would be applying for a position in copy or design, ask what sort of portfolio you would need to develop and how you should present your work.

Search Online! Discovering More About Landing the Job

Use InfoTrac College Edition to discover more about landing a job in advertising. Try these phrases and others for Key Words and Subject Guide searches: *career objectives, job resume, job cover letter, advertising agency hiring trends, hiring trends in advertising, advertising jobs, networking + jobs, advertising portfolio, interviewing.*

The following Web sites offer advice on the job search:

www.10minuteresume.com

www.collegegrad.com

www.talentzoo.com

ITT Industries' Corporate Advertising Campaign: Putting a Face on a Large Corporation

By Sue Westcott Alessandri, S. I. Newhouse School of Public Communications, Syracuse University

Corporate advertising promotes the company itself rather than any individual product brands. Often, a company develops a corporate advertising campaign because it feels the public is not fully aware of what it does. Such was the case with New York–based ITT Industries. The company launched a campaign in September 1998 in an attempt to raise the level of awareness of itself as an engineering and manufacturing company.

The campaign was intended to reach several audiences, including vendors, the financial community, and ITT's own employees, and ITT wanted to promote itself "in a memorable way," according to Thomas Martin, senior vice president and director of Corporate Relations, who oversaw the campaign's development.

ITT found the solution to educating the company's diverse audiences beneath the surface—quite literally beneath the surface. The broadcast component of the campaign was launched with a television ad featuring an assortment of marine life singing Handel's "Hallelujah Chorus." From a strategic perspective, this ad accomplished the goal of any corporate advertising campaign: It promoted the corporate brand by giving an otherwise abstract company a personality. In ITT's case, this particular ad educated the public about the importance of clean water, which ITT can deliver with the help of its Fluid Technology Division.

Additional television spots took a slice-of-life approach, and each was successful in explaining a very complicated business in a simple yet creative way. Also, media was chosen that would reach the diverse audiences that ITT needed to educate. Ads aired on CNN, CNBC, and on local news programs in major markets such as New York; Washington, DC: Boston; and Chicago.

Over time, ITT adopted a print campaign that used full-color, vivid photography to highlight its four divisions: Fluid Technology, Electronic Components, Defense Electronics and Services, and Motion and Flow Control. For example, an ad for ITT's Defense Electronics and Services division features the image of a fighter pilot walking away from his jet and into the sunset.

Courtesy of ITT Industries.

He has no idea ITT Industries
helps track his missions.
But at Mach 1.2,
he knows exactly where he is.

Knifing through a mile of sky every five
seconds tightens tolerances. GPS responds
with positioning information accurate to the
foot. ITT satellite transmitters send GPS
information not just to fighter jets, but to
every receiver that flies, floats, rolls or walks
across the planet.
　　ITT believes that technology should work
undetectably. In this case, keeping everybody
from jet pilots to hikers in the right place.
Out of the proverbial woods.

DEFENSE ELECTRONICS AND SERVICES
ELECTRONIC COMPONENTS
FLUID TECHNOLOGY
MOTION AND FLOW CONTROL

ITT Industries
Engineered for life

www.itt.com

Strategically, the ad shows how ITT is capable of delivering a global positioning system (GPS) that "responds with positioning information accurate to the
foot." An ad for the Motion and Flow Control division features the headline
"Over 6,000,000 boaters don't know ITT Industries helps keep them on an
even keel." The strategy of using the simple image of a sailor aboard a small
vessel illustrates a company that can help keep "water safely at arm's length
or comfortably within reach."

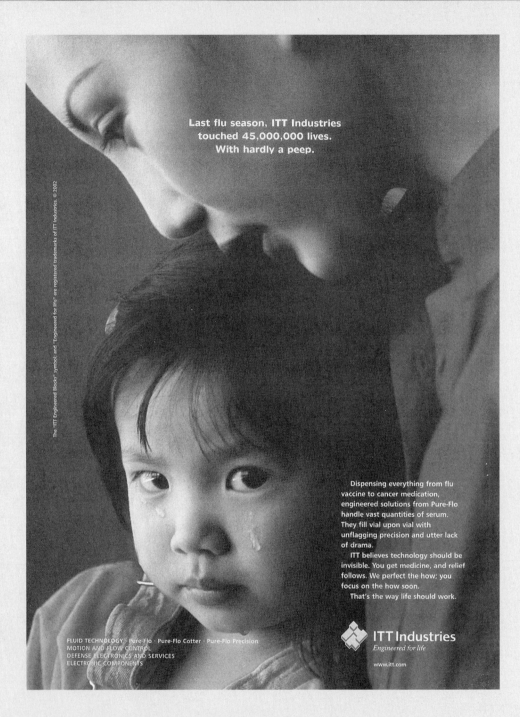

Last flu season, **ITT Industries**
touched 45,000,000 lives.
With hardly a peep.

The "ITT Engineered Blocks" symbol, and "Engineered for life" are registered trademarks of ITT Industries. © 2002

Dispensing everything from flu
vaccine to cancer medication,
engineered solutions from Pure-Flo
handle vast quantities of serum.
They fill vial upon vial with
unflagging precision and utter lack
of drama.
    ITT believes technology should be
invisible. You get medicine, and relief
follows. We perfect the how; you
focus on the how soon.
    That's the way life should work.

FLUID TECHNOLOGY · Pure-Flo · Pure-Flo Cotter · Pure-Flo Precision
MOTION AND FLOW CONTROL
DEFENSE ELECTRONICS AND SERVICES
ELECTRONIC COMPONENTS

ITT Industries
Engineered for life

www.itt.com

During the several years the campaign ran, it became apparent to ITT
executives that television was less practical than print in terms of reaching a
targeted audience, so in 2002 the company decided not to run additional TV
spots. Instead, ITT began to put its media budget to use running the print
ads in vehicles that would achieve the company's reach and frequency goals.

ITT and its agency developed a media plan that included a combination of horizontal trades, including *Business Week, Barron's, Forbes, Fortune,* and mainstream titles such as *Time* and *Newsweek.* And because 30 percent of ITT's revenues are derived from its defense division, the company placed ads in some vertical trades meant to target the Washington leadership, including *Congressional Quarterly* and *National Journal.* The company also used similar trade publications for additional key markets, such as water technology, irrigation, and communication.

During a campaign and certainly at the end of the campaign, a company measures its true success by measuring results. Because it is nearly impossible to make cause-and-effect arguments based on advertising, it is also nearly impossible to directly link the advertising to an increased stock price, but ITT does look at the relationship between the two.

In addition, ITT also uses several other methods to quantify the success of its advertising efforts. For example, in addition to calculating the actual reach and frequency of its chosen media vehicles, the company analyzes the media vehicles' own surveys that measure recall and message retention. By analyzing these two measures, the company is able to prove it is reaching the right audience with the appropriate frequency. More important, these efforts reinforce to the company that the appropriate audience is paying attention. To track more specific results, the company employs familiarity and favorability surveys to measure its success in reaching targeted audience segments.

Finally, the company's own employees represent the company's largest single block of shareholders and therefore were an important audience for the ITT corporate advertising campaign. To reach this target, ITT packaged the campaign on a CD and distributed it to all employees. To measure success among this constituency, the company tracked employees' knowledge of the ads over time in a creative and interactive way. ITT received several hundred responses to a "favorite ad" contest that simultaneously measured recognition and likeability of the ads.

APPENDIX
ASSIGNMENTS

Build a Campaign Step by Step

Get a recent copy of *Advertising Age* and turn to the "Account Action" section. Select a client who is looking for a new agency and complete the following assignments as you read each of the following chapters.

Chapter 1: Critique the client's current advertising campaign. Does it meet the definition of *creativity* as discussed in this book? What are the strengths of the current campaign? The weaknesses? How do the client's ads compare to the competitions' ads? Why do you think the client wants a new agency?

Chapter 2: Does the client's current campaign reflect diversity? If so, does it do it in a positive way, or does it perpetuate stereotypes?

Chapter 3: Conduct primary and secondary research for this client. Address the following:

- What are trends in the client's industry?
- How does the client compare to its competitors?
- What do consumers think of the client and its competitors?
- What real or perceived differences make the client special?

Chapter 4: Using the research you compiled in the previous assignment, write a strategy statement for the client.

Chapter 5: Using the strategy statement you completed in the previous assignment, develop 20 ideas for ads for the client. These ideas can be sketches or described briefly in words. Present your ideas to the class for feedback. When critiquing other students' ideas, be sure to use the suggestions in the chapter on effective use of criticism.

Chapter 6: Taking the best idea developed in the previous assignment, write copy for a print ad and describe what the visual will look like.

Chapter 7: Draw thumbnail sketches using the copy you just completed. Choose the best thumbnail and develop a detailed layout. Depending upon your computer skills, you may want to scan photos for a more finished look.

Chapter 8: Determine if the idea for your print campaign can translate effectively into radio. If the print ad relies on a visual to be understood, will you be able to communicate that image through sound? If not, develop a new concept for radio, still following the strategy statement you completed in Chapter 4. Then write a :30 or :60 spot.

Chapter 9: Determine if the idea for your print campaign can translate effectively into television. If the print ad uses long copy, will you be able to communicate the same points into a visual medium? If not, develop a new concept for TV, still following the strategy statement you completed in Chapter 4. Then develop a storyboard for a :30 spot.

Chapter 10: Develop a direct-mail piece for your client. A letter with an envelope will work best for such clients as credit card companies and nonprofit organizations who need longer copy to make their pitch. A catalog makes sense for retailers and business-to-business organizations. Postcards work for restaurants, hair salons, and other service-oriented clients who don't need much copy to remind consumers that they're ready to be of service. An offer in a print ad or free-standing insert (FSI) works for clients who sell personal care products or packaged foods.

Chapter 11: Look at your client's current Web site. Does it reflect the brand image of your client? Is it easy to navigate? Develop a site map and look for the home page that reflects the new image you've created for the client.

Chapter 12: Determine which alternatives to traditional advertising work best for your client. Then develop at least one of these ideas. It's not necessary to actually produce things such as store displays, special packaging, or premiums—just illustrate an image of what they will look like on an 8½- by 11-inch sheet of paper.

Chapter 13: Take the individual ads you've just completed and refine them, using feedback from your professor and classmates. As you revise your work, make certain that your ads have continuity and work as a campaign. Once you've revised your work, make a pitch to the class, pretending that they are the client. Address the following:

- What insights you have uncovered about the client's business and consumers
- The campaign theme and why it works
- Three to five examples from the campaign
- Why the client should hire you as its new agency

Chapter 14: Write a cover letter and self-promotion piece trying to get a job with the client or the agency that actually wins the business in the real world.

Ideas for Clients

American Classic Tea

More than 100 years ago, tea planters brought their finest ancestral tea bushes from China, India, and Ceylon to the Low Country of South Carolina. Now the direct descendants of those very plants have been lovingly restored to their former grandeur at the Charleston Tea Plantation, the only farm in the nation that grows tea. The owners of the farm, Mark Fleming and Bill Hall, have spent their working lives steeped in tea. Hall is a third-generation tea taster who apprenticed in London. Fleming, a horticulturist, began working on the plantation while it was a research-and-development facility for Thomas J. Lipton, Inc. Both owners insist on purity and use no pesticides or fungicides to grow the premium black pekoe tea.

Cascade Plastic 2-in-1 Booster

Have you ever tried to wash a plastic container after you stored spaghetti or lasagna in it? The sauce leaves a disgusting orange film that's impossible to remove. Until now. Just add 3 tablespoons of Cascade Plastic Booster to your dishwasher and presto! The plastic container comes out looking new. It's also a great way to clean and freshen your dishwasher.

This product contains benzoyl peroxide. It is not for hand dishwashing, and the label advises against prolonged skin contact. Cost is about $3 for a 6.8-ounce tube. That's a lot cheaper than replacing a Tupperware bowl. But how will you be able to convince people it beats buying the disposable containers and just tossing them if they get stained?

Fizzies Drink Tablets

Okay, this is definitely not for those with champagne tastes. It's for kids. Adolescents. Those seventh- and eighth-graders who love to do "yucky" things. And it's called Fizzies. Fizzies are instant sparkling-water drink tablets in cherry, grape, root beer, and orange.

Fizzies have a strong nostalgic appeal for folks who were around in the late 1950s—the "golden age of bomb shelters"—for this is when they were originally introduced. In the intervening years, they faded from the shelves. Now revived, they're an unusual novelty item for children (or perhaps for their parents—or even grandparents—who remember "the good ole days").

One particularly disgusting aspect of a Fizzie—you don't even need a glass of water to get in on the fun—is to just stick a tablet on your tongue;

soon you'll "spew blue goo" and have "colored foam oozing out of your mouth." Now how would you advertise this?

Gotta Go

Got a nuisance phone caller but you're too embarrassed to end the one-way conversation? An electronic device called Gotta Go can simulate the clicking sound made by the phone company's call-waiting service. The gadget is a small white box activated by pushing a button. It can be hooked up to any single-line phone. Its inventor came up with the idea after trying to find a polite way to end rambling phone conversations with his rather chatty girl-friend. She was calling every day at his busiest times and just gabbing. One day she actually offered to end the conversation after she heard the click-click sound of call waiting and realized he had another call coming through. It struck him that he was very relieved when someone else would call and he'd hear the click, because he didn't have to end the call himself. Gotta Go sells for $14.95, less than some call-waiting services provided by the telephone companies, which usually charge a recurring monthly fee for the service.

Hill Pet Drinks

Think of them as a cross between Gatorade, Evian, and Ensure . . . for dogs and cats. Dr. George Hill Pet Drinks are beef-flavored concoctions for dogs and cats (two formulations). They can be added to dry food or lapped up as a treat. Both are fortified with twelve vitamins and minerals and with brewer's yeast, commonly used to control fleas.

The products are packaged in 32- and 64-ounce "milk jug" bottles. The smaller ones sell for $1.39. Dr. Hill is a veterinarian from Salisbury, North Carolina, who thinks that dogs and cats don't get a balanced diet.

Meanwhile a competitor, Original Pet Drink Co., has signed four beverage bottlers to make and distribute its Thirsty Dog! and Thirsty Cat! products. These vitamin- and mineral-enriched waters are intended to replace tap water in a pet's bowl. A 1-liter bottle of either the Crispy Beef flavor Thirsty Dog! or the Tangy Fish flavor Thirsty Cat! sells for $1.79. Two new flavors are in the making, as are formulations for puppies, kittens, and older pets. Research shows that many pet owners give Evian and Perrier to their pets. "Once you give people more than water to drink, they do. Why shouldn't pets have that option, too?" asks president Marc Duke.

The Koolatron Portable Refrigerator

It looks like a cooler. It's just as portable, but it's really a refrigerator and food warmer all in one. NASA developed the technology for the Koolatron. They needed something less bulky and more dependable than traditional refrigeration coils and compressors. They found it in a solid-state component called the thermoelectric module, no bigger than a matchbook, that delivers the cooling power of a 10-pound block of ice. Aside from a small fan, this electronic fridge has no moving parts to wear out or break down. It costs the same as a good cooler plus one or two season's supply of ice (about the same as five family dinners out).

With the switch of a plug, the Koolatron becomes a food warmer for a casserole, burger, or baby bottle. It heats up to 125 degrees. Empty, it weighs only 12 pounds. Full, it holds up to forty 12-ounce cans. On motor trips, plug the Koolatron into your cigarette lighter. For picnics or fishing, it holds its cooling capacity for 24 hours. If you leave it plugged into your battery with the engine off, it consumes only 3 amps of power. $99 plus $12 shipping and handling. An optional ac adapter lets you use it in your recreation room, patio, or motel room. 1-800-number for orders.

Lawn Makeup

Possibly inspired by those infomercials for spray-on hair, this aerosol can of colored spray is for folks who don't want their lawns to look "browned out" come fall and winter. You can even choose the color to match your lawn or your mood, from Palm Green to Cedar Green to Spring Green to Kentucky Blue. The label promises that Lawn Makeup is virtually nontoxic and suggests that you spray a test area for color match. Definitely not for nature purists, so don't target them. Find your market and convince them it's better to have a healthy-looking lawn than a healthy lawn (just kidding).

Lipton Kettle Creations Home-Style Soup Mix

Cooks in 30 minutes. Just add water. A fresh way to make soup. Makes 32 fluid ounces, or four servings. No soup tastes better than homemade, but these days nobody's got the time. So just choose Lipton—their home-style soup mix is a wholesome mix of beans, grains, and pastas with herbs and spices. In other words, the ingredients are mixed for you. You add the water and let it simmer for 30 minutes. Four varieties: chicken with pasta and beans, bean medley with pasta, minestrone, and chicken and onion with long grain and wild rice. Packaged in attractive sealed bags with windows to show ingredients. Sell against canned soups, which heat in about 5 minutes.

Pizza Chef Gourmet Pizza

Locally owned and operated. Recipes prepared fresh on premises. Fresh herbs and spices used in sauce and on pizzas. Gourmet salads of fresh romaine lettuce are tossed with homemade salad dressings. Bake their own sub buns and offer pizzas on freshly made whole-wheat dough or traditional hand-tossed dough. All pizzas available baked or unbaked. All made to order.

Eat in, delivery, or pickup. Beer and wine on premises. Traditional pizza toppings plus "designer pizzas." Garden, Caesar, antipasto, southwestern chicken salads. Set this operation apart from the giants: Pizza Hut, Domino's, and so on.

Soundmate Personal Safety Device

Out with the old-fashioned way to locate your lost youngster—that is, by shouting his or her name at a volume that blows out store windows. You can now track your child electronically. The Child Safety Corporation of Miami markets a child-tracking monitor system. The system consists of a battery-operated transmitter, attached with a safety pin to the child, and a receiver carried by the parent. Each system sells for $99.

The device allows parents to log in an alarm range of 30 to 60 feet on the child's transmitter, which he or she wears like a pendant about the size of a silver dollar. If the child wanders farther than the preset range, an alarm is triggered on the parent's receiver. The alarm also sounds if the transmitter is switched off or immersed in water.

Tabasco 7-Spice Chili Recipe

For more than 100 years, the world's premier marketer of red-pepper sauce has been churning out its mainstay product with no sense of urgency about diversifying its line. The family-owned McIlhenny Co., makers of the Tabasco sauce that all but owns the hot-sauce market, started marketing other products only in 1973, when they introduced a Bloody Mary mix, followed by a picante sauce in 1982. Now they offer Tabasco Brand 7-Spice Chili Recipe mix, which plays off the strong heritage and widespread awareness of the Tabasco brand.

Tabasco is to red-pepper sauce what Xerox is to copiers. Despite repeated buyout offers, the McIlhenny family has remained dedicated to preserving the old family recipe. The sauce is aged in oaken vats on remote Avery Island, deep in Louisiana Cajun country and headquarters for the company. The fiery sauce is difficult to duplicate because of the Central American capsicum peppers used in the aging process, which involves mixing them with the local salt and vinegar.

Tabasco got its start in 1865 when Henry McIlhenny used peppers brought from Mexico's Yucatan Peninsula to create the sauce. For four generations, each patriarch has taken a daily walk, dressed in suit and tie, through the fields of peppers during the fall harvest to personally inspect the crop's quality, examine the mash in the vats, and watch the shipment of bottles. For more than a century, neither the bottle, the name, nor the logo has changed.

The chili is made from the finest vine-ripened tomatoes, green chilies, diced onions, genuine Tabasco pepper sauce, and a blend of seven herbs and spices known only to the company. All you add is fresh beef. The sauce comes in a "spaghetti sauce" jar. The label reads, "Tabasco Brand 7-Spice Chili Recipe. McIlhenny Co."

Tabasco dominates the hot-sauce category with 30 percent of the market. It is a growing market, riding the crest of a wave of popularity for spicy foods.

The Value of Independent Higher Education

America's private (or independent) colleges are doing well but see that they must strive to increase enrollment. So they have decided to pool funds to advertise their advantages and thereby increase inquiries and enrollments. One region, the Midwest, is combining its efforts through the Midwest Partnership of Independent Colleges (Illinois, Indiana, Michigan, Ohio, and Wisconsin) and needs to develop a print campaign.

The facts will run in regional editions of national newsweeklies, which have agreed to run some of the ads as a public service. This information on private colleges is not well known:

- Independent colleges perform an important service to our society, although many of their contributions go unrecognized, perhaps because of the stronger "clout" of major state-funded colleges and universities.

- They have an average faculty–student ratio of 14 to 1. Their enrollments represent all races and income brackets.

- The Midwest group enrolls 390,000 students, of which 48,000 are minorities. Eighty percent of students receive some form of financial aid, 20 percent of which comes from the schools' budgets—double that of ten years ago.

- They award 30 percent of all bachelor's degrees in the region, and 66 percent of their students go on to postgraduate studies.

- They contribute an estimated $10 billion and 350,000 jobs each year to their local economies.

- Six out of ten Fortune 500 CEOs attended an independent college.

It is therefore clear that these colleges are strong contributors to the educational, cultural, and economic well-being of our society.

The audience: Several choices are appropriate, but for this campaign think in terms of parents of junior and senior high school students in the Midwest region served by this group of colleges. Because financial aid is available, it is important to reach middle- and low-middle-income families, especially those who find it difficult to believe they can afford to send their children to anything but a large state university, where tuition tends to be more affordable and where grants are often available for lower-income levels. Because roughly 5 out of 40 college students are minorities, this is an audience that should not be overlooked. Essentially, the message should appeal to whites and minorities who believe in the value of diversity and who see or can be made to see the value in low faculty–student ratios and other appealing features of these schools that set them apart from the competition.

The competition: This is a broad category. People in the target market might consider the competition to be large state universities and community and technical colleges (lower cost). But you might also think of the competition as not going to college at all. Remember, this is an era of inflated costs for everything, and education is no exception. Students from this pool will almost certainly have to finance part of their education, either by working or through grants and scholarships. The general perception is that the smaller and more private the school, the less opportunity for any sort of financial support.

Create and Market a New Product

Think up a new product that satisfies certain needs of a particular group of consumers. Use the following guidelines to help you determine what your new product should offer. Then develop an advertising campaign for it.

1. What is the nature of the product? Give uses, description of packaging, approximate selling price, type of store carrying it, sizes available, and general shape and appearance.
2. What is its name? What does the name signify?
3. Who is the target audience, in demographic, lifestyle, and relationship terms? Is there a secondary audience?
4. What products will this one replace for this audience? In what ways will it be better than the products they were using before?
5. What is the key selling idea for this product?

SUGGESTED READINGS

Creativity

Aitchison, Jim. *Cutting Edge Advertising.* Singapore: Prentice Hall, 1999.

———. *Cutting Edge Commercials.* Singapore: Prentice Hall, 2001.

Baldwin, Huntley. *How to Create Effective TV Commercials.* Lincolnwood, IL: NTC Business Books, 1989.

Bendinger, Bruce. *The Copy Workshop Workbook.* Chicago: The Copy Workshop, 1993.

Bernbach, Evelyn, and Bob Levenson. *Bill Bernbach's Book.* New York: Villard Books, 1987.

Berger, Warren. *Advertising Today.* London: Phaidon Press Limited, 2001.

Bond, Jonathan, and Richard Kirshenbaum. *Under the Radar (Talking to Today's Cynical Consumer).* New York: Wiley, 1998.

The Book of Gossage. Chicago: The Copy Workshop, 1995.

Brady, Philip. *Using Type Right.* Lincolnwood, IL: NTC Business Books, 1988.

The Design and Art Directors Association of the United Kingdom. *The Copywriter's Bible.* Singapore: RotoVision, 1995.

Garchik, Morton. *Creative Visual Thinking: How to Think Up Ideas Fast.* New York: Art Direction Book Company, 1982.

Garfield, Bob. *And Now a Few Words from Me.* New York: McGraw Hill, 2003.

Haag, Dan. *Advertising Practitioners: One-on-One.* Boston: Houghton Mifflin, 1999.

Higgins, Denis. *The Art of Writing Advertising: Conversations with Masters of the Craft.* Lincolnwood, IL: NTC Business Books, 1989.

Jaffe, Andrew. *Casting for Big Ideas.* New York: Wiley, 2003.

Kanner, Bernice. *The 100 Best TV Commercials . . . and Why They Worked.* New York: Random House, 1999.

Keding, Ann, and Thomas Bivins. *How to Produce Creative Advertising: Proven Techniques and Computer Applications.* Lincolnwood, IL: NTC Business Books, 1991.

Keil, John M. *How to Zig in a Zagging World.* New York: Wiley, 1988.

Lawrence, Mary Wells. *A Big Life (in Advertising).* New York: Knopf. 2002

Lewis, Herschell Gordon, and Carol Nelson. *World's Greatest Direct Mail Sales Letters.* Lincolnwood, IL: NTC Business Books, 1996.

Marra, James L. *Advertising Creativity: Techniques for Generating Ideas.* Englewood Cliffs, NJ: Prentice Hall, 1990.

Newman, Michael. *Creative Leaps: 10 Lessons in Effective Advertising Inspired at Saatchi & Saatchi.* New York: Wiley, 2003.

Norins, Hanley. *The Young & Rubicam Traveling Creative Workshop.* Englewood Cliffs, NJ: Prentice Hall, 1990.

Ogilvy, David. *Confessions of an Advertising Man.* New York: Atheneum, 1963.

———. *Ogilvy on Advertising.* New York: Random House, 1985.

O'Toole, John. *The Trouble with Advertising.* New York: Random House, 1985.

Pricken, Mario. *Creative Advertising: Ideas and Techniques from the World's Best Campaigns.* London: Thames & Hudson, 2002.

Roman, Kenneth, and Jane Maas. *The New How to Advertise.* New York: St. Martin's Press, 1992.

Sroge, Maxwell. *How to Create Successful Catalogs.* Lincolnwood, IL: NTC Business Books, 1995.

Sullivan, Luke. *Hey Whipple, Squeeze This: A Guide to Creating Great Ads.* New York: Wiley, 1998.

US Ad Review: 10th Anniversary Book. New York: Visual Reference Publications, 2001.

Von Oech, Roger. *A Kick in the Seat of the Pants.* New York: Harper Perennial, 1986.

———. *A Whack on the Side of the Head.* New York: Warner Books, 1990.

Weinberger, Marc G., Leland Campbell, and Beth Brody. *Effective Radio Advertising.* New York: Lexington Books, 1994.

Diversity

Demographics of Minority Markets. Ithaca, NY: American Demographics Press, 1993.

Dunn, William. *The Baby Bust: A Generation Comes of Age.* Ithaca, NY: American Demographics Books, 1993.

Guber, Selina S., and Jon Berry. *Marketing to and Through Kids.* New York: McGraw-Hill, 1993.

Halter, Marilyn. *Shopping for Identity: The Marketing of Ethnicity.* New York: Schocken Books, 2000.

Lazer, William. *Handbook of Demographics for Marketing and Advertising.* New York: Lexington Books, 1994.

Lukenbill, Grant. *Untold Millions: Positioning Your Business for the Gay and Lesbian Consumer Revolution.* New York: Harper, 1995.

McNeal, James U. *Kids as Customers.* New York: Lexington Books. 1992.

Morgan, Carol M., and Doran J. Levy. *Segmenting the Mature Market: Identifying and Reaching America's Diverse, Booming Senior Markets.* Chicago: Probus, 1993.

Moschis, George P. *Gerontographics: Life-Stage Segmentation for Marketing Strategy Development.* Westport, CT: Quorum Books, 1996.

———. *Marketing Strategies for the Mature Market.* Westport, CT: Quorum Books, 1994.

Reedy, Joel. *Marketing to Consumers with Disabilities.* Chicago: Probus, 1993.

Ritchie, Karen. *Marketing to Generation X.* New York: Lexington Books, 1995.

Rossman, Marlene L. *Multicultural Marketing: Selling to a Diverse America.* New York: American Management Association, 1994.

Seelye, Ned, and James Alan Seelye. *Culture Clash: Managing in a Multicultural World.* Lincolnwood, IL: NTC Business Books, 1995.

Wolfe, David B. *Marketing to Boomers and Beyond.* New York: McGraw-Hill, 1993.

Wong, Angi Ma. *Target the U.S. Asian Market. A Practical Guide to Doing Business.* Los Angeles: Pacific Heritage Books, 1993.

Woods, Gail Baker. *Advertising and Marketing to the New Majority: A Case Study Approach.* Belmont, CA: Wadsworth, 1995.

Research

Alreck, Pamela L., and Robert B. Settle. *The Survey Research Handbook: Guidelines and Strategies for Conducting a Survey.* Burr Ridge, IL: Irwin Professional, 1995.

Berkman, Robert I. *Find It Fast: How to Uncover Expert Information on Any Subject.* New York: Harper & Row, 1990.

Greenbaum, Thomas L. *The Handbook for Focus Group Research.* New York: Lexington Books, 1993.

Haskins, Jack B., and Alice Kendrick. *Successful Advertising Research Methods.* Lincolnwood, IL: NTC Business Books, 1992.

Krueger, Richard A. *Focus Groups: A Practical Guide for Applied Research.* Newbury Park, CA: Sage, 1994.

Morrison, Margaret A., Eric Haley, Kim Bartel Sheenhan, and Ronald E. Taylor. *Using Qualitative Research in Advertising: Strategies, Techniques and Applications.* Thousand Oaks, CA: Sage, 2002.

Piirto, Rebecca. *Beyond Mind Games: The Marketing Power of Psychographics.* Ithaca, NY: American Demographics Books, 1991.

Sutherland, Max, and Alice K. Sylvester. *Advertising and the Mind of the Consumer.* Sydney, Australia: Griffin Press. 2000.

Strategy

Aaker, David A. *Managing Brand Equity.* New York: Free Press, 1991.

Bogart, Leo. *Strategy in Advertising.* Lincolnwood, IL: NTC Business Books, 1996.

Jones, Susan K. *Creative Strategy in Direct Marketing.* Lincolnwood, IL: NTC Business Books, 1991.

Loden, D. John. *Megabrands: How to Build Them, How to Beat Them.* Homewood, IL: Business One Irwin, 1992.

Marconi, Joe. *Beyond Branding: How Savvy Marketers Build Brand Equity to Create Products and Open New Markets.* Chicago: Probus, 1994.

Murphy, John M. *Brand Strategy.* Englewood Cliffs, NJ: Prentice Hall, 1990.

Randazzo, Sal. *Mythmaking on Madison Avenue: How Advertisers Apply the Power of Myth and Symbolism to Create Leadership Brands.* Chicago: Probus, 1993.

Rothenberg, Randall. *Where the Suckers Moon: The Life and Death of an Advertising Campaign.* New York: Vintage Books, 1995.

Schultz, Don E., Stanley Tannenbaum, and Anne Allison. *Essentials of Advertising Strategy.* Lincolnwood, IL: NTC Business Books, 1992.

Steel, Jon. *Truth, Lies and Advertising.* New York: Wiley, 1998.

Integrated Marketing Communications

Clow, Kenneth E., and Donald Baack. *Integrated Advertising, Promotion, and Marketing Communications.* Upper Saddle River, NJ: Pearson Prentice Hall, 2004.

Ries, Al, and Laura Ries. *The Fall of Advertising & The Rise of PR.* New York: HarperCollins, 2002.

Schultz, Don E., Stanley Tannenbaum, and Robert R. Lauterborn. *Integrated Marketing Communications.* Lincolnwood, IL: NTC Business Books, 1992.

Zyman, Sergio, *The End of Advertising as We Know It.* Hoboken, NJ: Wiley, 2002.

Presentations

Fletcher, Leon. *How to Speak Like a Pro.* New York: Ballantine Books, 1983.

Hoff, Ron. *I Can See You Naked.* Kansas City: Andrews and McMeel, 1992.

Moriarty, Sandra, and Tom Duncan. *Creating and Delivering Winning Advertising and Marketing Presentations.* Lincolnwood, IL: NTC Business Books, 1995.

Schloff, Laurie, and Marcia Yudkin. *Smart Speaking.* New York: Plume, 1992.

Stuart, Cristina. *How to Be an Effective Speaker.* Lincolnwood, IL: NTC Business Books, 1989.

Advertising Careers

Barry, Ann Marie. *The Advertising Portfolio.* Lincolnwood, IL: NTC Business Books, 1990.

Field, Shelby. *Career Opportunities in Advertising and Public Relations.* New York: Facts on File, 1990.

Minski, Laurence, and Emily Thorton Calvo. *How to Succeed in Advertising When All You Have Is Talent.* Lincolnwood, IL: NTC Business Books, 1994.

Morgan, Bradley J. *Marketing and Sales Career Directory.* Detroit: Invisible Ink Press, 1993.

Paetro, Maxine. *How to Put Your Book Together and Get a Job in Advertising.* Chicago: The Copy Workshop, 1990.

Pattis, S. William. *Careers in Advertising.* Lincolnwood, IL: NTC Business Books, 1996.

References

Ammer, Christine. *Have a Nice Day—No Problem: A Dictionary of Clichés.* New York: Dutton, 1992.

Encyclopedia of Consumer Brands. Detroit: St. James Press, 1994.

Hulbert, James. *Dictionary of Symbolism.* New York: Meridian, 1993.

Moran, Hal. *Symbols of America.* New York: Penguin Books, 1986.

Wiechmann, Jack G. *NTC's Dictionary of Advertising.* Lincolnwood, IL: NTC Business Books, 1993.

Index